AF426272

Enhancing Tech Theory

T. T. Samuels

Published by Masterworks, 2024.

ENHANCING TECH THEORY

First edition. June 20, 2024.

ISBN: 979-8227503039

Written by T. T. Samuels.

CONTENT
Artificial Intelligence (AI)
1. **Machine Learning**: Algorithms that enable computers to learn from data.
2. **Neural Networks**: Computing systems inspired by the human brain.
3. **Deep Learning**: A subset of machine learning with neural networks.
4. **Natural Language Processing (NLP)**: AI for understanding and generating human language.
5. **Computer Vision**: AI that enables machines to interpret and make decisions based on visual data.
6. **Autonomous Systems**: Self-operating machines like drones and self-driving cars.
7. **AI Ethics**: Moral implications and guidelines for AI development and deployment.
Cybersecurity
8. **Encryption**: Techniques for securing data by converting it into code.
9. **Firewalls**: Security systems that monitor and control network traffic.
10. **Cyber Threats**: Potential dangers like viruses, malware, and phishing.
11. **Blockchain**: Distributed ledger technology for secure transactions.
12. **Penetration Testing**: Simulated cyber attacks to identify vulnerabilities.
13. **Cryptography**: Methods of protecting information through encoding.
14. **Zero Trust Security**: Security model that requires strict identity verification.
Virtual Reality (VR) and Augmented Reality (AR)
15. **Immersive Experiences**: Fully engaging environments in VR and AR.
16. **Haptic Feedback**: Technology that simulates touch in virtual environments.
17. **Mixed Reality (MR)**: Combining VR and AR to interact with both virtual and real objects.
18. **360-Degree Videos**: Videos that allow viewing from every angle.
19. **Head-Mounted Displays (HMDs)**: Devices worn on the head for VR and AR experiences.
20. **Spatial Computing**: Technology that blends digital and physical spaces.
Cyber Culture
21. **Digital Identity**: Online representation of individuals.
22. **Memes**: Cultural elements that spread rapidly online.
23. **Internet Subcultures**: Communities with shared interests and practices online.
24. **Online Privacy**: Protection of personal information on the internet.
25. **Social Media**: Platforms for online communication and content sharing.
Computing and Technology
26. **Quantum Computing**: Advanced computing using quantum-mechanical phenomena.
27. **Cloud Computing**: Delivery of computing services over the internet.
28. **Edge Computing**: Processing data near its source rather than in a centralized data center.
29. **Internet of Things (IoT)**: Network of physical objects connected to the internet.
30. **Big Data**: Large and complex data sets analyzed computationally.
31. **Digital Twins**: Virtual replicas of physical systems for simulation and analysis.
Digital Art and Computer Graphics
32. **Generative Art**: Art created using algorithms and computational processes.
33. **Procedural Graphics**: Creating images algorithmically rather than manually.
34. **Digital Sculpting**: Using software to create 3D models.
35. **Virtual Galleries**: Online spaces for displaying digital art.
36. **Interactive Art**: Art that responds to the viewer's actions.
Communications and Media

37. **Digital Literacy**: The ability to use and understand digital tools and media.

38. **Media Convergence**: Blending of different media forms and platforms.

39. **Virtual Influencers**: AI-generated characters influencing social media.

40. **Streaming Services**: Platforms delivering digital content in real-time.

41. **Digital Journalism**: News and information disseminated online.

Futurism and Speculative Concepts

42. **Singularity**: Hypothetical point when AI surpasses human intelligence.

43. **Transhumanism**: Enhancing human capabilities through technology.

44. **Biotechnology**: Using living systems and organisms in technology.

45. **Nanotechnology**: Manipulating matter on an atomic or molecular scale.

46. **Cybernetics**: Study of systems, including biological and mechanical, for control and communication.

Additional Concepts

47. **Deconstruction**: Analyzing cultural texts and media to reveal assumptions and contradictions.

48. **Postmodernism**: Critique of grand narratives and embrace of fragmented, diverse perspectives.

49. **Simulation Theory**: The hypothesis that reality could be an artificial simulation.

50. **Digital Ecosystems**: Interconnected digital environments and platforms.

Artificial Intelligence (AI)

Artificial Intelligence (AI) is a transformative field of technology that has significantly impacted various sectors, from healthcare to finance, and continues to shape the future of human-computer interaction. At its core, AI is about creating systems that can perform tasks that would typically require human intelligence. These tasks include learning, reasoning, problem-solving, perception, and language understanding. Key components of AI include machine learning, neural networks, deep learning, natural language processing, computer vision, autonomous systems, and AI ethics.

Machine learning is a foundational aspect of AI, involving algorithms that enable computers to learn from and make decisions based on data. Unlike traditional programming, where a computer follows explicit instructions, machine learning allows the system to identify patterns and improve its performance over time. There are various types of machine learning, including supervised learning, where the model is trained on a labeled dataset; unsupervised learning, which involves finding hidden patterns in unlabeled data; and reinforcement learning, where an agent learns to make decisions by interacting with its environment and receiving feedback.

Neural networks are computing systems inspired by the human brain's structure and function. These networks consist of interconnected nodes, or neurons, which process and transmit information. Neural networks are particularly effective in tasks that involve recognizing patterns and making predictions. They are the backbone of many AI applications, including image and speech recognition, language translation, and game playing. The complexity of neural networks can vary, with some models having just a few layers of neurons, while others, known as deep neural networks, can have dozens or even hundreds of layers.

Deep learning is a subset of machine learning that focuses on neural networks with many layers, also known as deep neural networks. This approach has revolutionized AI by enabling systems to handle large amounts of data and perform highly complex tasks. Deep learning models excel in areas such as computer vision, natural language processing, and speech recognition. The ability of deep learning algorithms to automatically discover representations and features from raw data has led to significant advancements in various fields, including autonomous driving, medical image analysis, and recommendation systems.

Natural language processing (NLP) is a branch of AI that focuses on the interaction between computers and human language. NLP enables machines to understand, interpret, and generate human language in a way that is both meaningful and useful. Applications of NLP include language translation, sentiment analysis, chatbots, and voice assistants. By leveraging techniques such as tokenization, parsing, and machine translation, NLP systems can process large volumes of text data and extract valuable insights. Recent advancements in NLP, such as the development of transformer models like BERT and GPT, have significantly improved the accuracy and efficiency of language-based AI applications.

Computer vision is another critical area of AI, enabling machines to interpret and make decisions based on visual data. This field involves techniques for acquiring, processing, and analyzing images and videos to extract meaningful information. Computer vision applications include facial recognition, object detection, image classification, and autonomous navigation. By using deep learning algorithms, computer vision systems can achieve high levels of accuracy and performance, making them essential in various industries, including healthcare, automotive, and security.

Autonomous systems are self-operating machines that can perform tasks without human intervention. Examples of autonomous systems include drones, self-driving cars, and robotic process automation. These systems rely on a combination of machine learning, computer vision, and sensor data to navigate and make decisions in real-time. Autonomous systems have the potential to transform industries by increasing efficiency, reducing costs, and enhancing safety. For instance, self-driving cars can potentially reduce traffic accidents and improve transportation efficiency, while drones can be used for tasks such as delivering goods, inspecting infrastructure, and monitoring crops.

AI ethics is a critical aspect of AI development and deployment, focusing on the moral implications and guidelines for creating and using AI systems. As AI becomes increasingly integrated into society, ethical considerations become paramount to ensure that these technologies are used responsibly and for the benefit of all. Key issues in AI ethics include bias and fairness, transparency, accountability, and privacy. Bias in AI systems can arise from the data used to train them, leading to discriminatory outcomes. Ensuring fairness involves creating models that are free from bias and represent diverse perspectives. Transparency in AI involves making the decision-making processes of AI systems understandable to users and stakeholders. Accountability ensures that there are mechanisms in place to address any harm caused by AI systems. Privacy concerns revolve around the collection, storage, and use of personal data by AI technologies.

In conclusion, AI encompasses a broad range of technologies and applications that are transforming various aspects of our lives. Machine learning provides the foundation for AI systems to learn from data and improve over time. Neural networks and deep learning enable the creation of models capable of performing complex tasks. Natural language processing allows machines to understand and generate human language, while computer vision enables them to interpret visual data. Autonomous systems are revolutionizing industries by performing tasks without human intervention. Finally, AI ethics ensures that these technologies are developed and used in a way that is fair, transparent, and accountable. As AI continues to advance, it holds the promise of driving innovation and solving some of the world's most pressing challenges.

1. **Machine Learning**: Algorithms that enable computers to learn from data.

Machine learning is a transformative field within artificial intelligence (AI) that focuses on developing algorithms capable of learning from data. Unlike traditional programming, where explicit instructions are given to the computer to perform a specific task, machine learning allows systems to improve their performance over time by learning from their experiences. This paradigm shift has led to significant advancements across various domains, including healthcare, finance, transportation, and entertainment.

At its core, machine learning is about creating models that can generalize from a given dataset to make predictions or decisions without being explicitly programmed to perform those tasks. These models are built using algorithms that process data, identify patterns, and adjust their parameters to improve their accuracy. The learning process typically involves three main types of learning: supervised learning, unsupervised learning, and reinforcement learning.

Supervised learning is the most common type of machine learning. In supervised learning, the algorithm is trained on a labeled dataset, meaning that each training example is paired with an output label. The goal of the algorithm is to learn a mapping from inputs to outputs that can be used to predict the labels of new, unseen examples. Common algorithms used in supervised learning include linear regression, logistic regression, support vector machines, decision trees, and neural networks. For example, in a spam email classification task, a supervised learning algorithm would be trained on a dataset of emails labeled as "spam" or "not spam" and would learn to classify new emails based on the patterns it identifies.

Unsupervised learning, on the other hand, deals with unlabeled data. The algorithm tries to identify inherent structures in the data without any guidance on what the outputs should be. Common techniques in unsupervised learning include clustering and dimensionality reduction. Clustering algorithms, such as k-means and hierarchical clustering, group similar data points together based on their features. This approach is often used in market segmentation, where businesses group customers with similar purchasing behaviors. Dimensionality reduction techniques, like principal component analysis (PCA) and t-distributed stochastic neighbor embedding (t-SNE), aim to reduce the number of features in the data while preserving its essential structure. These methods are useful for visualizing high-dimensional data and for improving the performance of other machine learning algorithms by removing noise and redundancy.

Reinforcement learning is a type of machine learning that is inspired by behavioral psychology. In reinforcement learning, an agent learns to make decisions by interacting with its environment and receiving feedback in the form of rewards or penalties. The agent's goal is to learn a policy that maximizes the cumulative reward over time. This type of learning is particularly well-suited for problems where the consequences of actions are not immediately apparent and where long-term planning is required. Reinforcement learning has been successfully applied to various domains, including robotics, game playing, and autonomous driving. Notable examples include DeepMind's AlphaGo, which defeated the world champion Go player, and various applications in robotic control where agents learn to perform complex tasks through trial and error.

The success of machine learning algorithms depends heavily on the quality and quantity of the data used for training. Data preprocessing is a crucial step in the machine learning pipeline, involving tasks such as data cleaning, normalization, and feature extraction. Data cleaning involves removing or correcting errors and inconsistencies in the data, while normalization ensures that the features have a consistent scale. Feature extraction is the process of transforming raw data into a set of meaningful attributes that can be used by the learning algorithm. This step often requires domain knowledge and can significantly impact the performance of the model.

Once the data is prepared, the next step is to select an appropriate model and algorithm. The choice of algorithm depends on various factors, including the nature of the problem, the size and complexity of the dataset, and the desired trade-off between accuracy and interpretability. Some algorithms, like decision trees, are highly interpretable but may not perform well on complex datasets. Others, like deep neural networks, can achieve state-of-the-art performance on a wide range of tasks but are often seen as "black boxes" due to their complexity.

After selecting the model, the training process begins. During training, the algorithm iteratively adjusts its parameters to minimize a loss function, which measures the difference between the predicted and actual outputs. This process is often facilitated by optimization algorithms such as gradient descent, which compute the gradients of the loss function with respect to the model parameters and update them in the direction that reduces the loss. The training process continues until the model converges to a set of parameters that produce the lowest possible loss on the training data.

One of the key challenges in machine learning is ensuring that the model generalizes well to new, unseen data. Overfitting occurs when the model learns the training data too well, capturing noise and random fluctuations instead of the underlying patterns. This results in poor performance on new data. To mitigate overfitting, various techniques can be employed, such as cross-validation, regularization, and early stopping. Cross-validation involves splitting the dataset into multiple folds and training the model on different subsets while evaluating it on the remaining data. Regularization adds a penalty term to the loss function that discourages overly complex models, while early stopping halts the training process when the model's performance on a validation set starts to degrade.

Another important aspect of machine learning is model evaluation. Once the model is trained, it needs to be evaluated on a separate test set to assess its performance. Common evaluation metrics for classification tasks include accuracy, precision, recall, and the F1 score. For regression tasks, metrics such as mean squared error (MSE) and mean absolute error (MAE) are used. These metrics provide insights into how well the model is performing and can guide further improvements.

Machine learning has a wide range of applications across different industries. In healthcare, machine learning algorithms are used for disease diagnosis, drug discovery, and personalized medicine. For instance, machine learning models can analyze medical images to detect tumors or predict patient outcomes based on electronic health records. In finance, machine learning is used for fraud detection, algorithmic trading, and risk management. By analyzing transaction data, machine learning models can identify suspicious activities and help prevent financial crimes. In the automotive industry, machine learning powers advanced driver-assistance systems (ADAS) and autonomous vehicles. These systems use data from sensors and cameras to make real-time decisions and improve safety on the roads.

In addition to these applications, machine learning is also making significant contributions to fields such as natural language processing (NLP), computer vision, and recommendation systems. NLP techniques enable machines to understand and generate human language, leading to applications such as language translation, sentiment analysis, and chatbots. Computer vision algorithms allow machines to interpret and make decisions based on visual data, with applications in facial recognition, object detection, and image classification. Recommendation systems use machine learning to provide personalized content and product suggestions, enhancing user experiences on platforms like Netflix, Amazon, and Spotify.

Despite its many successes, machine learning also faces several challenges and limitations. One of the primary challenges is the need for large amounts of labeled data, which can be expensive and time-consuming to obtain. Additionally, machine learning models can be sensitive to the quality of the data, and issues such as bias and fairness must be carefully addressed to ensure that the models do not perpetuate or amplify existing inequalities. Another challenge is the interpretability of complex models, particularly deep neural networks, which can make it difficult to understand how decisions are being made and to ensure accountability.

To address these challenges, researchers and practitioners are developing new techniques and tools for data augmentation, transfer learning, and explainable AI. Data augmentation involves generating additional training examples by applying transformations to the existing data, while transfer learning leverages pre-trained models on related tasks to improve performance on new tasks with limited data. Explainable AI aims to make machine learning models more transparent and interpretable, enabling users to understand and trust the decisions made by these systems.

In conclusion, machine learning is a powerful and versatile field that enables computers to learn from data and make intelligent decisions. Its applications span a wide range of domains, from healthcare and finance to transportation and entertainment. By leveraging algorithms that can identify patterns and improve over time, machine learning is transforming industries and driving innovation. However, challenges such as data quality, model interpretability, and ethical considerations must be carefully addressed to ensure that the benefits of machine learning are realized in a responsible and equitable manner. As the field continues to evolve, ongoing research and development will likely lead to even more sophisticated and impactful applications, further enhancing our ability to harness the power of data and technology.

2. **Neural Networks**: Computing systems inspired by the human brain.

Neural networks, often referred to as artificial neural networks (ANNs), are a subset of machine learning algorithms modeled after the human brain's structure and function. The fundamental concept behind neural networks is to simulate the way biological neurons communicate with one another, thereby enabling machines to process data and learn patterns in a manner akin to human cognition.

At the heart of a neural network are its basic units: neurons. These artificial neurons, also known as nodes or units, are designed to mimic the behavior of biological neurons. Each neuron receives one or more input signals, processes these signals, and generates an output. The connections between neurons are referred to as synapses, and in artificial neural networks, these are represented by weights. These weights determine the strength and significance of the input signals being transmitted.

The architecture of neural networks typically consists of multiple layers of neurons. The simplest form of a neural network is a single-layer perceptron, which contains only one layer of output neurons connected to input neurons. However, more complex neural networks, known as deep neural networks (DNNs), have multiple hidden layers between the input and output layers. These hidden layers allow the network to learn and represent complex patterns and relationships within the data.

The process of training a neural network involves adjusting the weights of the connections between neurons to minimize the error in the network's predictions. This is typically achieved through a process called backpropagation, combined with an optimization algorithm like gradient descent. During backpropagation, the error is calculated at the output and propagated backward through the network, updating the weights to reduce the error.

One of the key advantages of neural networks is their ability to learn from data. Unlike traditional algorithms that rely on predefined rules, neural networks can learn to perform tasks by being exposed to large amounts of data. This learning capability is what makes neural networks particularly powerful for tasks such as image recognition, natural language processing, and speech recognition.

Neural networks have seen a significant resurgence in recent years due to advancements in computational power and the availability of large datasets. This resurgence has led to remarkable breakthroughs in various fields. For instance, in computer vision, convolutional neural networks (CNNs) have achieved state-of-the-art performance in image classification, object detection, and image segmentation tasks. CNNs are designed to automatically and adaptively learn spatial hierarchies of features from input images, making them highly effective for visual data.

In the realm of natural language processing (NLP), recurrent neural networks (RNNs) and their variants, such as long short-term memory (LSTM) networks and gated recurrent units (GRUs), have proven to be highly effective. RNNs are particularly well-suited for sequential data, such as text, because they maintain a memory of previous inputs, allowing them to capture context and dependencies in language. This has enabled significant advancements in machine translation, text generation, sentiment analysis, and more.

Another notable development in neural networks is the emergence of generative models, such as generative adversarial networks (GANs) and variational autoencoders (VAEs). GANs consist of two networks: a generator and a discriminator. The generator creates fake data, while the discriminator evaluates the authenticity of the data. The two networks are trained simultaneously in a competitive manner, resulting in the generation of highly realistic synthetic data. VAEs, on the other hand, are probabilistic models that learn to represent data in a continuous latent space, allowing for the generation of new data samples.

Neural networks have also found applications in reinforcement learning, where they are used to train agents to make sequential decisions in complex environments. Deep reinforcement learning, which combines neural networks with reinforcement learning algorithms, has achieved notable success in various domains, including game playing, robotics, and autonomous driving. For instance, the AlphaGo program, developed by DeepMind, used deep reinforcement learning to defeat human world champions in the game of Go.

Despite their successes, neural networks are not without challenges. One major challenge is the need for large amounts of labeled data for training. Acquiring and annotating such data can be time-consuming and expensive. Additionally, neural networks can be computationally intensive, requiring specialized hardware, such as graphics processing units (GPUs) or tensor processing units (TPUs), to accelerate training and inference.

Another challenge is the interpretability of neural networks. While neural networks are capable of learning complex patterns, the learned representations are often difficult to interpret, leading to a lack of transparency in decision-making. This has prompted research into explainable AI (XAI), which aims to develop methods for making neural networks more interpretable and understandable to humans.

Overfitting is another concern when training neural networks. Overfitting occurs when a neural network learns to memorize the training data rather than generalizing to new, unseen data. Techniques such as dropout, regularization, and early stopping are commonly used to mitigate overfitting and improve the generalization performance of neural networks.

Moreover, the ethical implications of neural networks and AI, in general, have become a topic of increasing importance. The deployment of AI systems in critical areas such as healthcare, finance, and criminal justice raises questions about fairness, accountability, and bias. Ensuring that neural networks are developed and deployed in an ethical and responsible manner is crucial to addressing these concerns.

Looking forward, the field of neural networks continues to evolve, with ongoing research focused on addressing these challenges and pushing the boundaries of what is possible. Areas of active research include unsupervised and self-supervised learning, which aim to reduce the dependence on labeled data, and federated learning, which enables collaborative training of neural networks across decentralized data sources while preserving privacy.

Another exciting area of research is neuromorphic computing, which seeks to develop hardware inspired by the brain's structure and function. Neuromorphic chips, such as IBM's TrueNorth and Intel's Loihi, are designed to mimic the parallel and event-driven nature of biological neural networks, offering the potential for more energy-efficient and scalable neural network implementations.

Quantum computing is also emerging as a potential game-changer for neural networks. Quantum neural networks leverage the principles of quantum mechanics to perform computations, potentially offering exponential speedups for certain tasks. While still in its early stages, research in quantum neural networks holds promise for addressing some of the computational challenges associated with classical neural networks.

In conclusion, neural networks, inspired by the human brain, have revolutionized the field of artificial intelligence and machine learning. Their ability to learn from data and recognize complex patterns has led to significant advancements across a wide range of applications, from image recognition and natural language processing to reinforcement learning and generative modeling. Despite the challenges, ongoing research and development in neural networks continue to drive innovation, with the potential to transform various industries and reshape our understanding of intelligence. As we move forward, it is essential to address the ethical and societal implications of neural networks to ensure their responsible and equitable deployment in the real world.

3. **Deep Learning**: A subset of machine learning with neural networks.

Deep learning, a subset of machine learning, represents a significant advancement in the field of artificial intelligence (AI). At its core, deep learning leverages neural networks to simulate the human brain's ability to process data and recognize patterns, enabling machines to perform complex tasks with remarkable accuracy and efficiency.

The foundation of deep learning is built upon artificial neural networks, specifically those with many layers, hence the term "deep." These layers consist of nodes, or neurons, that mimic the neurons in a biological brain. Each neuron receives input, processes it, and passes it to the next layer. The more layers there are, the deeper the network, and the more sophisticated the representations and abstractions it can learn.

Deep learning has its roots in the early neural networks of the 1950s and 1960s, but it wasn't until the advent of more powerful computational resources and the availability of vast amounts of data that it truly began to flourish. The resurgence of deep learning in the 2010s was marked by significant breakthroughs, particularly in the areas of image and speech recognition.

One of the most notable developments in deep learning is the convolutional neural network (CNN). CNNs are particularly effective for image processing tasks because they can automatically and adaptively learn spatial hierarchies of features from input images. The convolutional layers within a CNN apply filters to the input image, capturing essential features such as edges, textures, and patterns. These features are then passed through pooling layers that reduce the dimensionality of the data, making the network more efficient and less prone to overfitting. Finally, fully connected layers interpret these features to make predictions or classifications.

The impact of CNNs has been profound in fields such as computer vision. For example, CNNs have achieved human-level performance in image classification tasks, as demonstrated by their success in the ImageNet competition, a benchmark for evaluating the accuracy of image recognition algorithms. Beyond image classification, CNNs are also used in object detection, where the goal is to identify and locate objects within an image, and in image segmentation, which involves partitioning an image into meaningful regions.

Another critical development in deep learning is the recurrent neural network (RNN), which excels at handling sequential data. RNNs are designed to recognize patterns in sequences of data, making them ideal for tasks such as time series prediction, natural language processing (NLP), and speech recognition. Unlike traditional neural networks, RNNs have connections that form cycles, allowing them to maintain a memory of previous inputs. This capability enables RNNs to capture temporal dependencies and contextual information in sequential data.

However, traditional RNNs suffer from limitations such as the vanishing gradient problem, which makes it difficult for them to learn long-range dependencies. To address these issues, advanced variants of RNNs, such as long short-term memory (LSTM) networks and gated recurrent units (GRUs), were developed. LSTMs and GRUs incorporate mechanisms called gates that regulate the flow of information, enabling them to capture long-term dependencies more effectively.

The advancements in NLP driven by RNNs and their variants have been remarkable. For instance, LSTMs have been successfully applied to machine translation, where they have significantly improved the accuracy and fluency of translations. Additionally, they have been used in text generation, sentiment analysis, and speech synthesis, among other applications.

In recent years, a new architecture known as the transformer has revolutionized deep learning, particularly in the field of NLP. Transformers, introduced in the seminal paper "Attention is All You Need," rely entirely on a mechanism called self-attention to capture relationships between elements in a sequence, without the need for recurrent connections. This self-attention mechanism allows transformers to process entire sequences in parallel, leading to significant improvements in training efficiency and performance.

Transformers have enabled the development of powerful language models such as BERT (Bidirectional Encoder Representations from Transformers) and GPT (Generative Pre-trained Transformer). These models have set new benchmarks in a wide range of NLP tasks, including language understanding, text generation, and question answering. The success of transformers has extended beyond NLP to areas such as image processing and reinforcement learning, showcasing their versatility and effectiveness.

Generative models represent another exciting frontier in deep learning. Generative adversarial networks (GANs) and variational autoencoders (VAEs) are two prominent types of generative models that have demonstrated the ability to create realistic synthetic data. GANs consist of two networks: a generator that creates fake data and a discriminator that evaluates the authenticity of the data. The two networks are trained simultaneously in a competitive manner, resulting in the generation of highly realistic data samples.

VAEs, on the other hand, are probabilistic models that learn to represent data in a continuous latent space. They consist of an encoder that maps input data to a latent space and a decoder that reconstructs the data from the latent space. VAEs are particularly useful for tasks such as data generation, anomaly detection, and dimensionality reduction.

The applications of GANs and VAEs are vast and varied. For instance, GANs have been used to generate realistic images, enhance image resolution, and create art. They have also been applied in fields such as healthcare for generating synthetic medical data and in finance for modeling stock market behavior. VAEs have been employed in drug discovery, where they are used to generate novel molecular structures, and in recommendation systems, where they help to capture the underlying preferences of users.

Deep learning has also made significant strides in reinforcement learning, where it is used to train agents to make sequential decisions in complex environments. Deep reinforcement learning combines neural networks with reinforcement learning algorithms, enabling agents to learn optimal policies through trial and error. Notable successes in deep reinforcement learning include AlphaGo, which defeated human world champions in the game of Go, and DeepMind's AlphaStar, which achieved Grandmaster level performance in the real-time strategy game StarCraft II.

Despite the remarkable achievements of deep learning, several challenges remain. One major challenge is the need for large amounts of labeled data for training. Acquiring and annotating such data can be time-consuming and expensive. Techniques such as transfer learning, where models pre-trained on large datasets are fine-tuned on smaller, task-specific datasets, have been developed to mitigate this challenge. Additionally, research into unsupervised and semi-supervised learning aims to reduce the reliance on labeled data.

Another challenge is the interpretability of deep learning models. While deep learning models can achieve high performance, their inner workings are often opaque, making it difficult to understand how they arrive at their predictions. This lack of transparency has implications for trust and accountability, particularly in critical applications such as healthcare and autonomous driving. Efforts to develop explainable AI (XAI) seek to address this challenge by creating methods and tools that make deep learning models more interpretable and understandable.

Overfitting is another concern when training deep learning models. Overfitting occurs when a model learns to memorize the training data rather than generalizing to new, unseen data. Regularization techniques, such as dropout, weight decay, and data augmentation, are commonly used to mitigate overfitting and improve the generalization performance of deep learning models.

The computational demands of deep learning are also significant. Training deep learning models, particularly large ones, requires substantial computational resources, including specialized hardware such as graphics processing units (GPUs) and tensor processing units (TPUs). Research into more efficient algorithms and hardware architectures aims to address these computational challenges.

Looking ahead, the field of deep learning continues to evolve, with ongoing research focused on addressing these challenges and exploring new frontiers. One promising area of research is neuromorphic computing, which seeks to develop hardware inspired by the brain's structure and function. Neuromorphic chips, such as IBM's TrueNorth and

Intel's Loihi, are designed to mimic the parallel and event-driven nature of biological neural networks, offering the potential for more energy-efficient and scalable deep learning implementations.

Quantum computing is another emerging field that holds potential for deep learning. Quantum neural networks leverage the principles of quantum mechanics to perform computations, potentially offering exponential speedups for certain tasks. While still in its early stages, research in quantum neural networks is exploring how quantum computing can address some of the computational challenges associated with classical deep learning.

In conclusion, deep learning, as a subset of machine learning, has revolutionized the field of artificial intelligence by leveraging neural networks to process data and recognize patterns. Its ability to learn from large amounts of data and represent complex relationships has led to significant advancements across various domains, including image and speech recognition, natural language processing, generative modeling, and reinforcement learning. Despite the challenges, ongoing research and development in deep learning continue to push the boundaries of what is possible, with the potential to transform industries and reshape our understanding of intelligence. As we move forward, it is essential to address the ethical and societal implications of deep learning to ensure its responsible and equitable deployment in the real world.

4. **Natural Language Processing (NLP)**: AI for understanding and generating human language.

Natural Language Processing (NLP) is a branch of artificial intelligence (AI) that focuses on the interaction between computers and humans through natural language. The ultimate goal of NLP is to enable computers to understand, interpret, and generate human language in a way that is both meaningful and useful. This technology has become a cornerstone in the development of various applications that require the understanding and generation of human language, including voice-activated assistants, translation services, and sentiment analysis tools.

The foundation of NLP lies in the ability of computers to process large amounts of natural language data. This process involves several steps, starting with the collection and preprocessing of data. Preprocessing typically includes tasks such as tokenization, which divides text into individual words or phrases; stemming and lemmatization, which reduce words to their base or root form; and removing stop words, which are common words that do not contribute significant meaning to a sentence, such as "and," "the," and "is."

Once the data is preprocessed, the next step is to analyze the structure and meaning of the text. This involves syntactic analysis, which examines the grammatical structure of sentences, and semantic analysis, which focuses on understanding the meaning of words and sentences. Syntactic analysis can involve parsing, where the structure of a sentence is represented as a parse tree, showing the relationship between different words and phrases. Semantic analysis, on the other hand, deals with word sense disambiguation, resolving the meanings of words based on context, and named entity recognition, identifying and classifying entities such as names, dates, and locations within the text.

A critical component of NLP is the ability to model language statistically. Language models, which are probabilistic frameworks that predict the likelihood of a sequence of words, play a key role in many NLP applications. Early language models, such as n-gram models, were relatively simple and relied on the frequency of word sequences in a given dataset. However, modern NLP techniques often employ more sophisticated models, such as those based on neural networks, which can capture more complex patterns in language data.

One of the most significant advancements in NLP in recent years has been the development of transformer models, such as BERT (Bidirectional Encoder Representations from Transformers) and GPT (Generative Pre-trained Transformer). These models have revolutionized the field by achieving state-of-the-art performance on a wide range of NLP tasks. Transformers are designed to handle long-range dependencies in text, allowing them to understand the context of words more effectively. BERT, for example, uses a bidirectional approach to process text, meaning it considers both the left and right context of a word, leading to a deeper understanding of language. GPT, on the other hand, is primarily focused on text generation, using a unidirectional approach to predict the next word in a sequence.

The applications of NLP are vast and varied, spanning multiple industries and impacting everyday life. One of the most common applications is in virtual assistants, such as Amazon's Alexa, Apple's Siri, and Google's Assistant. These assistants rely on NLP to understand and respond to user queries, enabling tasks such as setting reminders, answering questions, and controlling smart home devices. The ability to accurately interpret and generate human language is crucial for these systems to provide a seamless user experience.

In the realm of translation, NLP has enabled significant advancements in machine translation systems. Tools like Google Translate and DeepL utilize sophisticated NLP algorithms to translate text from one language to another with increasing accuracy. These systems are trained on vast amounts of bilingual text data, allowing them to learn the nuances and complexities of different languages. While machine translation is not yet perfect, ongoing improvements in NLP continue to enhance the quality and reliability of these services.

Sentiment analysis is another important application of NLP, particularly in the fields of marketing and customer service. By analyzing the sentiment expressed in customer reviews, social media posts, and other forms of text, companies can gain valuable insights into customer opinions and preferences. Sentiment analysis can help businesses identify trends, gauge public perception, and make data-driven decisions to improve products and services.

NLP also plays a crucial role in information retrieval and search engines. When users enter queries into a search engine, NLP algorithms analyze the query to understand the user's intent and retrieve the most relevant results. This involves not only keyword matching but also understanding the context and semantics of the query. Advanced NLP techniques, such as semantic search, can provide more accurate and meaningful results by considering the overall context and meaning of the query rather than relying solely on keyword matching.

In healthcare, NLP is being used to analyze medical records, research papers, and other text-based data to improve patient care and outcomes. For example, NLP can be used to extract relevant information from electronic health records (EHRs), identify potential diagnoses, and recommend treatment options. By automating the analysis of large volumes of text data, NLP can help healthcare professionals make more informed decisions and provide personalized care to patients.

Another emerging application of NLP is in the field of legal technology. Legal professionals often deal with large amounts of text, including contracts, case law, and legal documents. NLP can assist in automating the review and analysis of these documents, helping to identify relevant information, flag potential issues, and streamline the legal research process. This can significantly reduce the time and effort required for legal work, allowing professionals to focus on more complex and strategic tasks.

Despite the significant advancements in NLP, there are still many challenges that researchers and developers face. One of the primary challenges is the inherent complexity and ambiguity of human language. Words can have multiple meanings, sentences can be structured in various ways, and context plays a crucial role in interpretation. Developing algorithms that can accurately capture and understand these nuances is an ongoing area of research.

Another challenge is the need for large amounts of labeled data to train NLP models. While there is a vast amount of text data available, obtaining high-quality labeled data for specific tasks can be time-consuming and expensive. Researchers are exploring techniques such as transfer learning and unsupervised learning to address this challenge, allowing models to leverage existing knowledge and learn from unlabeled data.

Bias in NLP models is also a significant concern. Language models are trained on large datasets that often contain biases present in human language. These biases can be inadvertently learned by the models, leading to biased or unfair outcomes in applications. Addressing this issue requires careful consideration of the data used for training, as well as the development of techniques to detect and mitigate bias in NLP models.

Privacy and security are additional considerations in NLP applications, particularly when dealing with sensitive information. Ensuring that NLP systems handle data responsibly and securely is crucial to maintaining user trust and complying with regulatory requirements. Techniques such as differential privacy and secure multi-party computation are being explored to enhance the privacy and security of NLP systems.

Looking to the future, the field of NLP is likely to continue evolving rapidly, driven by advancements in machine learning, computational power, and the availability of data. Researchers are exploring new architectures and techniques to further improve the performance and capabilities of NLP models. For example, there is ongoing work on developing models that can better understand and generate human language in a more context-aware and conversational manner.

One promising direction is the integration of multimodal data, where NLP models incorporate not only text but also other forms of data such as images, audio, and video. This can enhance the ability of NLP systems to understand and generate language in more complex and dynamic contexts. For example, a multimodal NLP system could analyze both the text and visual content of a social media post to better understand the sentiment and intent behind it.

Another exciting area of research is the development of more interactive and adaptive NLP systems. These systems can engage in more natural and dynamic interactions with users, learning from their inputs and adapting to their preferences over time. This can lead to more personalized and engaging user experiences, whether in virtual assistants, customer service chatbots, or other applications.

In conclusion, Natural Language Processing is a rapidly advancing field that is transforming the way humans interact with computers. By enabling computers to understand, interpret, and generate human language, NLP is driving innovation across various industries and applications. From virtual assistants and machine translation to sentiment analysis and healthcare, NLP is making it possible to leverage the power of language in new and impactful ways. Despite the challenges, the future of NLP holds immense potential, promising to bring even more sophisticated and human-like language capabilities to AI systems.

5. **Computer Vision**: AI that enables machines to interpret and make decisions based on visual data.

Computer Vision is a fascinating and rapidly evolving field within artificial intelligence (AI) that focuses on enabling machines to interpret and make decisions based on visual data. At its core, computer vision aims to replicate the remarkable capabilities of human vision by equipping computers with the ability to see, understand, and analyze the visual world around them. This technology has profound implications across various industries, revolutionizing the way we interact with machines and how they interact with their environments.

One of the key challenges in computer vision is the complexity of visual data. Unlike textual or numerical data, which can be easily structured and processed, visual data is inherently unstructured and rich in information. It consists of millions of pixels, each with its own color and intensity values, forming intricate patterns that convey meaningful information. To extract useful insights from such data, computer vision systems rely on sophisticated algorithms and models capable of recognizing and interpreting these patterns.

The foundation of computer vision lies in image processing, a field that has been studied for decades. Image processing involves a series of techniques to enhance, manipulate, and analyze images to extract relevant features. Basic operations like filtering, edge detection, and segmentation form the building blocks of more complex computer vision tasks. For instance, edge detection algorithms help identify the boundaries of objects within an image, while segmentation techniques partition an image into meaningful regions.

As the field progressed, the advent of machine learning and, more recently, deep learning has brought about significant advancements in computer vision. Traditional image processing methods, while effective for simple tasks, often struggled with the complexity and variability of real-world images. Machine learning introduced the idea of training models on large datasets to recognize patterns and make predictions, enabling more robust and flexible solutions.

Deep learning, a subset of machine learning, has been particularly transformative in computer vision. Deep learning models, such as convolutional neural networks (CNNs), have demonstrated unprecedented performance in a wide range of visual tasks. CNNs are designed to mimic the visual processing mechanisms of the human brain, with multiple layers of interconnected neurons that learn to detect hierarchical features in images. These models excel at tasks like image classification, object detection, and image segmentation, achieving accuracy levels that were previously thought unattainable.

Image classification is one of the fundamental tasks in computer vision, where the goal is to assign a label to an entire image based on its content. For example, given an image of a cat, an image classification model should correctly identify it as a cat. This seemingly simple task requires the model to recognize various features of the cat, such as its shape, color, and texture, and distinguish it from other objects. CNNs have achieved remarkable success in this area, surpassing human-level performance in some benchmarks.

Object detection goes a step further by not only classifying objects within an image but also locating them. This involves drawing bounding boxes around each object and assigning labels to them. Object detection is crucial for applications like autonomous driving, where the system needs to identify and track multiple objects, such as pedestrians, vehicles, and road signs, in real-time. Advanced object detection models, like the YOLO (You Only Look Once) and SSD (Single Shot MultiBox Detector), have made significant strides in achieving real-time performance with high accuracy.

Image segmentation, on the other hand, involves partitioning an image into distinct regions corresponding to different objects or surfaces. Unlike object detection, which uses bounding boxes, image segmentation assigns a label to each pixel, providing a more detailed understanding of the image. This task is essential in medical imaging, where precise segmentation of anatomical structures can aid in diagnosis and treatment planning. Techniques like U-Net and Mask R-CNN have shown great promise in achieving accurate and efficient image segmentation.

Beyond these traditional tasks, computer vision has expanded into various specialized domains, each with its unique challenges and applications. Facial recognition is one such domain that has garnered significant attention due to its potential for security and surveillance. Facial recognition systems analyze facial features and match them against a database to identify individuals. Despite their widespread use, these systems face ethical and privacy concerns, particularly regarding their potential for misuse and bias.

Another exciting application of computer vision is in augmented reality (AR) and virtual reality (VR). AR overlays digital information onto the real world, enhancing our perception and interaction with our surroundings. VR, on the other hand, creates immersive virtual environments that simulate real-world experiences. Both technologies rely heavily on computer vision to track and understand the user's environment, enabling seamless integration of virtual and real elements.

In the realm of healthcare, computer vision has the potential to revolutionize diagnostics and treatment. Medical imaging techniques, such as X-rays, MRIs, and CT scans, generate vast amounts of visual data that require expert interpretation. Computer vision algorithms can assist radiologists by automatically detecting anomalies and highlighting areas of concern, thereby improving accuracy and reducing the workload. Moreover, computer vision can aid in surgical procedures by providing real-time guidance and enhancing precision.

The field of agriculture also benefits from computer vision through precision farming. By analyzing aerial images captured by drones, computer vision systems can monitor crop health, detect pests and diseases, and optimize irrigation and fertilization. This data-driven approach enables farmers to make informed decisions, increase yields, and reduce resource wastage.

Autonomous vehicles represent one of the most high-profile and challenging applications of computer vision. Self-driving cars rely on a combination of sensors, including cameras, to perceive their surroundings and make real-time decisions. Computer vision algorithms analyze the visual data to detect lanes, obstacles, and traffic signs, ensuring safe and efficient navigation. The development of robust and reliable computer vision systems is crucial for the widespread adoption of autonomous vehicles.

Despite the remarkable progress, computer vision still faces several challenges. One major hurdle is the need for large amounts of labeled data for training. Deep learning models, in particular, require vast datasets with accurate annotations to learn effectively. Acquiring and labeling such data can be time-consuming and expensive. Additionally, computer vision systems must generalize well to different environments and conditions, such as varying lighting, weather, and camera perspectives.

Another challenge is the interpretability of deep learning models. While these models achieve high accuracy, they often operate as black boxes, making it difficult to understand how they arrive at their decisions. This lack of transparency can be problematic in critical applications where trust and accountability are paramount. Researchers are actively working on techniques to improve the interpretability and explainability of computer vision models.

Moreover, ethical considerations play a significant role in the deployment of computer vision systems. Issues related to privacy, bias, and fairness must be addressed to ensure that these technologies are used responsibly. For instance, facial recognition systems have been criticized for their potential to infringe on individual privacy and their susceptibility to bias against certain demographic groups. Ensuring fairness and avoiding discriminatory outcomes requires careful design, testing, and regulation.

Looking ahead, the future of computer vision holds immense potential. Continued advancements in AI and machine learning are expected to drive further improvements in accuracy, efficiency, and robustness. Integration with other AI technologies, such as natural language processing and robotics, will enable more sophisticated and versatile systems. For example, combining computer vision with natural language processing can facilitate the development of multimodal AI systems that understand and interact with both visual and textual information.

Furthermore, the proliferation of edge computing and the Internet of Things (IoT) is likely to accelerate the adoption of computer vision in various applications. Edge computing involves processing data locally on devices rather than relying solely on centralized servers. This approach reduces latency and bandwidth requirements, making real-time computer vision feasible in resource-constrained environments. IoT devices equipped with computer vision capabilities can enable smart cities, intelligent surveillance, and automated industrial processes.

In conclusion, computer vision is a transformative technology that empowers machines to interpret and make decisions based on visual data. From image classification and object detection to specialized applications in healthcare, agriculture, and autonomous vehicles, computer vision is reshaping industries and enhancing our interaction with technology. While challenges related to data, interpretability, and ethics remain, ongoing research and innovation promise to unlock new possibilities and drive the field forward. As computer vision continues to evolve, it will undoubtedly play a pivotal role in shaping the future of AI and its impact on society.

6. **Autonomous Systems**: Self-operating machines like drones and self-driving cars.

Autonomous systems are self-operating machines that function without human intervention, transforming various industries through their advanced capabilities. These systems include a range of technologies such as drones, self-driving cars, and robotics. Autonomous systems leverage artificial intelligence (AI), machine learning, sensors, and data analytics to perform tasks that traditionally required human control. The development and deployment of these systems are reshaping industries, from transportation and logistics to agriculture and healthcare, promising significant improvements in efficiency, safety, and productivity.

One of the most well-known applications of autonomous systems is in the realm of self-driving cars. These vehicles use a combination of sensors, cameras, radar, and lidar to perceive their surroundings. They process vast amounts of data in real-time to navigate roads, recognize traffic signals, avoid obstacles, and ensure the safety of passengers and pedestrians. Companies like Tesla, Waymo, and Uber have been at the forefront of developing autonomous driving technology, aiming to revolutionize transportation by reducing accidents, easing traffic congestion, and providing mobility solutions for those unable to drive.

The core technology behind self-driving cars includes AI algorithms and machine learning models that enable the vehicle to make decisions based on sensory input. These algorithms are trained on extensive datasets that include various driving scenarios, helping the vehicle to understand and react to complex situations. The continuous learning aspect of these systems allows them to improve over time, adapting to new environments and enhancing their decision-making capabilities.

Drones, or unmanned aerial vehicles (UAVs), represent another significant category of autonomous systems. Initially developed for military applications, drones are now widely used in commercial, industrial, and recreational settings. They are equipped with advanced navigation systems, cameras, and sensors, enabling them to perform tasks such as aerial photography, surveying, delivery services, and environmental monitoring. The ability of drones to reach remote or hazardous areas makes them invaluable tools in disaster response, infrastructure inspection, and agriculture.

In agriculture, drones are revolutionizing farming practices through precision agriculture. They provide farmers with detailed aerial imagery and data on crop health, soil conditions, and irrigation needs. This information allows farmers to make informed decisions about planting, fertilization, and pest control, leading to increased yields and reduced resource usage. Autonomous drones can also perform tasks like planting seeds, spraying crops, and monitoring livestock, further enhancing agricultural efficiency.

Autonomous systems extend beyond land and air; they also operate underwater. Autonomous underwater vehicles (AUVs) are used for oceanographic research, underwater exploration, and inspection of underwater infrastructure such as pipelines and cables. These vehicles are equipped with sensors and cameras to navigate and collect data in challenging underwater environments. AUVs play a crucial role in marine biology, environmental monitoring, and underwater archaeology, providing valuable insights into the world beneath the sea.

In industrial settings, autonomous robots are transforming manufacturing and logistics. Collaborative robots, or cobots, work alongside human workers, assisting with tasks such as assembly, packaging, and quality control. These robots are designed to be safe and adaptable, able to learn new tasks and operate in dynamic environments. By taking over repetitive and physically demanding tasks, cobots improve productivity and reduce the risk of workplace injuries.

Autonomous systems also enhance warehouse operations through automated guided vehicles (AGVs) and autonomous mobile robots (AMRs). AGVs follow predefined paths to transport goods within a warehouse, while AMRs use sensors and AI to navigate dynamically, avoiding obstacles and optimizing routes. These systems streamline inventory management, reduce operational costs, and enable faster order fulfillment, meeting the demands of modern e-commerce.

The healthcare industry is increasingly adopting autonomous systems to improve patient care and operational efficiency. Autonomous robots are used for tasks such as medication delivery, disinfection, and patient monitoring. For example, robots equipped with UV light can autonomously disinfect hospital rooms, reducing the spread of infections. In surgical settings, autonomous robotic systems assist surgeons with precision tasks, improving the accuracy and outcomes of procedures.

The integration of autonomous systems in healthcare extends to telemedicine and home care. Autonomous robots can assist elderly and disabled individuals with daily activities, providing companionship and monitoring their health. These systems enable remote patient care, reducing the need for hospital visits and allowing healthcare providers to monitor patients' conditions in real-time.

The development of autonomous systems is driven by advancements in AI and machine learning. These technologies enable machines to process sensory data, learn from experiences, and make decisions. For instance, reinforcement learning, a type of machine learning, allows autonomous systems to learn optimal behaviors through trial and error. This approach is particularly useful in dynamic and unpredictable environments, such as self-driving cars navigating city streets.

The use of neural networks, particularly deep learning, has significantly improved the performance of autonomous systems. Deep learning models can analyze complex patterns in sensory data, enabling machines to recognize objects, understand scenes, and predict outcomes. These models are trained on large datasets, allowing them to generalize from training data to real-world scenarios.

Despite the remarkable progress, the deployment of autonomous systems faces several challenges. One major challenge is ensuring the safety and reliability of these systems. Autonomous vehicles, for example, must operate flawlessly in diverse and unpredictable conditions to gain public trust. Rigorous testing, simulation, and validation are essential to ensure that autonomous systems can handle a wide range of scenarios without causing accidents or failures.

Ethical considerations also play a critical role in the development of autonomous systems. Decisions made by these systems can have significant consequences, raising questions about accountability, transparency, and fairness. For instance, in the case of autonomous vehicles, ethical dilemmas arise when deciding how a vehicle should respond in unavoidable accident scenarios where harm is likely regardless of the chosen action. These ethical considerations necessitate careful design and the establishment of guidelines and regulations to ensure that autonomous systems operate in a manner that aligns with societal values and priorities.

Privacy concerns are another significant issue, particularly with autonomous systems that collect and process vast amounts of data. For example, drones used for surveillance and data collection can potentially infringe on individuals' privacy rights if not properly regulated. Ensuring that data is collected, stored, and used responsibly is crucial to maintaining public trust in autonomous technologies.

The regulatory landscape for autonomous systems is still evolving. Governments and regulatory bodies around the world are working to develop frameworks that ensure the safe and ethical deployment of these technologies. For instance, the development and testing of self-driving cars require adherence to strict safety standards and thorough validation processes. Similarly, the use of drones is subject to aviation regulations that govern their operation to prevent accidents and misuse.

The integration of autonomous systems into existing infrastructure also poses technical challenges. For self-driving cars, this includes the development of smart road systems, vehicle-to-infrastructure communication, and the establishment of dedicated lanes or zones for autonomous vehicles. For drones, it involves creating air traffic management systems that can safely accommodate the increasing number of unmanned aerial vehicles sharing the skies.

Collaboration between industry stakeholders, academia, and governments is essential to address these challenges and foster innovation. Public-private partnerships can facilitate the development of standardized technologies, promote best practices, and accelerate the adoption of autonomous systems. Research institutions play a crucial role in advancing the underlying technologies, while industry players drive commercialization and large-scale deployment.

Despite these challenges, the potential benefits of autonomous systems are immense. In transportation, self-driving cars have the potential to drastically reduce traffic accidents, which are often caused by human error. They can also improve mobility for individuals who are unable to drive, such as the elderly or disabled, and reduce the need for parking space in urban areas through efficient ride-sharing models.

In logistics, autonomous systems can significantly enhance efficiency and reduce costs. Autonomous delivery drones and ground vehicles can expedite last-mile delivery, providing faster and more reliable services. Warehouses equipped with autonomous robots can operate around the clock, optimizing inventory management and order fulfillment processes.

In agriculture, the use of autonomous systems can lead to more sustainable and productive farming practices. Precision agriculture enabled by drones and autonomous tractors allows for targeted application of inputs, reducing waste and environmental impact. Autonomous systems can also help monitor crop health and manage resources more effectively, contributing to food security and resilience against climate change.

In healthcare, autonomous systems can improve patient outcomes and operational efficiency. Robots that assist with surgery, patient care, and logistics can reduce the workload on healthcare professionals, allowing them to focus on more complex and critical tasks. Autonomous systems also enable continuous monitoring and data collection, providing valuable insights for personalized medicine and preventive care.

The future of autonomous systems is closely tied to advancements in AI, machine learning, and sensor technologies. Continued research and development in these areas will lead to more capable, reliable, and versatile autonomous systems. The integration of AI with other emerging technologies, such as the Internet of Things (IoT) and 5G networks, will further enhance the capabilities of autonomous systems by enabling real-time data processing and communication.

In urban environments, the concept of smart cities is gaining traction, where autonomous systems play a central role in enhancing urban living. Smart cities leverage autonomous systems for transportation, energy management, waste management, and public safety. Autonomous vehicles can reduce traffic congestion and emissions, while autonomous drones can monitor infrastructure and deliver essential services. The integration of autonomous systems with IoT devices and smart infrastructure can lead to more efficient and sustainable urban environments.

In the realm of defense and security, autonomous systems are being developed for a wide range of applications, from surveillance and reconnaissance to search and rescue missions. Autonomous drones and ground robots can operate in hazardous environments, providing critical support to military and emergency response teams. These systems can also enhance border security and infrastructure protection, leveraging advanced sensors and AI for threat detection and response.

The deployment of autonomous systems also has significant economic implications. The automation of tasks across various industries can lead to increased productivity and economic growth. However, it also raises concerns about job displacement and the need for workforce adaptation. Ensuring that workers are equipped with the skills needed to thrive in an automated world is essential. This may involve reskilling programs, education initiatives, and policies that support workforce transitions.

In conclusion, autonomous systems represent a transformative technology with the potential to revolutionize numerous industries. From self-driving cars and drones to industrial robots and healthcare assistants, these systems offer unprecedented opportunities for efficiency, safety, and innovation. While challenges related to safety, ethics, privacy, and regulation must be addressed, the benefits of autonomous systems are substantial. As research and development continue to advance, the integration of AI, machine learning, and sensor technologies will drive the evolution of autonomous systems, shaping the future of transportation, logistics, agriculture, healthcare, and beyond. The collaborative efforts of industry stakeholders, academia, and governments will be crucial in realizing the full potential of autonomous systems and ensuring their responsible and beneficial deployment in society.

7. **AI Ethics**: Moral implications and guidelines for AI development and deployment.

AI ethics is a crucial field that addresses the moral implications and guidelines for the development and deployment of artificial intelligence (AI). As AI technologies become increasingly integrated into various aspects of society, it is essential to consider the ethical challenges they pose and establish frameworks to ensure their responsible use. This involves a multidisciplinary approach, combining insights from philosophy, law, computer science, and social sciences to navigate the complex landscape of AI ethics.

One of the primary ethical concerns in AI is the potential for bias and discrimination. AI systems learn from data, and if the training data contains biases, the AI can perpetuate and even amplify these biases in its decisions. This can result in unfair treatment of individuals or groups based on race, gender, age, or other characteristics. For example, biased algorithms in hiring processes can disadvantage certain demographic groups, while biased facial recognition systems can lead to higher rates of misidentification for minorities. Addressing bias requires rigorous testing, diverse and representative datasets, and ongoing monitoring to ensure fairness and equity.

Transparency and accountability are also critical ethical considerations in AI. Many AI systems operate as "black boxes," meaning their decision-making processes are not easily understandable or explainable. This lack of transparency can lead to mistrust and hinder the ability to hold AI systems accountable for their actions. To mitigate this, there is a growing emphasis on developing explainable AI (XAI) that provides insights into how decisions are made. Additionally, establishing clear lines of responsibility for AI decisions is essential, ensuring that developers, users, and organizations can be held accountable for the outcomes of AI systems.

Privacy is another significant ethical concern in AI. AI systems often rely on vast amounts of data, including personal and sensitive information, to function effectively. The collection, storage, and use of this data raise questions about individuals' privacy rights. Ensuring that AI systems adhere to data protection regulations, such as the General Data Protection Regulation (GDPR) in the European Union, is vital to safeguarding privacy. Moreover, developing privacy-preserving AI techniques, such as differential privacy and federated learning, can help minimize the risks associated with data usage.

The potential for AI to be used in surveillance and monitoring poses further ethical challenges. AI-powered surveillance systems can track individuals' movements, behaviors, and interactions, raising concerns about state and corporate overreach and the erosion of civil liberties. Balancing the benefits of AI in enhancing security and public safety with the need to protect individual freedoms is a delicate task. Establishing robust oversight mechanisms and legal safeguards can help prevent the misuse of AI for intrusive surveillance.

Autonomy and decision-making by AI systems also raise ethical questions. As AI systems become more capable of making decisions autonomously, it is crucial to consider the implications of delegating decision-making authority to machines. This is particularly important in high-stakes domains such as healthcare, criminal justice, and autonomous vehicles, where AI decisions can have significant consequences for individuals' lives and well-being. Ensuring that AI systems are designed with appropriate levels of human oversight and intervention is essential to maintain ethical standards and protect human dignity.

The impact of AI on employment and the workforce is another critical ethical issue. While AI has the potential to increase productivity and create new job opportunities, it also poses a risk of job displacement and economic inequality. Automation of routine tasks can lead to significant job losses in certain sectors, disproportionately affecting low-skilled workers. Addressing these challenges requires proactive measures, such as investing in education and reskilling programs, to prepare the workforce for the changing job landscape. Policymakers and organizations must also consider the broader economic and social implications of AI deployment to ensure inclusive growth.

AI's role in decision-making and governance also warrants ethical consideration. AI systems are increasingly being used to assist or even replace human decision-makers in various contexts, from financial services to public administration. While AI can enhance efficiency and objectivity, it also raises concerns about the erosion of human agency and the potential for technocratic governance. Ensuring that AI is used as a tool to augment human decision-making, rather than replace it, is crucial for maintaining democratic values and empowering individuals.

The ethical implications of AI extend to the design and development process itself. Ensuring that AI systems are built with ethical considerations in mind from the outset is essential for responsible AI deployment. This involves incorporating ethical principles, such as fairness, transparency, and accountability, into the design and development phases. Ethical AI development also requires interdisciplinary collaboration, bringing together experts from various fields to address the multifaceted challenges posed by AI.

International collaboration and governance are vital for addressing the ethical challenges of AI on a global scale. As AI technologies transcend national borders, there is a need for coordinated efforts to establish international norms and standards. Organizations such as the United Nations, the European Union, and the OECD are working to develop frameworks for AI governance that promote ethical principles and ensure the responsible use of AI worldwide. These efforts include the establishment of ethical guidelines, regulatory frameworks, and mechanisms for international cooperation.

Public engagement and awareness are also crucial components of AI ethics. Ensuring that the public is informed about the benefits and risks of AI technologies is essential for fostering trust and promoting responsible use. Public consultations, education initiatives, and transparent communication can help demystify AI and address concerns. Engaging diverse stakeholders, including marginalized communities, in discussions about AI ethics can ensure that different perspectives are considered and that AI systems are designed to serve the needs of all members of society.

Ethical considerations in AI also encompass the long-term implications and potential existential risks associated with advanced AI. As AI systems become more powerful and autonomous, there is a need to consider the potential for unintended consequences and the broader impact on humanity. Ensuring that AI development is aligned with human values and that safeguards are in place to prevent harmful outcomes is critical for the future of AI. This includes ongoing research into AI safety and the development of frameworks for the ethical oversight of AI technologies.

In conclusion, AI ethics is a multifaceted field that addresses the moral implications and guidelines for the development and deployment of AI technologies. It encompasses a wide range of issues, including bias and discrimination, transparency and accountability, privacy, surveillance, autonomy, employment, governance, and long-term risks. Addressing these challenges requires a multidisciplinary approach, combining insights from philosophy, law, computer science, and social sciences. International collaboration, public engagement, and interdisciplinary collaboration are essential for establishing ethical frameworks and ensuring the responsible use of AI. As AI continues to evolve and integrate into various aspects of society, it is crucial to prioritize ethical considerations to harness the benefits of AI while mitigating its risks and ensuring that it serves the greater good.

Cybersecurity

Cybersecurity is a critical aspect of modern technology, aiming to protect systems, networks, and data from digital attacks. As cyber threats become increasingly sophisticated, the methods and tools used to secure information must also evolve. Key components of cybersecurity include encryption, firewalls, cyber threat management, blockchain technology, penetration testing, cryptography, and zero trust security. Each of these plays a unique role in creating a robust defense against cyber attacks.

Encryption is one of the fundamental techniques used in cybersecurity to secure data by converting it into a code that can only be deciphered with a specific key. This process ensures that even if data is intercepted during transmission or accessed by unauthorized individuals, it remains unreadable without the decryption key. There are two main types of encryption: symmetric and asymmetric. Symmetric encryption uses the same key for both encryption and decryption, making it fast and efficient for encrypting large amounts of data. However, the key must be securely shared between the sender and receiver. Asymmetric encryption, on the other hand, uses a pair of keys: a public key for encryption and a private key for decryption. This method enhances security by eliminating the need to share the private key, but it is computationally more intensive.

Firewalls are another essential component of cybersecurity, acting as security systems that monitor and control incoming and outgoing network traffic based on predetermined security rules. They serve as barriers between trusted internal networks and untrusted external networks, such as the internet. Firewalls can be hardware-based, software-based, or a combination of both. They use various techniques to filter traffic, including packet filtering, stateful inspection, and proxy services. Packet filtering examines individual packets of data and allows or blocks them based on source and destination IP addresses, port numbers, and protocols. Stateful inspection tracks the state of active connections and makes decisions based on the context of the traffic. Proxy services act as intermediaries between users and the internet, filtering requests and responses to ensure they meet security criteria.

Cyber threats are potential dangers that can compromise the security of systems and data. These threats come in many forms, including viruses, malware, and phishing attacks. Viruses are malicious programs that replicate themselves by attaching to other software and can cause significant damage to systems and data. Malware is a broader category that includes viruses, worms, Trojans, ransomware, and spyware. Each type of malware has a specific method of attack and potential impact. Phishing attacks involve tricking individuals into revealing sensitive information, such as passwords or credit card numbers, by pretending to be a trustworthy entity in electronic communications. These attacks often use email or fake websites to deceive victims.

Blockchain technology offers a novel approach to cybersecurity through its distributed ledger system, which ensures secure and transparent transactions. Blockchain records transactions across multiple computers in a decentralized network, making it difficult for any single entity to alter the data without consensus from the entire network. Each block in the chain contains a cryptographic hash of the previous block, a timestamp, and transaction data. This structure creates an immutable and tamper-evident record of transactions. Blockchain is particularly useful in financial services, supply chain management, and any application requiring secure, verifiable transactions.

Penetration testing, also known as ethical hacking, involves simulating cyber attacks to identify vulnerabilities in systems, networks, and applications. These tests are conducted by security professionals who use the same techniques as malicious hackers to find weaknesses that could be exploited. Penetration testing can be performed internally by the organization's own IT staff or externally by third-party firms. The process typically includes reconnaissance, scanning, gaining access, maintaining access, and covering tracks. By identifying and addressing vulnerabilities before they can be exploited, organizations can significantly improve their security posture.

Cryptography encompasses various methods of protecting information through encoding, ensuring that only authorized parties can access the data. Beyond encryption, cryptography includes techniques such as hashing and digital signatures. Hashing involves converting data into a fixed-size string of characters, which acts as a unique identifier for the data. Even a small change in the original data will produce a significantly different hash value, making it useful for verifying data integrity. Digital signatures use a combination of hashing and asymmetric encryption to verify the authenticity and integrity of digital messages or documents. They provide a way to ensure that the data has not been altered and that it originated from a legitimate source.

Zero trust security is a modern security model that requires strict identity verification for every user and device attempting to access resources, regardless of their location within or outside the network. Unlike traditional security models that assume users within the network can be trusted, zero trust operates on the principle of "never trust, always verify." This approach involves continuous monitoring and validation of all access requests, ensuring that only authenticated and authorized users and devices can access sensitive resources. Key components of zero trust security include multi-factor authentication, micro-segmentation, and the principle of least privilege. Multi-factor authentication requires users to provide multiple forms of verification, such as a password and a fingerprint, before gaining access. Micro-segmentation involves dividing the network into smaller, isolated segments to limit the lateral movement of attackers. The principle of least privilege ensures that users and devices have the minimum level of access necessary to perform their tasks, reducing the risk of unauthorized access.

The integration of these components creates a comprehensive cybersecurity strategy. Encryption protects data both at rest and in transit, ensuring that sensitive information remains secure even if it is intercepted. Firewalls act as the first line of defense, filtering traffic and preventing unauthorized access to the network. Effective management of cyber threats involves continuous monitoring and updating of security measures to detect and respond to new threats. Blockchain technology provides a secure framework for transactions, ensuring data integrity and transparency. Penetration testing helps organizations proactively identify and address vulnerabilities before they can be exploited by malicious actors. Cryptography provides the foundational tools for securing data, verifying integrity, and authenticating sources. Zero trust security ensures that access to resources is tightly controlled and continuously monitored, reducing the risk of breaches.

The importance of cybersecurity cannot be overstated, as cyber attacks can have devastating consequences for individuals, businesses, and governments. Data breaches can result in the loss of sensitive information, financial losses, reputational damage, and legal liabilities. Ransomware attacks can disrupt operations and extort money from victims. State-sponsored cyber attacks can threaten national security and critical infrastructure. Therefore, it is essential for organizations to implement robust cybersecurity measures and stay vigilant against evolving threats.

Education and training are also critical components of a successful cybersecurity strategy. Employees should be aware of the common tactics used by cyber attackers, such as phishing, and know how to recognize and respond to potential threats. Regular training sessions and simulated phishing attacks can help reinforce good security practices and reduce the risk of human error.

Collaboration and information sharing among organizations, industries, and governments are essential for effective cybersecurity. By sharing threat intelligence and best practices, entities can better defend against common threats and respond more quickly to emerging attacks. Public-private partnerships and international cooperation are vital for addressing the global nature of cyber threats and developing coordinated responses.

In conclusion, cybersecurity is a multifaceted field that requires a combination of technologies, practices, and policies to protect systems, networks, and data from cyber threats. Encryption, firewalls, cyber threat management, blockchain, penetration testing, cryptography, and zero trust security each play a crucial role in building a robust defense against cyber attacks. As cyber threats continue to evolve, it is essential for organizations to stay informed, implement comprehensive security measures, and foster a culture of cybersecurity awareness. By doing so, they can protect their assets, maintain trust, and ensure the resilience of their operations in the face of an increasingly complex and dangerous cyber landscape.

8. **Encryption**: Techniques for securing data by converting it into code.

Encryption is a fundamental technique in cybersecurity, essential for protecting sensitive information by converting it into a coded format that can only be deciphered by those who possess the appropriate decryption key. This process ensures the confidentiality, integrity, and authenticity of data, whether it is stored or transmitted across networks. As cyber threats continue to evolve, encryption remains a critical defense mechanism against unauthorized access, data breaches, and various forms of cyberattacks.

The concept of encryption is not new; it has been used for centuries to secure communication. The earliest forms of encryption, known as classical encryption, involved simple techniques such as substitution ciphers and transposition ciphers. One of the most famous historical examples is the Caesar cipher, named after Julius Caesar, who used it to encrypt his military commands. In the Caesar cipher, each letter in the plaintext is shifted by a fixed number of positions down the alphabet. While effective in its time, classical encryption methods are easily broken by modern standards.

Modern encryption techniques are far more sophisticated and can be broadly classified into two categories: symmetric-key encryption and asymmetric-key encryption. Each of these categories has its own set of algorithms and use cases, offering varying levels of security and performance.

Symmetric-key encryption, also known as secret-key encryption, involves a single key for both encryption and decryption. This means that both the sender and the receiver must possess the same key and keep it secret. The security of symmetric-key encryption relies heavily on the secrecy of the key. Some of the most widely used symmetric-key algorithms include the Data Encryption Standard (DES), Triple DES (3DES), and the Advanced Encryption Standard (AES).

AES, in particular, is the most widely adopted symmetric-key algorithm today. It was established by the U.S. National Institute of Standards and Technology (NIST) in 2001, replacing DES due to its vulnerabilities. AES operates on fixed-size blocks of data (128 bits) and supports key sizes of 128, 192, and 256 bits. Its robustness and efficiency make it suitable for a wide range of applications, from securing financial transactions to protecting data on personal devices.

While symmetric-key encryption is efficient, it has a significant drawback: key distribution. The need to securely share the encryption key between parties presents a challenge, especially over untrusted networks. This limitation led to the development of asymmetric-key encryption, which uses a pair of keys: a public key and a private key.

Asymmetric-key encryption, also known as public-key encryption, involves two mathematically related keys. The public key is used for encryption and can be shared openly, while the private key is used for decryption and must be kept secret. This key pair mechanism eliminates the key distribution problem inherent in symmetric-key encryption. RSA (Rivest-Shamir-Adleman) is one of the most well-known asymmetric-key algorithms and has been widely used since its introduction in the late 1970s.

RSA's security is based on the mathematical difficulty of factoring large prime numbers. It supports key lengths of 1024 bits, 2048 bits, and higher, with longer keys providing increased security. However, RSA is computationally intensive, making it less suitable for encrypting large amounts of data. Instead, it is often used to encrypt small pieces of data, such as encryption keys, which can then be used in symmetric-key encryption for bulk data.

Another important asymmetric-key algorithm is Elliptic Curve Cryptography (ECC). ECC offers similar levels of security to RSA but with much shorter key lengths, resulting in faster computations and lower resource consumption. This makes ECC particularly attractive for use in mobile devices and other environments where computational efficiency is crucial.

In practice, modern encryption systems often use a combination of symmetric and asymmetric encryption in a hybrid approach. For example, during a secure web transaction (HTTPS), asymmetric encryption is used to securely exchange a symmetric session key. This session key is then used to encrypt the bulk of the data exchanged between the client and the server, leveraging the efficiency of symmetric encryption while benefiting from the secure key exchange provided by asymmetric encryption.

Encryption not only protects the confidentiality of data but also plays a crucial role in ensuring data integrity and authenticity. This is achieved through techniques such as hashing and digital signatures. Hashing involves transforming data into a fixed-size hash value or digest using a hash function. Popular hash functions include SHA-256 (Secure Hash Algorithm 256-bit) and MD5 (Message Digest Algorithm 5). Even a small change in the input data results in a significantly different hash value, making it useful for verifying data integrity.

Digital signatures combine hashing and asymmetric encryption to provide both data integrity and authenticity. When a sender signs a message, they create a hash of the message and then encrypt the hash with their private key. The resulting digital signature can be verified by the recipient using the sender's public key. If the hash of the received message matches the decrypted hash from the signature, it confirms that the message has not been altered and indeed originated from the sender.

While encryption is a powerful tool for securing data, it is not without challenges. One of the primary concerns is key management. Ensuring that encryption keys are securely generated, distributed, stored, and eventually destroyed is critical to maintaining the security of the encrypted data. Compromised keys can lead to unauthorized access, rendering the encryption useless.

Another challenge is the balance between security and performance. Strong encryption algorithms and long key lengths provide higher security but also require more computational resources, which can impact performance. This trade-off must be carefully managed, especially in resource-constrained environments such as IoT devices.

Additionally, the emergence of quantum computing poses a significant threat to current encryption algorithms. Quantum computers have the potential to break widely used algorithms like RSA and ECC through their ability to solve complex mathematical problems much faster than classical computers. This has led to the development of post-quantum cryptography, which aims to create encryption algorithms that are resistant to quantum attacks. Researchers are actively working on new cryptographic techniques to ensure the long-term security of data in the face of quantum computing advancements.

Encryption is also subject to legal and regulatory considerations. Governments and regulatory bodies around the world have established laws and standards to govern the use of encryption, often requiring organizations to implement encryption for protecting sensitive data. For example, the General Data Protection Regulation (GDPR) in the European Union mandates the use of encryption to protect personal data. However, there is also ongoing debate over the balance between strong encryption for privacy and security and the need for lawful access by authorities for national security and law enforcement purposes.

In conclusion, encryption is a vital technique for securing data by converting it into code that can only be deciphered by authorized parties. It encompasses a range of methods and algorithms, from symmetric-key and asymmetric-key encryption to hashing and digital signatures, each with its own strengths and applications. While encryption provides robust protection for data confidentiality, integrity, and authenticity, it also presents challenges related to key management, performance, and evolving threats such as quantum computing. As cyber threats continue to grow, the importance of encryption in safeguarding information and maintaining trust in digital systems cannot be overstated. Ongoing research, development, and collaboration among industry, academia, and regulatory bodies are essential to advancing encryption technologies and ensuring their effective and responsible use in an increasingly digital world.

9. **Firewalls**: Security systems that monitor and control network traffic.

Firewalls are essential security systems that monitor and control network traffic based on predetermined security rules. They serve as barriers between trusted internal networks and untrusted external networks, such as the internet, effectively acting as gatekeepers that manage data flow and protect against unauthorized access, cyberattacks, and other security threats. Firewalls are a critical component of any robust cybersecurity strategy, ensuring that only legitimate traffic is allowed while malicious or suspicious activity is blocked.

The concept of firewalls dates back to the late 1980s when the growing interconnectedness of networks led to increased security concerns. Early firewalls were relatively simple, using basic packet filtering techniques to control access. However, as cyber threats have evolved, so too have firewall technologies, becoming more sophisticated and capable of handling a wide range of security functions.

Modern firewalls can be categorized into several types, each offering different levels of protection and features. These include packet-filtering firewalls, stateful inspection firewalls, proxy firewalls, and next-generation firewalls (NGFWs).

Packet-filtering firewalls are the most basic type and operate at the network layer of the OSI model. They inspect each packet of data that enters or leaves the network, checking the packet headers against a set of predefined rules. These rules typically involve criteria such as source and destination IP addresses, port numbers, and protocols. If a packet matches the rules, it is allowed to pass through; if not, it is blocked. While packet-filtering firewalls are efficient and straightforward, they have limitations. They do not inspect the payload of packets, making them vulnerable to attacks that use allowed protocols and ports.

Stateful inspection firewalls, also known as dynamic packet-filtering firewalls, offer a more advanced level of security. They not only inspect packet headers but also track the state of active connections. By maintaining a state table, these firewalls can make decisions based on the context of the traffic rather than just individual packets. For example, they can recognize whether an incoming packet is part of an established connection or an unsolicited attempt to access the network. This capability allows stateful inspection firewalls to provide more accurate filtering and protection against attacks.

Proxy firewalls, also known as application-level gateways, operate at the application layer of the OSI model. They act as intermediaries between internal and external networks, processing requests on behalf of users. When a user makes a request to access an external resource, the proxy firewall evaluates the request and, if deemed safe, forwards it to the destination. The response from the external resource is similarly inspected before being sent back to the user. This process effectively isolates the internal network from direct contact with external servers, providing an additional layer of security. Proxy firewalls can perform deep packet inspection, examining the content of packets to detect and block malicious activity at the application level.

Next-generation firewalls (NGFWs) represent the latest evolution in firewall technology, integrating traditional firewall capabilities with advanced features such as intrusion prevention systems (IPS), deep packet inspection, application awareness, and control, and user identity management. NGFWs can inspect traffic at multiple layers, from the network to the application layer, and use advanced threat detection techniques to identify and block sophisticated attacks. They can also enforce security policies based on the specific applications being used, the identity of users, and other contextual factors. This comprehensive approach enables NGFWs to provide more granular control and better protection against modern threats.

Firewalls can be implemented as hardware appliances, software solutions, or cloud-based services. Hardware firewalls are dedicated devices installed at the network perimeter, providing high performance and reliability. They are typically used in enterprise environments where they can handle large volumes of traffic and offer robust protection. Software firewalls, on the other hand, are installed on individual devices or servers. They are often used in smaller networks or to provide an additional layer of security on end-user devices. Cloud-based firewalls, also known as firewall-as-a-service (FWaaS), offer flexible and scalable protection for cloud environments and remote users. They can be managed and updated centrally, ensuring consistent security policies across distributed networks.

The primary function of firewalls is to enforce security policies by filtering traffic based on predefined rules. These rules can be tailored to meet the specific needs of an organization, allowing for precise control over what traffic is allowed or blocked. For example, rules can be set to allow traffic only from trusted IP addresses, block access to known malicious sites, or permit specific applications while denying others. Firewalls can also be configured to detect and respond to suspicious activity, such as attempts to exploit vulnerabilities or conduct denial-of-service (DoS) attacks.

Firewalls play a crucial role in protecting against various cyber threats. They can prevent unauthorized access by blocking inbound traffic from untrusted sources and limiting outbound traffic to approved destinations. This helps to mitigate the risk of data breaches, malware infections, and other security incidents. Firewalls can also protect against attacks that target specific vulnerabilities in network protocols or applications, such as SQL injection or cross-site scripting (XSS). By inspecting and filtering traffic at multiple layers, firewalls can detect and block these attacks before they reach their targets.

In addition to their role in network security, firewalls can also provide valuable insights into network activity. They generate logs and reports that can be analyzed to identify patterns, detect anomalies, and investigate security incidents. This information can be used to fine-tune security policies, improve threat detection, and enhance overall network visibility. Many firewalls also offer integration with security information and event management (SIEM) systems, enabling centralized monitoring and correlation of security events across the entire network.

Despite their many benefits, firewalls are not a silver bullet and must be used in conjunction with other security measures to provide comprehensive protection. For example, firewalls cannot protect against threats that bypass the network perimeter, such as insider threats or malware delivered via removable media. They also cannot prevent users from falling victim to social engineering attacks, such as phishing or pretexting. Therefore, it is essential to implement a multi-layered security strategy that includes endpoint protection, intrusion detection and prevention, secure access controls, regular security training, and other best practices.

The effectiveness of a firewall depends on proper configuration and management. Misconfigured firewalls can create security gaps that can be exploited by attackers. It is crucial to regularly review and update firewall rules to ensure they align with current security policies and address emerging threats. Regular audits and vulnerability assessments can help identify and remediate weaknesses in firewall configurations. Additionally, keeping firewall software and firmware up to date is essential to protect against known vulnerabilities and ensure optimal performance.

In recent years, the rise of cloud computing, remote work, and the Internet of Things (IoT) has introduced new challenges for firewall management. Traditional perimeter-based security models are becoming less effective as the network perimeter becomes more diffuse and dynamic. To address these challenges, organizations are adopting new approaches, such as zero trust security and software-defined perimeter (SDP) solutions. These approaches emphasize the importance of verifying the identity and integrity of every device, user, and application, regardless of their location, and dynamically controlling access based on real-time risk assessments.

Firewalls continue to evolve to meet the changing threat landscape and the needs of modern networks. Advanced technologies such as artificial intelligence (AI) and machine learning (ML) are being integrated into firewalls to enhance their threat detection and response capabilities. These technologies can analyze vast amounts of network data to identify patterns and anomalies that may indicate malicious activity. By continuously learning from new data, AI-powered firewalls can adapt to evolving threats and improve their effectiveness over time.

Another emerging trend is the use of micro-segmentation to enhance network security. Micro-segmentation involves dividing the network into smaller, isolated segments, each with its own security policies and controls. This approach limits the lateral movement of attackers within the network and reduces the potential impact of a security breach. Firewalls play a key role in implementing micro-segmentation by enforcing traffic controls between segments and ensuring that only authorized communication is allowed.

In conclusion, firewalls are indispensable tools for securing networks by monitoring and controlling traffic based on predefined rules. They have evolved significantly from simple packet filters to sophisticated next-generation firewalls that offer comprehensive protection against modern cyber threats. By enforcing security policies, detecting and blocking malicious activity, and providing valuable insights into network activity, firewalls help organizations safeguard their data and systems. However, to be truly effective, firewalls must be part of a multi-layered security strategy that includes other protective measures and best practices. As technology continues to advance and the threat landscape evolves, firewalls will remain a critical component of cybersecurity, adapting to new challenges and helping to ensure the security and resilience of networks worldwide.

10. **Cyber Threats**: Potential dangers like viruses, malware, and phishing.

Cyber threats encompass a wide range of potential dangers that pose significant risks to the security, integrity, and availability of information systems and data. These threats include viruses, malware, phishing attacks, ransomware, and more. As our reliance on digital technology grows, so too does the sophistication and frequency of cyber threats, making it imperative for individuals, organizations, and governments to understand and mitigate these risks.

Viruses are one of the earliest and most well-known forms of cyber threats. A virus is a type of malicious software, or malware, that attaches itself to legitimate programs or files and replicates itself when those programs or files are executed. Once activated, a virus can corrupt, delete, or steal data, disrupt system operations, and spread to other systems. Early computer viruses, such as the Brain virus in 1986, were relatively simple, but modern viruses can be highly complex and damaging. To protect against viruses, it is essential to use up-to-date antivirus software, implement regular system scans, and avoid downloading or opening unknown files and email attachments.

Malware, a broader category of malicious software, includes viruses, worms, Trojans, ransomware, spyware, adware, and more. Each type of malware has its unique method of operation and impact. Worms, for instance, are self-replicating programs that spread independently across networks, exploiting vulnerabilities to infect multiple systems. Unlike viruses, worms do not need to attach themselves to a host file. The infamous Mydoom worm, which appeared in 2004, is an example of a fast-spreading and highly disruptive worm that caused extensive damage worldwide.

Trojans, or Trojan horses, disguise themselves as legitimate software to trick users into executing them. Once installed, a Trojan can create backdoors, allowing attackers to gain unauthorized access to the infected system. Trojans can also be used to steal sensitive information, log keystrokes, or download additional malware. One notorious example is the Zeus Trojan, which targeted banking credentials and caused significant financial losses.

Ransomware is a particularly insidious type of malware that encrypts a victim's data and demands a ransom payment in exchange for the decryption key. This form of cyber extortion has become increasingly prevalent, with high-profile attacks on businesses, healthcare institutions, and government agencies. The WannaCry ransomware attack in 2017, which exploited a vulnerability in Microsoft Windows, affected hundreds of thousands of computers across more than 150 countries. Ransomware attacks can result in significant financial losses, operational disruptions, and reputational damage. To defend against ransomware, it is crucial to maintain regular data backups, implement robust security measures, and educate users about the risks of phishing and malicious downloads.

Phishing attacks are a common method used by cybercriminals to deceive individuals into divulging sensitive information, such as usernames, passwords, and credit card details. Phishing typically involves sending fraudulent emails or messages that appear to come from legitimate sources, such as banks, social media platforms, or trusted contacts. These messages often contain urgent or enticing content, prompting recipients to click on malicious links or download infected attachments. Once the victim provides the requested information, the attacker can use it for identity theft, financial fraud, or further cyberattacks.

Spear phishing is a more targeted form of phishing, where attackers tailor their messages to specific individuals or organizations. By using personal information gathered from social media or other sources, spear phishers increase the likelihood of success. For example, a spear-phishing email might appear to come from a colleague or supervisor, making it more convincing and harder to detect. To protect against phishing and spear phishing, individuals and organizations should be cautious of unsolicited messages, verify the authenticity of requests for sensitive information, and use email filtering and authentication technologies.

Apart from these common types of cyber threats, there are several other sophisticated and emerging threats that pose significant risks. Advanced Persistent Threats (APTs) are prolonged and targeted cyberattacks, often orchestrated by state-sponsored or highly skilled adversaries. APTs aim to gain and maintain unauthorized access to a network over an extended period, typically to steal sensitive data or intellectual property. Unlike conventional cyberattacks that focus on immediate damage, APTs are stealthy and can remain undetected for months or even years. They employ a combination of techniques, including social engineering, malware, and exploiting zero-day vulnerabilities. Organizations must implement advanced security measures, continuous monitoring, and threat intelligence to detect and mitigate APTs effectively.

Zero-day vulnerabilities refer to security flaws in software or hardware that are unknown to the vendor and have not been patched. Cybercriminals exploit these vulnerabilities before they can be addressed, making zero-day attacks highly effective and dangerous. Zero-day exploits are often sold on the dark web, making them accessible to a wide range of threat actors. Protecting against zero-day attacks requires a proactive approach, including regular software updates, vulnerability assessments, and employing advanced threat detection technologies.

Distributed Denial of Service (DDoS) attacks are another significant cyber threat, aiming to overwhelm a target's network or website with a flood of traffic, rendering it inaccessible. DDoS attacks are typically carried out using a botnet, a network of compromised devices controlled by the attacker. These attacks can cause severe disruptions to online services, leading to financial losses and reputational damage. Mitigating DDoS attacks involves using DDoS protection services, implementing network redundancy, and employing rate limiting and traffic filtering techniques.

Social engineering is a psychological manipulation technique used by cybercriminals to trick individuals into divulging confidential information or performing actions that compromise security. Social engineering attacks exploit human behavior and emotions, such as curiosity, fear, or trust. Common social engineering tactics include pretexting, baiting, and tailgating. Pretexting involves creating a fabricated scenario to obtain sensitive information, while baiting uses enticing offers, such as free software or USB drives, to lure victims into downloading malware or providing credentials. Tailgating, also known as piggybacking, involves an attacker physically following an authorized person into a restricted area. Organizations should conduct regular security awareness training to help employees recognize and respond to social engineering attempts.

Insider threats pose significant risks, as they involve individuals within an organization who have authorized access to systems and data. Insiders can be employees, contractors, or business partners who misuse their access for malicious purposes, such as stealing sensitive information, disrupting operations, or sabotaging systems. Insider threats can be difficult to detect, as insiders often have legitimate access and knowledge of the organization's security measures. Mitigating insider threats requires a combination of technical controls, such as monitoring and access management, and organizational measures, such as background checks, employee training, and fostering a culture of security.

Cyber threats are continually evolving, with attackers developing new techniques and exploiting emerging technologies. The rise of the Internet of Things (IoT) has introduced new vulnerabilities, as many IoT devices lack robust security features and can be easily compromised. Attackers can use these devices as entry points to infiltrate networks or as part of a botnet for DDoS attacks. Ensuring the security of IoT devices involves implementing strong authentication, encryption, regular firmware updates, and network segmentation.

Artificial intelligence (AI) and machine learning (ML) have also become both tools and targets in the realm of cybersecurity. Cybercriminals can use AI and ML to automate attacks, develop sophisticated malware, and evade detection. For example, AI-powered malware can adapt its behavior to avoid traditional signature-based detection methods. On the other hand, AI and ML can enhance cybersecurity by improving threat detection, automating response actions, and analyzing large volumes of data to identify patterns and anomalies. Organizations must leverage AI and ML responsibly, while also being aware of the potential risks and implementing safeguards to prevent misuse.

In response to the growing cyber threat landscape, governments and regulatory bodies worldwide have implemented laws and frameworks to enhance cybersecurity. Regulations such as the General Data Protection Regulation (GDPR) in the European Union and the California Consumer Privacy Act (CCPA) in the United States mandate organizations to protect personal data and report data breaches. Compliance with these regulations requires robust cybersecurity measures, including data encryption, access controls, incident response plans, and regular security assessments.

Collaboration and information sharing among organizations, industries, and governments are crucial for effective cybersecurity. By sharing threat intelligence, best practices, and lessons learned, entities can enhance their collective defense against cyber threats. Public-private partnerships, such as the Cybersecurity and Infrastructure Security Agency (CISA) in the United States, facilitate collaboration and coordination in responding to cyber incidents.

In conclusion, cyber threats represent a diverse and constantly evolving set of dangers that require a comprehensive and proactive approach to cybersecurity. Understanding the various types of threats, including viruses, malware, phishing, APTs, zero-day vulnerabilities, DDoS attacks, social engineering, and insider threats, is essential for developing effective defense strategies. Implementing strong access controls, network segmentation, endpoint security, vulnerability assessments, incident response planning, and leveraging threat intelligence are critical components of a robust cybersecurity strategy. Fostering a culture of cybersecurity awareness, collaborating with industry peers, complying with regulations, and embracing emerging technologies are also vital for protecting against cyber threats. As the digital landscape continues to grow and evolve, organizations must remain vigilant, adaptive, and committed to ensuring the security and resilience of their information systems and data.

11. **Blockchain**: Distributed ledger technology for secure transactions.

Blockchain is a revolutionary technology that underpins the world of cryptocurrencies and beyond. At its core, blockchain is a type of distributed ledger technology (DLT) that ensures the secure and transparent recording of transactions. Unlike traditional ledgers, which are centralized and controlled by a single entity, blockchains are decentralized and maintained by a network of computers, known as nodes. This decentralization is one of the key features that makes blockchain secure and resilient to tampering.

The basic structure of a blockchain consists of a chain of blocks, each containing a list of transactions. When a new transaction is initiated, it is broadcast to the network of nodes. These nodes then validate the transaction through a consensus mechanism, which can vary depending on the type of blockchain. Once validated, the transaction is added to a block. When the block is full of transactions, it is added to the chain in a way that is cryptographically linked to the previous block, ensuring the integrity and chronological order of the entire chain.

One of the most well-known consensus mechanisms is Proof of Work (PoW), which is used by Bitcoin, the first and most prominent blockchain. In PoW, nodes, also known as miners, compete to solve a complex mathematical problem. The first node to solve the problem gets to add the new block to the chain and is rewarded with newly minted cryptocurrency. This process is computationally intensive and ensures that adding a block to the blockchain requires significant effort, making it difficult for any single entity to control the network.

Another popular consensus mechanism is Proof of Stake (PoS), used by blockchains like Ethereum 2.0. In PoS, validators are chosen to add new blocks based on the amount of cryptocurrency they hold and are willing to "stake" as collateral. This method is less energy-intensive than PoW and aims to achieve the same level of security and decentralization.

Blockchain's security is further enhanced by its cryptographic nature. Each block contains a unique cryptographic hash of the previous block, creating an immutable chain of records. If an attacker tries to alter any transaction in a block, they would need to change the hash of that block and all subsequent blocks, which is computationally infeasible given the decentralized nature of the network. This immutability is a critical feature that ensures the trustworthiness of the blockchain.

Beyond cryptocurrencies, blockchain technology has numerous applications across various industries. One significant use case is in supply chain management. By recording every transaction and movement of goods on a blockchain, companies can achieve unparalleled transparency and traceability. This helps in combating fraud, counterfeiting, and inefficiencies in the supply chain. For instance, consumers can verify the authenticity of a product by tracing its journey from the manufacturer to the retailer.

In the financial sector, blockchain technology has the potential to revolutionize the way transactions are conducted. Traditional banking systems are often slow, costly, and prone to errors due to the involvement of multiple intermediaries. Blockchain can streamline this process by enabling peer-to-peer transactions without the need for intermediaries, reducing costs and increasing efficiency. Moreover, blockchain-based smart contracts, which are self-executing contracts with the terms of the agreement directly written into code, can automate various financial processes, from loan approvals to insurance claims.

The healthcare industry also stands to benefit from blockchain technology. Patient records can be securely stored and shared on a blockchain, ensuring privacy and data integrity. Patients can have control over their health data, granting access to doctors and healthcare providers as needed. This can lead to better-coordinated care and reduce administrative burdens. Additionally, blockchain can help in the fight against counterfeit drugs by tracking the production and distribution of pharmaceuticals.

In the realm of digital identity, blockchain offers a robust solution for managing identities securely. Traditional identity systems are often fragmented and vulnerable to breaches. Blockchain can provide a decentralized and tamper-proof method of verifying identities, which can be particularly useful in areas such as online voting, access to services, and reducing identity theft.

The concept of decentralized finance (DeFi) has emerged as a significant innovation within the blockchain space. DeFi refers to a range of financial services, including lending, borrowing, trading, and earning interest, that operate on blockchain platforms without traditional intermediaries. By leveraging smart contracts, DeFi platforms can offer financial services that are more accessible, transparent, and inclusive. Users can participate in financial activities directly from their digital wallets, often with lower fees and higher efficiency than traditional banking systems.

Despite its many advantages, blockchain technology faces several challenges that need to be addressed for widespread adoption. One of the primary concerns is scalability. As the number of transactions on a blockchain network increases, so does the demand for computational resources, which can lead to slower transaction times and higher fees. Various solutions, such as sharding and layer-two protocols, are being explored to address this issue.

Regulatory and legal challenges also pose significant hurdles for blockchain adoption. Different countries have varying approaches to regulating blockchain and cryptocurrencies, leading to a fragmented regulatory landscape. Ensuring compliance with anti-money laundering (AML) and know-your-customer (KYC) regulations while maintaining the decentralized nature of blockchain is a complex task that requires careful consideration and collaboration between industry stakeholders and regulators.

Another challenge is the energy consumption associated with certain consensus mechanisms, particularly PoW. The computational power required for mining in PoW networks like Bitcoin has raised environmental concerns due to its significant energy usage. Transitioning to more energy-efficient consensus mechanisms, such as PoS, and exploring renewable energy sources for mining operations are potential ways to mitigate this issue.

Interoperability between different blockchain networks is also a crucial factor for the future of blockchain technology. Currently, many blockchains operate in silos, limiting their ability to communicate and interact with each other. Developing standards and protocols for interoperability can enable seamless transfer of assets and information across different blockchain networks, unlocking new possibilities for innovation and collaboration.

Despite these challenges, the potential of blockchain technology to transform various industries and create new opportunities is immense. The continued development and maturation of blockchain technology, coupled with advancements in related fields such as cryptography and distributed computing, will likely address many of the current limitations and pave the way for broader adoption.

In conclusion, blockchain is a groundbreaking technology that offers a secure, transparent, and decentralized method for recording transactions. Its potential applications extend far beyond cryptocurrencies, with significant implications for industries such as supply chain management, finance, healthcare, digital identity, and more. While challenges related to scalability, regulation, energy consumption, and interoperability exist, ongoing research and innovation in the blockchain space hold promise for overcoming these obstacles. As blockchain technology continues to evolve, it has the potential to reshape the way we conduct transactions, share information, and interact with digital systems, ushering in a new era of security, efficiency, and trust.

12. **Penetration Testing**: Simulated cyber attacks to identify vulnerabilities.

Penetration testing, often referred to as "pen testing," is a crucial process in the field of cybersecurity. It involves simulating cyber attacks on a system, network, or application to identify vulnerabilities that could be exploited by malicious actors. The primary objective of penetration testing is to proactively detect and fix security weaknesses before they can be leveraged in a real attack, thereby enhancing the overall security posture of an organization.

Penetration testing is typically conducted by ethical hackers, also known as penetration testers or white-hat hackers. These professionals use the same techniques and tools as malicious hackers, but with the permission of the organization being tested. By thinking and acting like attackers, penetration testers can uncover vulnerabilities that automated tools and traditional security measures might miss.

The penetration testing process generally follows a structured approach, beginning with planning and reconnaissance. During this phase, penetration testers gather information about the target system, network, or application. This can include publicly available information, such as domain names, IP addresses, and employee details, as well as data gathered through active scanning and probing. The goal is to understand the target's structure and identify potential entry points.

Once the reconnaissance phase is complete, penetration testers move on to the scanning and enumeration phase. This involves using various tools and techniques to identify open ports, services, and applications running on the target system. Vulnerability scanners are often used to detect known security issues, such as outdated software versions, misconfigurations, and weak passwords. The results of this phase provide a detailed map of the target's attack surface, highlighting areas that require further investigation.

The next phase is gaining access, where penetration testers attempt to exploit the identified vulnerabilities to gain unauthorized access to the target system. This can involve a range of attack techniques, including exploiting software bugs, leveraging social engineering tactics, and using brute force methods to crack passwords. The objective is to demonstrate the potential impact of a successful attack by gaining control over critical systems and data.

Once access is gained, penetration testers move on to the escalation of privileges phase. In many cases, initial access may be limited to a low-privilege account or a non-critical system. To fully understand the potential risk, penetration testers attempt to elevate their privileges to gain control over more sensitive parts of the network. This can involve exploiting additional vulnerabilities, such as misconfigured user permissions or weaknesses in the operating system, to achieve administrative or root-level access.

After gaining and escalating access, penetration testers focus on maintaining access to the compromised system. This involves deploying backdoors, rootkits, or other persistence mechanisms that allow them to retain control over the system even if initial vulnerabilities are patched. The goal is to understand how an attacker might establish a foothold within the target environment and maintain long-term access without detection.

Throughout the penetration testing process, ethical hackers maintain detailed documentation of their activities, findings, and the methods used to exploit vulnerabilities. This documentation is critical for the final phase of the process: reporting and remediation. In this phase, penetration testers compile a comprehensive report that outlines the vulnerabilities discovered, the methods used to exploit them, and the potential impact on the organization. The report also includes recommendations for remediation, such as patching software, improving configurations, and enhancing security policies.

The remediation process is where the organization takes action to address the identified vulnerabilities. This can involve updating software, changing configurations, strengthening access controls, and implementing additional security measures. Penetration testers may also conduct follow-up tests to verify that the vulnerabilities have been effectively mitigated and that no new issues have been introduced.

Penetration testing offers several significant benefits to organizations. First and foremost, it provides a realistic assessment of an organization's security posture by simulating actual attack scenarios. This helps organizations understand their vulnerabilities and prioritize remediation efforts based on the potential impact of different threats. Additionally, penetration testing can uncover vulnerabilities that might not be detected by automated security tools or routine security audits, providing a deeper level of insight into the organization's defenses.

Another key benefit of penetration testing is that it helps organizations meet regulatory and compliance requirements. Many industries, such as finance, healthcare, and government, have strict security standards that mandate regular penetration testing. By conducting these tests, organizations can demonstrate their commitment to security and ensure compliance with relevant regulations.

Penetration testing also plays a critical role in improving incident response capabilities. By understanding how attackers might exploit vulnerabilities and gain access to systems, organizations can develop more effective detection and response strategies. This includes implementing advanced monitoring and alerting mechanisms, training security teams to recognize attack patterns, and conducting regular incident response drills.

Despite its many benefits, penetration testing also presents several challenges. One of the primary challenges is the potential for disruptions to normal business operations. Because penetration testing involves actively probing and attacking systems, there is a risk that these activities could cause performance issues or outages. To mitigate this risk, organizations must carefully plan and coordinate testing activities, often conducting tests during off-peak hours or in isolated environments that mirror production systems.

Another challenge is the evolving nature of cyber threats. Attackers are constantly developing new techniques and tools, making it difficult for penetration testers to stay ahead of the curve. This requires continuous learning and adaptation, as well as leveraging threat intelligence to stay informed about emerging threats and vulnerabilities.

The complexity of modern IT environments also adds to the challenge of penetration testing. Organizations today rely on a diverse array of technologies, including cloud services, mobile devices, Internet of Things (IoT) devices, and legacy systems. Each of these technologies presents unique security challenges that must be considered during penetration testing. This requires penetration testers to have a broad and deep understanding of different technologies and their associated vulnerabilities.

Additionally, finding skilled penetration testers can be a challenge. Ethical hacking requires a unique blend of technical expertise, creativity, and problem-solving skills. As the demand for penetration testing services continues to grow, organizations may struggle to find qualified professionals with the necessary experience and certifications.

To address these challenges, organizations can adopt a combination of in-house and external penetration testing resources. In-house teams can provide ongoing security assessments and maintain a deep understanding of the organization's specific environment. External penetration testing firms can offer specialized expertise and an objective perspective, often bringing fresh insights and identifying vulnerabilities that internal teams might overlook.

In conclusion, penetration testing is a vital component of a comprehensive cybersecurity strategy. By simulating real-world attacks, penetration testing helps organizations identify and remediate vulnerabilities, enhance their security posture, and meet regulatory requirements. While penetration testing presents certain challenges, such as potential disruptions and the evolving threat landscape, the benefits far outweigh the risks. Through careful planning, continuous learning, and leveraging both internal and external resources, organizations can effectively use penetration testing to protect their critical assets and maintain a strong defense against cyber threats.

13. **Cryptography**: Methods of protecting information through encoding.

Cryptography is the science of securing information by transforming it into a format that is unreadable to unauthorized users. The primary goal of cryptography is to ensure the confidentiality, integrity, authenticity, and non-repudiation of information. By encoding data into an unreadable format, cryptography protects sensitive information from being accessed or altered by malicious actors.

Cryptography has a long history that dates back to ancient civilizations. One of the earliest known examples of cryptography is the use of the Caesar cipher by Julius Caesar to protect his military communications. The Caesar cipher is a simple substitution cipher in which each letter in the plaintext is shifted a fixed number of places down the alphabet. For example, with a shift of three, A becomes D, B becomes E, and so on. Although the Caesar cipher is relatively easy to break, it represents one of the first attempts to use mathematical techniques to secure information.

Modern cryptography is far more complex and relies on advanced mathematical principles and algorithms. There are two main types of cryptographic techniques: symmetric-key cryptography and asymmetric-key cryptography. In symmetric-key cryptography, the same key is used for both encryption and decryption. This key must be kept secret and shared only with authorized parties. One of the most widely used symmetric-key algorithms is the Advanced Encryption Standard (AES), which was established by the National Institute of Standards and Technology (NIST) in 2001. AES is known for its high level of security and efficiency, making it a popular choice for securing sensitive data.

In contrast, asymmetric-key cryptography uses a pair of keys: a public key and a private key. The public key is used for encryption, while the private key is used for decryption. This approach eliminates the need for securely sharing a single key, as the public key can be freely distributed without compromising security. The most well-known asymmetric-key algorithm is the RSA algorithm, named after its inventors Ron Rivest, Adi Shamir, and Leonard Adleman. RSA relies on the mathematical properties of large prime numbers and is widely used for securing communications over the internet, such as in the SSL/TLS protocols that protect web traffic.

Cryptographic techniques can be applied to various aspects of information security. One of the primary applications is ensuring the confidentiality of data. Confidentiality means that only authorized parties can access the information. Encryption is the process of converting plaintext into ciphertext, which is an unreadable format, using a cryptographic algorithm and a key. Decryption is the reverse process, in which the ciphertext is converted back into plaintext using the same algorithm and key. By encrypting data, organizations can protect sensitive information, such as financial records, personal data, and intellectual property, from unauthorized access.

Another critical aspect of cryptography is data integrity. Integrity ensures that the information has not been altered or tampered with. One common technique for ensuring data integrity is the use of cryptographic hash functions. A hash function takes an input (or message) and produces a fixed-size string of characters, typically a digest that uniquely represents the input. Even if a small change is made to the input, the resulting hash value will be significantly different. This property makes hash functions useful for verifying the integrity of data. For example, when downloading a file, the file's hash value can be compared to a known good hash value. If the values match, the file has not been altered. Common cryptographic hash functions include SHA-256 and SHA-3.

Authenticity is another crucial goal of cryptography. Authenticity ensures that the information comes from a legitimate source and has not been forged. Digital signatures are a common method for achieving authenticity. A digital signature is created by generating a hash of the message and then encrypting the hash with the sender's private key. The recipient can verify the signature by decrypting it with the sender's public key and comparing the resulting hash to a newly computed hash of the message. If the hashes match, the message is authentic and has not been altered. Digital signatures are widely used in software distribution, financial transactions, and legal agreements.

Non-repudiation is the concept that a party cannot deny having sent a message or performed an action. This is particularly important in legal and financial contexts, where it is crucial to have proof that a particular transaction or communication took place. Digital signatures also provide non-repudiation, as the sender cannot later deny having signed the message if their private key was the use of digital certificates and public-key cryptography to secure communications and verify identities over networks such as the internet. PKI involves several components, including Certificate Authorities (CAs), Registration Authorities (RAs), and digital certificates. CAs are trusted entities that issue digital certificates, which are used to associate a public key with the identity of an individual, organization, or device. RAs assist in the certificate issuance process by verifying the identities of certificate requesters.

Digital certificates play a vital role in establishing trust and enabling secure communications. When a user or system presents a digital certificate, the recipient can verify the certificate's authenticity and validity by checking the digital signature of the issuing CA and ensuring that the certificate has not expired or been revoked. This process helps to prevent impersonation and ensure that communications are with legitimate entities.

Cryptography also underpins many secure communication protocols used on the internet. The Secure Sockets Layer (SSL) and its successor, the Transport Layer Security (TLS), are cryptographic protocols designed to provide secure communication over a computer network. SSL/TLS ensures that data transmitted between clients and servers is encrypted and secure from eavesdropping and tampering. These protocols use a combination of symmetric and asymmetric encryption to establish a secure session and exchange data. For example, during an SSL/TLS handshake, the server presents its digital certificate to the client, which then verifies the certificate and uses the server's public key to securely exchange a session key for symmetric encryption.

Another critical application of cryptography is in securing wireless communications. The Wi-Fi Protected Access (WPA) and its successor, WPA2, are security protocols designed to secure wireless networks. These protocols use strong encryption methods, such as AES, to protect data transmitted over Wi-Fi networks from unauthorized access and eavesdropping. By using cryptographic techniques, WPA and WPA2 ensure that only authorized users can access the network and that data remains confidential.

Cryptographic techniques are also essential in the realm of secure storage. Encrypted file systems and databases protect sensitive information by encrypting data at rest. This means that even if an attacker gains physical access to the storage medium, they cannot read the encrypted data without the proper decryption key. Full-disk encryption solutions, such as BitLocker and FileVault, provide comprehensive protection for data stored on laptops and other devices, safeguarding against data breaches resulting from device theft or loss.

In recent years, cryptography has become increasingly important in the context of blockchain technology and cryptocurrencies. Blockchain is a decentralized ledger that records transactions across a network of computers. Cryptographic techniques are used to secure the integrity and authenticity of the data on the blockchain. For instance, transactions are grouped into blocks, and each block contains a cryptographic hash of the previous block, creating an immutable chain. This ensures that once a block is added to the blockchain, it cannot be altered without changing all subsequent blocks, making the blockchain tamper-resistant.

Cryptocurrencies like Bitcoin rely heavily on cryptographic principles to secure transactions and control the creation of new units. Bitcoin transactions are signed with the private keys of the sender, and these signatures can be verified using the corresponding public keys. Additionally, Bitcoin uses a Proof of Work (PoW) consensus mechanism, where miners compete to solve complex cryptographic puzzles to add new blocks to the blockchain. This process ensures the security and integrity of the cryptocurrency network.

Despite its many benefits, cryptography is not without challenges. One of the main challenges is key management. Cryptographic systems rely on keys to encrypt and decrypt data, and the security of these systems depends on the protection of these keys. Key management involves generating, distributing, storing, and revoking keys securely. Poor key management practices can lead to key exposure and compromise the security of the entire cryptographic system.

Another challenge is the threat of quantum computing. Quantum computers have the potential to break many of the cryptographic algorithms currently in use, such as RSA and ECC, by efficiently solving mathematical problems that are infeasible for classical computers. To address this threat, researchers are developing post-quantum cryptographic algorithms that are resistant to quantum attacks. These new algorithms aim to provide the same level of security in a post-quantum world, ensuring the continued protection of sensitive information.

The implementation of cryptographic algorithms also poses challenges. Even if an algorithm is theoretically secure, its implementation can introduce vulnerabilities if not done correctly. Side-channel attacks, for instance, exploit physical characteristics of the implementation, such as timing information or power consumption, to extract cryptographic keys. Ensuring that cryptographic implementations are resistant to such attacks requires careful design and testing.

In conclusion, cryptography is a fundamental aspect of information security that protects data through encoding. It encompasses a wide range of techniques and applications, from ancient ciphers to modern encryption algorithms and digital signatures. Cryptography ensures the confidentiality, integrity, authenticity, and non-repudiation of information, enabling secure communications, transactions, and storage in various contexts. While challenges such as key management, quantum computing, and secure implementation exist, ongoing research and development in cryptography continue to advance the field and address these issues. As the digital landscape evolves, cryptography will remain a critical tool in safeguarding information and maintaining trust in the digital age.

14. **Zero Trust Security**: Security model that requires strict identity verification.

Zero Trust Security is a cybersecurity model that operates on the principle that no entity, whether inside or outside an organization's network, should be trusted by default. Every access request, regardless of where it originates, must be verified before permission is granted. This strict identity verification approach is a significant departure from traditional security models, which often assume that entities within the network perimeter can be trusted. The Zero Trust model is particularly relevant in today's digital landscape, where cloud computing, mobile devices, and remote work have blurred the traditional network boundaries.

The concept of Zero Trust was first introduced by John Kindervag, a former Forrester Research analyst, in 2010. The model addresses the evolving threat landscape and the limitations of perimeter-based security. With the rise of sophisticated cyberattacks, insider threats, and the increasing complexity of IT environments, organizations can no longer rely solely on a strong perimeter defense. Instead, Zero Trust emphasizes continuous monitoring, strict access controls, and the assumption that breaches can and will occur.

A fundamental aspect of Zero Trust is the principle of "never trust, always verify." This means that every request to access resources, whether it comes from a user, device, or application, must be authenticated and authorized. Identity verification is central to this process, involving multi-factor authentication (MFA), context-aware access controls, and the use of least privilege principles.

Multi-factor authentication (MFA) is a critical component of Zero Trust. It requires users to provide multiple forms of verification before granting access. These factors typically include something the user knows (such as a password), something the user has (such as a mobile device), and something the user is (such as a biometric identifier like a fingerprint or facial recognition). By requiring multiple forms of authentication, MFA significantly reduces the risk of unauthorized access due to compromised credentials.

Context-aware access controls take identity verification a step further by considering additional factors such as the user's location, the device being used, and the time of the access request. For example, if a user attempts to access corporate resources from an unfamiliar location or an unrecognized device, the system may require additional verification steps or deny access altogether. This dynamic approach helps ensure that access decisions are based on the current context, reducing the likelihood of unauthorized access.

The principle of least privilege is another key element of Zero Trust. It dictates that users and devices should be granted the minimum level of access necessary to perform their tasks. This approach limits the potential damage that can occur if an account or device is compromised. For instance, if a user only needs read access to certain files, they should not be granted write or administrative access. By enforcing least privilege, organizations can minimize their attack surface and contain the impact of potential breaches.

Network segmentation is also essential in a Zero Trust architecture. Traditional networks often operate on a flat structure, where once inside, users have broad access to the network. In contrast, Zero Trust advocates for micro-segmentation, which involves dividing the network into smaller, isolated segments. Each segment is protected with its own set of security controls, and access between segments is strictly regulated. This segmentation limits lateral movement within the network, making it more difficult for attackers to spread if they gain access to one segment.

Zero Trust also emphasizes the importance of continuous monitoring and visibility. In a Zero Trust environment, security teams must have real-time visibility into all network traffic, user activities, and access requests. Advanced security tools such as Security Information and Event Management (SIEM) systems, Endpoint Detection and Response (EDR) solutions, and Network Traffic Analysis (NTA) tools play a crucial role in achieving this visibility. These tools help detect and respond to suspicious activities, enabling organizations to quickly identify and mitigate potential threats.

The Zero Trust model extends beyond just user access. It also applies to devices and workloads. With the proliferation of Internet of Things (IoT) devices, mobile devices, and virtual machines, organizations must ensure that every device connecting to the network is trusted and secure. Device authentication and posture assessment are critical in this regard. Before granting access, the system should verify that the device is recognized, has up-to-date security patches, and complies with the organization's security policies. This helps prevent compromised or non-compliant devices from introducing vulnerabilities into the network.

Workload security is another important consideration. In modern IT environments, applications and services often run in dynamic and distributed environments, such as cloud platforms and containerized environments. Zero Trust principles require that workloads are authenticated and authorized before they can communicate with each other. Service meshes and identity-based security controls help enforce these principles, ensuring that only trusted workloads can interact.

Implementing a Zero Trust model requires a strategic and phased approach. Organizations need to start by understanding their current security posture and identifying gaps that need to be addressed. This involves mapping out all assets, users, devices, and data flows within the organization. A comprehensive risk assessment helps prioritize areas that require immediate attention and guides the development of a Zero Trust roadmap.

One of the initial steps in implementing Zero Trust is establishing robust identity and access management (IAM) systems. IAM solutions provide the foundation for managing user identities, roles, and access permissions. Organizations should implement MFA and context-aware access controls to enhance identity verification processes. Additionally, integrating IAM with other security tools, such as SIEM and EDR, helps create a cohesive security ecosystem.

Network segmentation and micro-segmentation are critical next steps. Organizations should design their network architecture to isolate sensitive data and critical systems. Each segment should have its own set of security controls, and access between segments should be tightly controlled. This approach limits the potential impact of a breach and helps contain attackers within a single segment.

Continuous monitoring and visibility are essential for maintaining a Zero Trust environment. Organizations should deploy advanced security tools to monitor network traffic, user activities, and access requests in real-time. SIEM systems aggregate and analyze security events from various sources, providing valuable insights into potential threats. EDR solutions help detect and respond to endpoint threats, while NTA tools monitor network traffic for suspicious activities.

Device security is another crucial aspect of Zero Trust. Organizations should implement device authentication and posture assessment to ensure that only trusted devices can access the network. This involves verifying that devices are recognized, have up-to-date security patches, and comply with security policies. Mobile device management (MDM) solutions can help enforce security policies on mobile devices, ensuring they meet the required security standards.

Workload security is particularly important in cloud and containerized environments. Organizations should implement identity-based security controls to authenticate and authorize workloads. Service meshes can help enforce these controls by managing communications between microservices and ensuring that only trusted workloads can interact.

Education and awareness are also vital components of a successful Zero Trust implementation. Employees should be educated about the principles of Zero Trust and the importance of following security best practices. Regular training sessions and awareness programs help reinforce the importance of identity verification, secure access, and vigilant monitoring.

While Zero Trust offers significant security benefits, it is not without challenges. Implementing Zero Trust requires a cultural shift within the organization, as it challenges traditional notions of trust and access. Organizations must be prepared to invest in the necessary technologies, tools, and training to support the Zero Trust model.

Additionally, the dynamic and complex nature of modern IT environments means that Zero Trust is not a one-time effort but an ongoing process that requires continuous adaptation and improvement.

In conclusion, Zero Trust Security is a comprehensive and modern approach to cybersecurity that requires strict identity verification and continuous monitoring. By adopting the principles of "never trust, always verify," organizations can enhance their security posture, limit the potential impact of breaches, and protect their sensitive data and critical systems. Implementing Zero Trust involves a strategic and phased approach, including robust identity and access management, network segmentation, continuous monitoring, device and workload security, and ongoing education and awareness. While challenges exist, the benefits of Zero Trust in mitigating modern cyber threats make it an essential model for organizations aiming to secure their digital assets in an increasingly complex and interconnected world.

Virtual Reality (VR) and Augmented Reality (AR)

Virtual Reality (VR) and Augmented Reality (AR) are transformative technologies that are reshaping the way we interact with digital content and the physical world. By creating fully engaging environments and allowing users to interact with virtual and real objects in unprecedented ways, VR and AR offer immersive experiences that extend beyond traditional media formats. As these technologies evolve, they introduce new paradigms such as haptic feedback, mixed reality (MR), 360-degree videos, head-mounted displays (HMDs), and spatial computing, each contributing to a more enriched and interactive user experience.

Immersive experiences in VR and AR involve creating a sense of presence and engagement that transports users to new realities or enhances their perception of the real world. In VR, this is achieved by generating entirely virtual environments that users can explore and interact with, providing a feeling of being physically present in a different place. VR environments can range from realistic simulations of real-world locations to fantastical worlds that defy the laws of physics. AR, on the other hand, overlays digital content onto the real world, augmenting the user's perception and interaction with their physical surroundings. This can involve anything from simple informational overlays to complex interactive experiences that blend seamlessly with the environment.

A key component of these immersive experiences is haptic feedback, a technology that simulates touch and other physical sensations in virtual environments. Haptic feedback enhances the sense of realism and immersion by allowing users to feel textures, vibrations, and forces as they interact with virtual objects. This technology is often integrated into VR gloves, suits, and other wearable devices, providing a tactile dimension to the visual and auditory stimuli. For example, in a VR simulation of a medical procedure, haptic feedback can replicate the sensation of handling surgical instruments and interacting with tissues, offering a more realistic training experience for medical professionals.

Mixed Reality (MR) represents the convergence of VR and AR, enabling users to interact with both virtual and real objects in a unified environment. MR goes beyond simply overlaying digital content on the real world; it allows for dynamic interaction and integration between the physical and digital realms. In an MR environment, virtual objects can respond to changes in the physical environment and vice versa. This creates a more cohesive and interactive experience, where users can manipulate virtual objects as if they were real and see virtual elements react to physical actions. MR has significant applications in fields such as education, design, and entertainment, where it can provide a more engaging and interactive learning or creative process.

360-degree videos are another innovation that contributes to the immersive experience in VR and AR. These videos capture a complete view of the surroundings, allowing users to look in any direction and feel as though they are actually present in the recorded environment. By wearing an HMD, users can explore these videos by simply moving their heads, providing a more natural and intuitive way to experience content. 360-degree videos are particularly effective for storytelling, travel experiences, and live events, where they can transport viewers to distant places or provide a sense of being part of a live audience. The ability to view the action from multiple angles enhances the depth and engagement of the experience.

Head-Mounted Displays (HMDs) are essential devices for delivering VR and AR experiences. These wearable devices position screens or transparent displays in front of the user's eyes, creating a visual interface for immersive content. In VR, HMDs completely cover the user's field of view, blocking out the real world and replacing it with a virtual environment. In AR, HMDs use transparent displays or cameras to overlay digital content onto the real world, allowing users to see and interact with both simultaneously. Modern HMDs are equipped with sensors that track the user's head movements, ensuring that the virtual content adjusts in real-time to maintain a consistent and realistic perspective. The development of lightweight, comfortable, and high-resolution HMDs has been crucial in advancing the adoption of VR and AR technologies.

Spatial computing is a broader concept that encompasses the technologies and techniques used to blend digital and physical spaces. It involves understanding and interacting with the spatial properties of the environment, allowing digital content to be anchored and manipulated in relation to the real world. Spatial computing relies on a combination of sensors, computer vision, and artificial intelligence to interpret the user's surroundings and provide context-aware interactions. This enables applications such as indoor navigation, object recognition, and spatially aware virtual assistants. In VR and AR, spatial computing allows for more natural and intuitive interactions, as users can use gestures, voice commands, and physical movement to control and manipulate virtual objects and information.

The integration of these technologies opens up a vast array of possibilities for various industries. In healthcare, VR and AR can provide immersive training simulations for medical professionals, enhance patient education, and support remote surgeries through AR overlays that guide surgeons in real-time. In education, these technologies can create interactive and engaging learning experiences, allowing students to explore historical events, conduct virtual science experiments, or visualize complex concepts in three dimensions. In the entertainment industry, VR and AR offer new forms of interactive storytelling, gaming, and live performances, where audiences can become active participants in the experience.

In retail, AR can enhance the shopping experience by allowing customers to visualize products in their own space before making a purchase, while VR can create virtual showrooms and immersive brand experiences. In architecture and design, these technologies can facilitate virtual walkthroughs of buildings and spaces, enabling clients to experience designs before they are built and make informed decisions. In manufacturing and engineering, VR and AR can improve design visualization, prototyping, and maintenance processes, reducing errors and increasing efficiency.

As VR and AR technologies continue to evolve, they are becoming more accessible and integrated into everyday life. Advances in hardware, such as lighter and more comfortable HMDs, improved haptic feedback devices, and more accurate spatial computing sensors, are enhancing the user experience and expanding the range of applications. At the same time, developments in software, including more realistic graphics, better user interfaces, and more sophisticated artificial intelligence, are enabling more complex and interactive experiences.

However, the widespread adoption of VR and AR also presents challenges. Ensuring user comfort and minimizing issues such as motion sickness, eye strain, and physical fatigue are crucial for creating sustainable and enjoyable experiences. Addressing privacy and security concerns, particularly with regard to the collection and use of spatial data and personal information, is also essential. Additionally, developing standardized protocols and interoperability between different VR and AR systems can help create a more cohesive ecosystem and facilitate broader adoption.

In conclusion, Virtual Reality and Augmented Reality are revolutionizing the way we interact with digital content and the physical world. Through immersive experiences, haptic feedback, mixed reality, 360-degree videos, head-mounted displays, and spatial computing, these technologies are creating new possibilities for engagement, interaction, and understanding. As they continue to advance, VR and AR have the potential to transform a wide range of industries and enhance many aspects of our daily lives, offering richer, more interactive, and more meaningful experiences. The ongoing development and integration of these technologies will shape the future of digital interaction, providing new opportunities for creativity, learning, and connection.

15. **Immersive Experiences**: Fully engaging environments in VR and AR.

Immersive experiences in Virtual Reality (VR) and Augmented Reality (AR) are transforming the way we engage with digital content, providing fully engaging environments that captivate and transport users into new realms of interaction and perception. These technologies create a sense of presence and involvement that traditional media cannot match, offering experiences that are not just seen and heard, but felt and lived. This essay explores the various aspects and implications of immersive experiences in VR and AR, focusing on their capabilities, applications, and the impact they have on users.

At the core of immersive experiences is the concept of presence—the sensation of being in a place other than where one physically resides. VR achieves this by creating entirely virtual environments that users can explore and interact with, while AR enhances the real world by overlaying digital content onto it. The goal is to make users feel as though they are truly part of these environments, engaging their senses and emotions in a profound way. This sense of presence is crucial for immersion, as it allows users to suspend disbelief and become fully absorbed in the experience.

One of the primary ways VR and AR create immersive experiences is through the use of head-mounted displays (HMDs). These devices position screens or transparent displays in front of the user's eyes, creating a visual interface for the virtual or augmented content. In VR, HMDs completely cover the user's field of view, blocking out the real world and replacing it with a virtual environment. This creates a sense of isolation and focus, allowing users to become fully immersed in the virtual world. In AR, HMDs use transparent displays or cameras to overlay digital content onto the real world, enabling users to see and interact with both simultaneously. The development of lightweight, comfortable, and high-resolution HMDs has been crucial in advancing the adoption of VR and AR technologies, as they enhance the visual fidelity and comfort of the experience.

Audio is another critical component of immersive experiences. Spatial audio techniques allow sounds to be placed and moved within a 3D space, creating a realistic soundscape that matches the visual environment. This enhances the sense of presence by providing auditory cues that correspond to the user's movements and interactions. For example, in a VR game, the sound of footsteps behind the user can create a sense of urgency and awareness, prompting them to turn around and investigate. In AR applications, spatial audio can provide context-aware information, such as navigation instructions or notifications, that blend seamlessly with the user's surroundings.

Haptic feedback further enhances immersion by simulating touch and other physical sensations in virtual environments. This technology uses actuators and sensors to create vibrations, forces, and textures that mimic the feeling of interacting with real objects. Haptic feedback can be integrated into VR gloves, suits, and other wearable devices, providing a tactile dimension to the visual and auditory stimuli. For instance, in a VR simulation of rock climbing, haptic feedback can replicate the sensation of gripping rough surfaces and the resistance of climbing holds, making the experience more realistic and engaging. By engaging the sense of touch, haptic feedback deepens the user's connection to the virtual environment, making interactions feel more natural and intuitive.

The ability to interact with virtual and augmented environments in a meaningful way is another crucial aspect of immersive experiences. Hand tracking, gesture recognition, and motion controllers allow users to manipulate objects, navigate spaces, and perform actions within the virtual or augmented world. These input methods provide a direct and intuitive way to interact with digital content, enhancing the sense of agency and involvement. For example, in a VR painting application, users can use hand gestures to select colors, brush strokes, and tools, creating artwork in a way that feels similar to real-world painting. In AR, users can interact with digital objects overlaid on the real world, such as placing virtual furniture in their living room and adjusting its position and orientation with hand movements.

Mixed reality (MR) represents the convergence of VR and AR, enabling users to interact with both virtual and real objects in a unified environment. MR goes beyond simply overlaying digital content on the real world; it allows for dynamic interaction and integration between the physical and digital realms. In an MR environment, virtual objects can respond to changes in the physical environment and vice versa. This creates a more cohesive and interactive experience, where users can manipulate virtual objects as if they were real and see virtual elements react to physical actions. MR has significant applications in fields such as education, design, and entertainment, where it can provide a more engaging and interactive learning or creative process.

360-degree videos are another innovation that contributes to the immersive experience in VR and AR. These videos capture a complete view of the surroundings, allowing users to look in any direction and feel as though they are actually present in the recorded environment. By wearing an HMD, users can explore these videos by simply moving their heads, providing a more natural and intuitive way to experience content. 360-degree videos are particularly effective for storytelling, travel experiences, and live events, where they can transport viewers to distant places or provide a sense of being part of a live audience. The ability to view the action from multiple angles enhances the depth and engagement of the experience.

Spatial computing is a broader concept that encompasses the technologies and techniques used to blend digital and physical spaces. It involves understanding and interacting with the spatial properties of the environment, allowing digital content to be anchored and manipulated in relation to the real world. Spatial computing relies on a combination of sensors, computer vision, and artificial intelligence to interpret the user's surroundings and provide context-aware interactions. This enables applications such as indoor navigation, object recognition, and spatially aware virtual assistants. In VR and AR, spatial computing allows for more natural and intuitive interactions, as users can use gestures, voice commands, and physical movement to control and manipulate virtual objects and information.

The integration of these technologies opens up a vast array of possibilities for various industries. In healthcare, VR and AR can provide immersive training simulations for medical professionals, enhance patient education, and support remote surgeries through AR overlays that guide surgeons in real-time. In education, these technologies can create interactive and engaging learning experiences, allowing students to explore historical events, conduct virtual science experiments, or visualize complex concepts in three dimensions. In the entertainment industry, VR and AR offer new forms of interactive storytelling, gaming, and live performances, where audiences can become active participants in the experience.

In retail, AR can enhance the shopping experience by allowing customers to visualize products in their own space before making a purchase, while VR can create virtual showrooms and immersive brand experiences. In architecture and design, these technologies can facilitate virtual walkthroughs of buildings and spaces, enabling clients to experience designs before they are built and make informed decisions. In manufacturing and engineering, VR and AR can improve design visualization, prototyping, and maintenance processes, reducing errors and increasing efficiency.

As VR and AR technologies continue to evolve, they are becoming more accessible and integrated into everyday life. Advances in hardware, such as lighter and more comfortable HMDs, improved haptic feedback devices, and more accurate spatial computing sensors, are enhancing the user experience and expanding the range of applications. At the same time, developments in software, including more realistic graphics, better user interfaces, and more sophisticated artificial intelligence, are enabling more complex and interactive experiences.

However, the widespread adoption of VR and AR also presents challenges. Ensuring user comfort and minimizing issues such as motion sickness, eye strain, and physical fatigue are crucial for creating sustainable and enjoyable experiences. Addressing privacy and security concerns, particularly with regard to the collection and use of spatial data and personal information, is also essential. Additionally, developing standardized protocols and interoperability between different VR and AR systems can help create a more cohesive ecosystem and facilitate broader adoption.

In conclusion, Virtual Reality and Augmented Reality are revolutionizing the way we interact with digital content and the physical world. Through immersive experiences, these technologies are creating new possibilities for engagement, interaction, and understanding. As they continue to advance, VR and AR have the potential to transform a wide range of industries and enhance many aspects of our daily lives, offering richer, more interactive, and more meaningful experiences. The ongoing development and integration of these technologies will shape the future of digital interaction, providing new opportunities for creativity, learning, and connection. Immersive experiences in VR and AR are not just a glimpse into the future; they are an evolving reality that is reshaping our world in profound and exciting ways.

16. **Haptic Feedback**: Technology that simulates touch in virtual environments.

Haptic feedback technology has revolutionized the way we interact with digital environments by simulating the sense of touch. This technology, also known as haptics, enhances the immersive experience of virtual reality (VR) and augmented reality (AR) by adding a tactile dimension that was previously absent. By providing physical sensations, haptic feedback allows users to feel and manipulate virtual objects as if they were real, significantly improving the realism and engagement of virtual experiences.

The basic principle of haptic feedback involves the use of actuators and sensors to create vibrations, forces, and motions that mimic the sensations of touch. These actuators can be integrated into various devices such as gloves, suits, controllers, and even handheld devices. When a user interacts with a virtual object, the haptic system responds by generating appropriate tactile feedback, enabling the user to feel textures, resistance, impacts, and other physical sensations.

One of the most common applications of haptic feedback is in VR gaming. In this context, haptic feedback can simulate the recoil of a firearm, the tension of drawing a bowstring, or the impact of a punch. This not only enhances the immersion but also provides a more intuitive and engaging way to interact with the virtual environment. For instance, when a player catches a ball in a VR game, the haptic feedback can simulate the sensation of the ball hitting their hand, making the experience more realistic.

Haptic feedback is also crucial in training simulations, particularly in fields such as medicine, aviation, and the military. In medical training, for example, haptic feedback can be used to simulate the sensation of performing surgery. Trainees can practice their skills on virtual patients, feeling the resistance of tissues and the texture of organs, which helps them develop a better understanding of the physical sensations involved in real surgical procedures. This type of training can enhance the learning experience and improve the trainees' skills without the need for live patients.

In aviation and military training, haptic feedback can simulate the forces experienced during flight or combat. Pilots can feel the vibrations and resistance of the controls, helping them to develop muscle memory and better prepare for real-world scenarios. Similarly, soldiers can train with haptic-enabled weapons and equipment, experiencing the physical sensations of firing, reloading, and handling gear in a safe and controlled virtual environment.

Beyond gaming and training, haptic feedback has significant applications in the field of remote operation and telepresence. In remote surgery, for example, surgeons can perform procedures on patients located far away by controlling robotic instruments. Haptic feedback allows the surgeon to feel the resistance and texture of tissues, providing a level of precision and control that is essential for delicate operations. This technology can also be used in remote maintenance and repair operations, where operators can feel the tools and equipment they are manipulating, improving accuracy and reducing the risk of errors.

In the consumer electronics industry, haptic feedback is used to enhance the user experience of smartphones, tablets, and wearable devices. For example, when typing on a virtual keyboard, haptic feedback can simulate the sensation of pressing physical keys, making the experience more intuitive and satisfying. Similarly, in wearable fitness devices, haptic feedback can provide tactile alerts and notifications, allowing users to stay informed without having to look at the screen.

Haptic feedback is also being explored in the realm of social interaction and communication. In VR and AR, haptic technology can enable users to feel handshakes, hugs, and other forms of physical contact with virtual avatars or remote users. This can enhance the sense of presence and connection in virtual meetings, social gatherings, and collaborative workspaces, making these interactions feel more natural and engaging.

The development of haptic feedback technology involves several challenges. One of the main challenges is creating realistic and accurate sensations that closely mimic real-world touch. This requires sophisticated algorithms and high-resolution actuators that can generate a wide range of tactile sensations. Another challenge is ensuring that the haptic feedback is synchronized with the visual and auditory stimuli in the virtual environment. Any delay or mismatch between the senses can break the immersion and reduce the effectiveness of the haptic feedback.

Another important aspect of haptic feedback technology is its impact on accessibility. For individuals with visual impairments, haptic feedback can provide a way to interact with digital content through touch. For example, haptic displays can convey information such as shapes, textures, and spatial arrangements, enabling visually impaired users to perceive and interact with graphical content. This can enhance their ability to use digital devices, access information, and participate in virtual experiences.

The potential of haptic feedback extends beyond simulating touch in virtual environments. Researchers are exploring the use of haptic technology in areas such as rehabilitation and therapy. For example, haptic devices can be used to help patients recover motor skills after a stroke or injury by providing tactile feedback that guides their movements and exercises. This can improve the effectiveness of rehabilitation programs and accelerate the recovery process.

In the field of robotics, haptic feedback is used to enhance the dexterity and precision of robotic systems. By providing tactile sensations to human operators, haptic-enabled robots can perform delicate tasks that require fine motor skills, such as assembling small components or handling fragile objects. This technology can also be used in collaborative robots, or cobots, that work alongside humans, providing them with a sense of touch and improving their ability to interact with their environment.

As haptic feedback technology continues to evolve, it is likely to become an integral part of our digital interactions. The development of new materials and actuator designs, along with advances in sensor technology and machine learning, will enable more sophisticated and realistic haptic experiences. This will open up new possibilities for applications in various fields, from entertainment and education to healthcare and industrial automation.

In conclusion, haptic feedback technology plays a crucial role in enhancing the realism and engagement of virtual and augmented reality experiences. By simulating the sense of touch, haptic feedback adds a tactile dimension to digital interactions, making them more intuitive and immersive. From gaming and training simulations to remote operation and social interaction, haptic feedback has a wide range of applications that improve the user experience and provide valuable benefits in various fields. As this technology continues to advance, it will further transform the way we interact with digital content, bridging the gap between the virtual and physical worlds and creating more meaningful and engaging experiences.

17. **Mixed Reality (MR)**: Combining VR and AR to interact with both virtual and real objects.

Mixed Reality (MR) represents an advanced technology paradigm that combines elements of both Virtual Reality (VR) and Augmented Reality (AR) to create environments where digital and real-world objects can coexist and interact in real time. This integration allows for a seamless blend of the physical and digital worlds, providing users with highly immersive and interactive experiences that go beyond the capabilities of VR or AR alone.

MR environments leverage the strengths of VR and AR to produce a cohesive and dynamic user experience. In a typical VR setup, users are completely immersed in a computer-generated environment, often losing sight of the real world around them. AR, on the other hand, overlays digital information onto the real world, enhancing the user's perception without fully replacing the physical environment. MR takes these concepts a step further by allowing virtual and real objects to interact in a shared space, providing users with a more integrated and holistic experience.

One of the key technologies that enable MR is advanced tracking and sensing systems. These systems use cameras, sensors, and computer vision algorithms to map the physical environment and track the user's movements and interactions. By accurately understanding the spatial layout and the position of objects, MR systems can anchor virtual elements in the real world with precision, ensuring that they remain fixed in place as the user moves around. This spatial awareness is crucial for creating a convincing and interactive MR experience, where virtual objects can respond to real-world actions and vice versa.

Head-mounted displays (HMDs) are essential devices for MR, providing the visual interface through which users perceive the blended environment. Unlike traditional VR headsets that completely cover the user's field of view, MR HMDs often incorporate transparent displays or pass-through cameras that allow users to see the real world while overlaying digital content. These devices are equipped with sensors and cameras that track the user's head movements and the environment, ensuring that virtual objects remain stable and responsive to changes in the real world. The development of lightweight, comfortable, and high-resolution MR HMDs has been a significant factor in advancing the adoption and usability of MR technology.

One of the primary applications of MR is in the field of education and training. MR can provide highly interactive and engaging learning experiences by allowing students to interact with both virtual and real objects. For example, in a medical training scenario, students can practice surgical procedures on virtual patients that are overlaid onto physical models. This combination allows them to develop their skills in a realistic and controlled environment, with the added benefit of receiving real-time feedback and guidance from the virtual system. Similarly, in engineering education, MR can enable students to explore and manipulate virtual models of complex machinery while still interacting with physical components, enhancing their understanding of the subject matter.

In the realm of industrial design and manufacturing, MR offers powerful tools for visualization, prototyping, and collaboration. Designers can create virtual prototypes of products and place them in the real world, allowing them to evaluate aesthetics, ergonomics, and functionality in a real-world context. This ability to see and interact with virtual prototypes alongside physical objects can significantly streamline the design process, reducing the need for multiple physical prototypes and accelerating time-to-market. MR also facilitates remote collaboration, where team members in different locations can work together on virtual prototypes, making adjustments and sharing feedback in real time as if they were in the same room.

MR has transformative potential in the healthcare industry, particularly in surgical planning and visualization. Surgeons can use MR to overlay patient-specific imaging data, such as MRI or CT scans, onto the patient during surgery. This allows for more precise and informed decision-making, as surgeons can see critical anatomical structures and plan their procedures with greater accuracy. MR can also be used for remote consultations, where specialists can collaborate and provide guidance to surgeons in different locations, enhancing the quality of care and access to expertise.

In the entertainment and gaming industry, MR provides new opportunities for creating immersive and interactive experiences that merge the digital and physical worlds. MR games can incorporate real-world objects and environments into the gameplay, allowing players to interact with both virtual characters and physical props. This can create a more engaging and dynamic gaming experience, where the boundaries between the game and the real world are blurred. MR can also be used in theme parks and live performances to create interactive attractions and shows that combine digital effects with physical sets and actors, offering audiences a unique and captivating experience.

Retail and e-commerce are other sectors where MR can have a significant impact. MR can enhance the shopping experience by allowing customers to visualize products in their own space before making a purchase. For example, customers can use MR to see how furniture would look in their living room or how clothes would fit on their body, helping them make more informed decisions and reducing the likelihood of returns. Retailers can also use MR to create interactive and personalized shopping experiences, where customers can explore virtual showrooms, try on virtual products, and receive customized recommendations based on their preferences and behavior.

One of the challenges of implementing MR is ensuring seamless and natural interactions between virtual and real objects. This requires sophisticated algorithms and user interfaces that can accurately interpret and respond to user actions. Hand tracking, gesture recognition, and voice commands are common input methods used in MR to provide intuitive and direct interactions. These input methods need to be highly responsive and precise to maintain the user's sense of presence and immersion. Developers must also consider the ergonomics and usability of MR devices, ensuring that they are comfortable to wear and easy to use for extended periods.

Privacy and security are important considerations in the development and deployment of MR technology. MR systems often require access to sensitive information, such as spatial data and personal user data, to function effectively. Protecting this data from unauthorized access and ensuring user privacy is crucial to gaining user trust and adoption. Developers must implement robust security measures and provide transparent policies regarding data collection and usage.

The potential of MR extends beyond the specific applications mentioned earlier, as it can be a transformative tool in numerous other fields. In architecture and urban planning, MR can allow stakeholders to visualize and interact with proposed buildings and infrastructure projects in their real-world locations. This can facilitate better decision-making and public engagement, as people can see how projects will impact their environment and provide feedback. In the arts, MR can enable new forms of expression and creativity, where artists can create immersive installations and performances that blend the digital and physical realms.

The future of MR holds exciting possibilities as technology continues to advance. Improvements in display technology, sensor accuracy, and computational power will enable even more realistic and seamless MR experiences. The integration of artificial intelligence and machine learning can enhance the responsiveness and adaptability of MR systems, providing more personalized and context-aware interactions. As MR devices become more affordable and accessible, we can expect wider adoption and innovative applications across various industries.

In conclusion, Mixed Reality represents a powerful and versatile technology that combines the best of VR and AR to create immersive and interactive environments where virtual and real objects can coexist and interact. By leveraging advanced tracking, sensing, and display technologies, MR provides users with a seamless blend of the physical and digital worlds, enhancing a wide range of applications from education and training to healthcare, entertainment, and beyond. As MR technology continues to evolve, it has the potential to transform the way we work, learn, play, and interact with our environment, offering new possibilities for creativity, productivity, and engagement.

18. **360-Degree Videos**: Videos that allow viewing from every angle.

360-degree videos are a dynamic and immersive form of media that allow viewers to explore video content from every angle, providing a comprehensive and engaging viewing experience. Unlike traditional videos, which present a fixed viewpoint, 360-degree videos capture the entire surrounding environment, enabling viewers to look around in all directions as if they were physically present at the scene. This technology has revolutionized the way stories are told and experienced, offering new opportunities for entertainment, education, journalism, and beyond.

The creation of 360-degree videos involves using special cameras equipped with multiple lenses arranged to capture footage in all directions simultaneously. These cameras, often referred to as omnidirectional or spherical cameras, stitch together the individual video feeds from each lens to create a seamless panoramic view. The resulting video allows viewers to freely explore the scene by panning, tilting, and zooming, either through the use of a mouse or touchscreen on a computer or mobile device, or by physically moving their heads when using a head-mounted display (HMD) for a more immersive experience.

One of the most significant impacts of 360-degree videos is their ability to provide a sense of presence and immersion that traditional videos cannot achieve. This immersive quality is particularly valuable in storytelling and journalism, where the goal is often to transport viewers to a different place and make them feel as if they are part of the action. For example, in documentary filmmaking, 360-degree videos can take viewers to remote or dangerous locations, allowing them to witness events and environments firsthand. This can create a deeper emotional connection and understanding of the subject matter, as viewers are able to explore the context and surroundings in a way that traditional videos do not allow.

In the realm of entertainment, 360-degree videos have opened up new possibilities for creating engaging and interactive content. Music videos, for instance, can now place viewers in the middle of a live concert, allowing them to look around the stage, audience, and venue, capturing the energy and atmosphere of the performance. Similarly, filmmakers can use 360-degree videos to create immersive scenes where viewers can choose their own perspective, adding an interactive element to the narrative. This format is also being explored in virtual reality (VR) gaming, where players can experience game environments in a fully immersive way, enhancing the sense of presence and engagement.

Education is another field where 360-degree videos have shown great potential. Virtual field trips, for example, can transport students to historical sites, natural wonders, or scientific laboratories, providing an interactive and engaging learning experience that goes beyond traditional classroom lectures. By exploring these environments in 360 degrees, students can gain a deeper understanding of the subject matter and develop a greater sense of curiosity and exploration. Additionally, 360-degree videos can be used in professional training, such as medical simulations or safety drills, where trainees can practice their skills in a realistic and controlled virtual environment.

In the tourism industry, 360-degree videos offer a unique way to showcase destinations and attractions. Potential travelers can explore hotels, landmarks, and scenic spots from the comfort of their own homes, getting a feel for the location before making a decision to visit. This can enhance marketing efforts and provide a more engaging way to attract visitors. For adventure tourism, 360-degree videos can capture experiences such as scuba diving, mountain climbing, or safari tours, allowing viewers to experience the thrill and beauty of these activities in an immersive way.

The technology behind 360-degree videos also enables more effective and engaging communication in the business world. Virtual tours of real estate properties, for example, can provide potential buyers with a comprehensive view of a home or commercial space, allowing them to explore every room and detail as if they were there in person. This can save time and resources by reducing the need for multiple physical visits. In corporate training and presentations, 360-degree videos can create more interactive and memorable experiences, helping to convey complex information in a more intuitive and engaging manner.

While the benefits of 360-degree videos are numerous, there are also several challenges and considerations involved in their production and consumption. One of the main challenges is the technical complexity of capturing and stitching together high-quality 360-degree footage. Ensuring that the video is seamless and free of distortions requires precise calibration of the camera lenses and sophisticated software algorithms. Additionally, the high resolution needed for a clear and detailed 360-degree video can result in large file sizes, posing challenges for storage, processing, and streaming.

Another important consideration is the user experience. While 360-degree videos offer a high degree of interactivity and immersion, they also require viewers to actively engage with the content by exploring the scene. This can be a double-edged sword, as it provides a more engaging experience but can also be overwhelming or confusing for some viewers. Content creators need to design their videos in a way that guides the viewer's attention and provides visual cues to important elements, ensuring that the experience is both intuitive and enjoyable.

The rise of 360-degree videos has also sparked discussions about the ethical implications of this technology. In journalism, for example, the immersive nature of 360-degree videos can blur the line between objective reporting and sensationalism. The ability to transport viewers to the scene of a conflict or disaster can create a powerful emotional impact, but it also raises questions about privacy, consent, and the potential for exploitation. Content creators need to be mindful of these ethical considerations and strive to balance the immersive qualities of 360-degree videos with responsible storytelling practices.

Looking ahead, the future of 360-degree videos is promising, with ongoing advancements in technology and increasing adoption across various industries. Improvements in camera technology, such as higher resolution sensors and more efficient stitching algorithms, will continue to enhance the quality and accessibility of 360-degree videos. Additionally, the integration of other emerging technologies, such as artificial intelligence and machine learning, can further enhance the interactivity and personalization of 360-degree video experiences. For example, AI algorithms can be used to automatically direct the viewer's attention to key elements in the scene, or to generate personalized content based on the viewer's preferences and behavior.

Moreover, the convergence of 360-degree videos with other immersive technologies, such as VR and AR, will open up new possibilities for creating even more engaging and interactive experiences. Hybrid applications that combine 360-degree videos with augmented reality overlays or virtual reality environments can provide users with a richer and more multifaceted experience, blending the best of both worlds. For instance, an educational app could use 360-degree videos to transport students to a historical site, while AR overlays provide additional context and information about the location.

In conclusion, 360-degree videos represent a significant advancement in the way we capture, share, and experience visual content. By allowing viewers to explore video scenes from every angle, this technology provides a level of immersion and interactivity that traditional videos cannot match. The applications of 360-degree videos are vast, ranging from entertainment and education to tourism, business, and beyond. Despite the challenges and considerations involved in their production and consumption, the potential of 360-degree videos to create engaging, informative, and transformative experiences is undeniable. As technology continues to evolve, we can expect to see even more innovative and impactful uses of 360-degree videos, shaping the future of media and communication in profound ways.

19. **Head-Mounted Displays (HMDs)**: Devices worn on the head for VR and AR experiences.

Head-mounted displays (HMDs) are transformative devices worn on the head to facilitate immersive experiences in virtual reality (VR) and augmented reality (AR). These devices play a crucial role in creating immersive environments by providing users with a visual interface that completely or partially covers their field of view, allowing them to interact with digital content in a way that feels natural and engaging. The development and refinement of HMDs have significantly advanced the capabilities and applications of VR and AR technologies, opening up new possibilities across various industries, including gaming, education, healthcare, and more.

At their core, HMDs are designed to provide a stereoscopic display that presents two slightly different images to each eye, creating a sense of depth and three-dimensionality. This stereoscopic effect, combined with head-tracking sensors that adjust the perspective based on the user's movements, enables users to feel as if they are truly present in the virtual or augmented environment. The visual fidelity and responsiveness of HMDs are critical for maintaining immersion and preventing issues such as motion sickness or visual discomfort.

One of the most well-known applications of HMDs is in the gaming industry, where they have revolutionized the way players interact with digital worlds. VR headsets like the Oculus Rift, HTC Vive, and PlayStation VR provide gamers with an immersive experience that goes beyond traditional screen-based gaming. By wearing an HMD, players can look around, move, and interact with the virtual environment as if they were physically present within the game. This level of immersion enhances the overall gaming experience, making it more engaging and thrilling. In addition to visual immersion, many VR headsets also incorporate spatial audio and haptic feedback, further enhancing the sense of presence and realism.

In the realm of augmented reality, HMDs like the Microsoft HoloLens and Magic Leap One offer a different approach by overlaying digital content onto the real world. These AR headsets use transparent or semi-transparent displays that allow users to see their physical surroundings while also interacting with virtual objects and information. This blending of the real and digital worlds has numerous practical applications. For example, in industrial settings, AR HMDs can provide workers with real-time information and instructions overlaid on their field of view, improving efficiency and reducing errors. In healthcare, AR HMDs can assist surgeons by overlaying patient data and imaging onto their view during procedures, enhancing precision and outcomes.

Education is another field where HMDs have shown great potential. VR and AR headsets can create immersive learning environments that make complex subjects more accessible and engaging. For instance, in a history class, students can use VR headsets to explore ancient civilizations and historical events, gaining a deeper understanding of the context and significance of what they are studying. In science education, AR headsets can bring abstract concepts to life by overlaying interactive simulations and visualizations onto the real world, allowing students to experiment and explore in ways that are not possible with traditional teaching methods.

HMDs are also making significant strides in the field of healthcare. In medical training, VR headsets can simulate surgical procedures and clinical scenarios, providing trainees with a realistic and risk-free environment to practice their skills. This hands-on training can improve competency and confidence, ultimately leading to better patient care. AR HMDs, on the other hand, can enhance real-time diagnostics and treatment. For example, AR headsets can assist doctors during surgeries by displaying vital information and imaging data directly in their line of sight, reducing the need to look away at monitors and improving focus and accuracy.

The business and enterprise sectors are also leveraging the capabilities of HMDs to enhance productivity and collaboration. In remote work and virtual meetings, VR headsets can create virtual offices and meeting rooms where participants feel as though they are in the same physical space, fostering a sense of presence and engagement. AR headsets can facilitate remote assistance and collaboration by allowing experts to guide workers through complex tasks with real-time visual instructions and annotations overlaid on their view. This can be particularly useful in fields like engineering, maintenance, and construction, where precise and timely guidance is critical.

While the potential of HMDs is vast, there are also several challenges and considerations in their development and adoption. One of the main challenges is ensuring user comfort and minimizing issues such as motion sickness, eye strain, and physical discomfort. The design of HMDs needs to balance performance and comfort, considering factors such as weight, fit, and ventilation. Advances in optics, display technology, and ergonomics are continuously improving the user experience, making HMDs more comfortable for extended use.

Another important consideration is the resolution and field of view of HMDs. High-resolution displays are essential for creating clear and detailed images that enhance immersion and reduce the screen-door effect, where individual pixels are visible. A wide field of view is also crucial for providing a more natural and encompassing visual experience. Innovations in display technology, such as the use of OLED and microLED panels, are helping to achieve higher resolutions and wider fields of view, enhancing the overall quality of the VR and AR experiences.

The integration of advanced tracking and sensing technologies is also vital for the effectiveness of HMDs. Accurate head-tracking is necessary for maintaining a consistent and responsive perspective, preventing disorientation and enhancing immersion. Additionally, the incorporation of eye-tracking technology can further improve the user experience by enabling foveated rendering, where the highest resolution is focused on the area the user is looking at, reducing the computational load and improving performance. Hand-tracking and gesture recognition are also becoming increasingly important, allowing for more natural and intuitive interactions with virtual and augmented content.

The development of HMDs is not limited to visual and tracking capabilities. Audio plays a significant role in creating immersive experiences, and many HMDs incorporate spatial audio technology to provide realistic and directional soundscapes. This enhances the sense of presence and can provide important cues in virtual environments, such as the direction of approaching objects or the location of sound sources. Haptic feedback is another area of innovation, with some HMDs integrating haptic elements to provide tactile sensations, further enhancing the realism and engagement of VR and AR experiences.

As HMD technology continues to evolve, it is likely to become more integrated into our daily lives, with applications extending beyond gaming and entertainment to areas such as communication, education, healthcare, and industry. The convergence of VR and AR, often referred to as mixed reality (MR), is expected to create new and hybrid experiences that seamlessly blend the real and virtual worlds. This convergence will enable more sophisticated and context-aware interactions, providing users with richer and more meaningful experiences.

In conclusion, head-mounted displays (HMDs) are pivotal devices that enable immersive VR and AR experiences by providing users with a visual interface that covers their field of view and tracks their movements. These devices have revolutionized various industries, including gaming, education, healthcare, and enterprise, by creating engaging and interactive environments. The ongoing advancements in display technology, optics, tracking, and sensing are continuously improving the performance and comfort of HMDs, making them more accessible and effective. As the technology evolves, HMDs are expected to play an increasingly significant role in our digital interactions, transforming the way we work, learn, play, and communicate, and shaping the future of immersive experiences.

20. **Spatial Computing**: Technology that blends digital and physical spaces.

Spatial computing is a revolutionary technology that seamlessly blends digital and physical spaces, allowing for more intuitive and interactive interactions between humans and machines. This technology encompasses a wide range of advancements, including augmented reality (AR), virtual reality (VR), mixed reality (MR), and other immersive technologies that rely on spatial awareness and contextual understanding to create new experiences. By integrating digital content with the real world, spatial computing enables users to interact with their environment in more meaningful and natural ways, transforming industries and everyday life.

At the heart of spatial computing is the concept of spatial awareness. This involves the ability of a computing system to understand and interpret the spatial properties of the physical world, such as the location, orientation, and movement of objects and people. This spatial understanding is achieved through a combination of sensors, cameras, and sophisticated algorithms that process and analyze data in real-time. These systems can map the physical environment, track the position and movements of users, and recognize objects and surfaces, creating a digital representation of the real world that can be overlaid with virtual content.

One of the most prominent applications of spatial computing is in the field of augmented reality. AR technology overlays digital information onto the real world, enhancing the user's perception and interaction with their surroundings. This can be achieved through various devices, including smartphones, tablets, and head-mounted displays (HMDs) like the Microsoft HoloLens and Magic Leap One. In an AR experience, users can see and interact with virtual objects that are anchored to specific locations in the physical environment. For example, AR can be used in retail to allow customers to visualize how furniture would look in their homes before making a purchase, or in education to bring historical events to life by overlaying virtual reconstructions onto real-world locations.

Virtual reality, another key component of spatial computing, creates entirely immersive digital environments that users can explore and interact with. VR headsets, such as the Oculus Rift and HTC Vive, provide a stereoscopic display and head-tracking capabilities that allow users to look around and move within the virtual space. While VR primarily focuses on creating immersive experiences within digital environments, it also relies on spatial computing principles to track user movements and interactions accurately. This ensures that the virtual world responds in real-time to the user's actions, maintaining a high level of immersion and realism.

Mixed reality (MR) represents the convergence of AR and VR, enabling users to interact with both virtual and real objects in a unified environment. MR systems, like the HoloLens, use advanced sensors and cameras to map the physical environment and integrate virtual objects seamlessly. This allows for dynamic interactions where virtual objects can respond to changes in the real world and vice versa. For example, in a mixed reality workspace, digital tools and documents can be placed on physical desks and manipulated as if they were real objects, enhancing productivity and collaboration.

One of the significant advancements in spatial computing is the development of spatial mapping and localization technologies. These technologies enable devices to create detailed 3D maps of the physical environment, which are essential for accurately placing and interacting with virtual objects. Simultaneous Localization and Mapping (SLAM) is a common technique used in spatial computing, allowing devices to build a map of an unknown environment while simultaneously tracking their own location within it. SLAM is widely used in AR, VR, and robotics to provide spatial awareness and ensure accurate interactions with the physical world.

Spatial computing also leverages computer vision and machine learning to enhance its capabilities. Computer vision algorithms analyze visual data from cameras and sensors to recognize objects, surfaces, and gestures. Machine learning models can be trained to understand complex spatial relationships and predict user behavior, enabling more intuitive and responsive interactions. For example, in a spatial computing application for interior design, computer vision can recognize the dimensions and layout of a room, while machine learning can suggest optimal furniture arrangements based on user preferences and spatial constraints.

The integration of spatial computing into various industries has led to numerous innovative applications and benefits. In healthcare, spatial computing is being used to enhance medical training, diagnostics, and treatment. AR and VR simulations allow medical professionals to practice surgical procedures and other complex tasks in a risk-free virtual environment, improving their skills and confidence. Spatial computing can also assist surgeons during operations by overlaying patient data, such as MRI or CT scans, onto the surgical field, providing real-time guidance and improving precision.

In manufacturing and industrial settings, spatial computing is transforming the way workers interact with machines and perform tasks. AR headsets can provide real-time instructions and information, overlaying step-by-step guides onto machinery and equipment to assist with assembly, maintenance, and repair. This can reduce errors, improve efficiency, and enhance worker safety. Spatial computing can also enable remote assistance, where experts can guide on-site workers through complex tasks using AR annotations and visual cues, reducing downtime and travel costs.

Education is another sector where spatial computing is making a significant impact. By creating immersive and interactive learning experiences, spatial computing can enhance student engagement and understanding. AR and VR can bring abstract concepts to life, allowing students to explore subjects such as history, science, and geography in a more tangible and experiential way. For example, students can take virtual field trips to historical sites, explore the human body in 3D, or conduct virtual science experiments, gaining a deeper understanding of the material and fostering curiosity and exploration.

The entertainment industry has also embraced spatial computing to create new forms of interactive and immersive experiences. AR and VR games provide players with a high level of immersion, allowing them to interact with digital worlds in ways that were previously impossible. Mixed reality experiences can blend physical and digital elements, creating unique and engaging attractions in theme parks, museums, and live performances. Spatial computing enables new storytelling techniques, where narratives can unfold dynamically based on the user's interactions and environment, offering personalized and adaptive experiences.

In the realm of architecture and construction, spatial computing is revolutionizing the design and building process. AR and VR can be used to create virtual walkthroughs of buildings and spaces, allowing architects, clients, and stakeholders to explore and visualize designs before they are built. This can improve decision-making, identify potential issues early in the process, and facilitate better communication and collaboration. Spatial computing can also assist with construction by overlaying blueprints and instructions onto the physical site, guiding workers and ensuring accuracy and consistency.

While the potential of spatial computing is vast, there are also challenges and considerations in its development and deployment. Ensuring accurate and reliable spatial mapping and tracking is crucial for maintaining the effectiveness and usability of spatial computing systems. Any inaccuracies or delays in tracking can break the immersion and reduce the overall experience. Advances in sensor technology, computer vision, and machine learning are continuously improving the accuracy and reliability of spatial computing, but ongoing research and development are needed to address these challenges fully.

Privacy and security are also important considerations in spatial computing. The ability of spatial computing systems to map and understand physical environments raises concerns about data privacy and security. Ensuring that spatial data is collected, stored, and used responsibly is essential to protect user privacy and build trust in spatial computing technologies. Developers must implement robust security measures and provide transparent policies regarding data collection and usage.

The future of spatial computing holds exciting possibilities as technology continues to evolve. Improvements in hardware, such as more advanced sensors and lightweight, high-resolution displays, will enhance the performance and usability of spatial computing devices. Integration with other emerging technologies, such as artificial intelligence,

5G connectivity, and the Internet of Things (IoT), will enable more sophisticated and context-aware interactions. For example, spatial computing could be used in smart cities to create dynamic, interactive environments that respond to the needs and behaviors of residents, enhancing urban living and sustainability.

One of the promising directions for spatial computing is its integration with artificial intelligence (AI). AI can enhance spatial computing by providing more personalized and adaptive experiences. For instance, AI algorithms can learn from user interactions to anticipate needs and preferences, making spatial computing applications more intuitive and efficient. In healthcare, AI-powered spatial computing systems could analyze patient data and provide personalized treatment recommendations in real-time. In retail, AI could enhance AR shopping experiences by suggesting products based on the customer's browsing history and preferences.

Another exciting development is the convergence of spatial computing with the Internet of Things (IoT). IoT devices, equipped with sensors and connectivity, can provide real-time data about the physical environment, which can be integrated into spatial computing systems. This synergy can create smart environments where digital and physical objects interact seamlessly. For example, in a smart home, AR could overlay information about the status of IoT-connected appliances, allowing users to control them through intuitive gestures or voice commands. In industrial settings, IoT sensors could provide real-time data about machinery performance, which AR systems could visualize to assist with maintenance and troubleshooting.

The advent of 5G connectivity will further enhance the capabilities of spatial computing by providing the high-speed, low-latency network required for real-time data processing and interaction. With 5G, spatial computing applications can access cloud-based resources and AI models, enabling more complex and data-intensive experiences. For example, 5G could support remote collaboration in mixed reality, where teams in different locations work together on virtual prototypes in real-time, with minimal latency and high fidelity.

The integration of spatial computing with blockchain technology also holds potential, particularly in ensuring the security and authenticity of spatial data. Blockchain can provide a decentralized and immutable record of spatial data transactions, enhancing trust and transparency. This could be particularly useful in industries like real estate and construction, where the provenance and accuracy of spatial data are crucial.

As spatial computing technology continues to evolve, it will likely become more integrated into our daily lives, transforming the way we interact with digital and physical environments. The potential applications are vast, from enhancing productivity and efficiency in the workplace to creating more engaging and personalized entertainment experiences. However, realizing this potential will require addressing several challenges, including technical limitations, privacy concerns, and the need for standardized protocols and interoperability.

In conclusion, spatial computing is a transformative technology that blends digital and physical spaces, creating more intuitive and interactive experiences. By leveraging advancements in augmented reality, virtual reality, mixed reality, and other immersive technologies, spatial computing enables users to interact with their environment in more meaningful ways. The integration of spatial computing into various industries, including healthcare, education, manufacturing, and entertainment, is opening up new possibilities and enhancing the way we live and work. As technology continues to advance, spatial computing will play an increasingly significant role in shaping the future, offering richer, more personalized, and more engaging interactions between humans and machines.

Cyber Culture

Cyber culture represents the evolving norms, behaviors, and practices that define the online world. This culture is marked by several key elements, including digital identity, memes, internet subcultures, online privacy, and social media. Each of these components plays a significant role in shaping how individuals interact with each other and with digital environments, creating a complex and dynamic landscape that influences both online and offline life.

Digital identity is a cornerstone of cyber culture, serving as the online representation of individuals. Unlike physical identities, which are generally stable and rooted in real-world attributes, digital identities are often fluid and multifaceted. People can present themselves in various ways depending on the platform and audience, allowing for experimentation with different aspects of their personality. This flexibility can be empowering, providing opportunities for self-expression and connection with like-minded individuals. However, it also raises issues around authenticity and accountability, as the anonymity of the internet can sometimes encourage behavior that people might avoid in face-to-face interactions.

Memes are another critical element of cyber culture. These are cultural elements that spread rapidly online, often taking the form of images, videos, or text that capture humorous or insightful commentary on various topics. Memes are a form of participatory media, where users not only consume content but also create and modify it, contributing to an ongoing cultural conversation. The viral nature of memes means that they can quickly reach a wide audience, influencing public discourse and popular culture. Memes can serve as a means of social commentary, political expression, or simply entertainment, reflecting the diverse interests and creativity of internet users.

Internet subcultures are communities with shared interests and practices that thrive online. These subcultures can range from fan groups dedicated to specific media franchises to niche communities centered around particular hobbies or ideologies. The internet provides a space for these groups to connect and communicate, often transcending geographical and social boundaries. Within these subcultures, members can find a sense of belonging and identity, sharing knowledge, experiences, and cultural artifacts that reinforce their community bonds. However, internet subcultures can also be insular and exclusive, sometimes leading to conflicts with mainstream culture or other subcultures.

Online privacy is a critical concern in cyber culture, encompassing the protection of personal information on the internet. As individuals increasingly live their lives online, sharing personal details, making transactions, and interacting with others, the potential for privacy breaches grows. Issues such as data mining, identity theft, and surveillance have become prominent, raising questions about how to balance the benefits of digital connectivity with the need to protect personal information. Privacy policies, encryption technologies, and user awareness are all part of the ongoing effort to safeguard online privacy. However, the evolving nature of technology and the internet means that new challenges and threats continuously emerge, requiring vigilance and adaptation.

Social media platforms are central to cyber culture, providing the infrastructure for online communication and content sharing. Platforms like Facebook, Twitter, Instagram, and TikTok have transformed how people interact, allowing for instant communication, content creation, and community building. Social media enables the rapid dissemination of information, making it a powerful tool for both individuals and organizations. It has played a significant role in social movements, marketing, and everyday social interactions. However, social media also presents challenges, including issues of misinformation, cyberbullying, and the impact on mental health. The algorithms that drive social media platforms often prioritize engagement over accuracy, sometimes amplifying divisive or harmful content.

The concept of digital identity encompasses various aspects, from usernames and avatars to social media profiles and personal blogs. People curate their digital identities based on how they want to be perceived, which can vary widely across different contexts. For instance, a professional LinkedIn profile might present a polished, career-focused image, while a personal Instagram account could highlight hobbies and social activities. This multiplicity allows for nuanced self-representation but also complicates the notion of a singular identity. The ability to create and manage multiple digital identities can lead to a more flexible and diverse online presence but also raises questions about consistency and authenticity.

Memes, as cultural artifacts, often reflect the collective consciousness of internet users. They can be highly ephemeral, with some memes going viral and then fading quickly, while others become enduring symbols within cyber culture. Memes often rely on humor, irony, and shared knowledge, creating a sense of in-group understanding among those who "get it." The creation and sharing of memes involve a participatory culture where users are not just passive consumers but active producers of content. This participatory nature democratizes cultural production, allowing anyone with an internet connection to contribute to and shape the cultural landscape.

Internet subcultures thrive on platforms that facilitate niche communities, such as Reddit, Discord, and specialized forums. These subcultures can develop their own norms, languages, and rituals, creating rich and diverse ecosystems of interaction. For example, gaming communities might have specific jargon, in-jokes, and customs that outsiders might find perplexing. The same goes for other subcultures, whether they are centered around music genres, political ideologies, or fandoms. These communities provide a sense of belonging and identity, allowing members to express themselves in ways that might not be possible in their offline lives. However, the insularity of some subcultures can lead to echo chambers, where dissenting opinions are marginalized, and groupthink prevails.

Online privacy remains a contentious and evolving issue within cyber culture. The amount of personal data generated and shared online has grown exponentially, leading to concerns about how this data is collected, stored, and used. Social media platforms, search engines, and other online services often rely on data collection to drive their business models, raising questions about user consent and data protection. Privacy advocates argue for stronger regulations and better user controls to protect personal information, while some companies have started to implement more robust privacy measures in response to public concern. Nonetheless, the tension between the convenience and benefits of digital services and the need for privacy continues to shape the discourse around online privacy.

Social media platforms have become the public squares of the digital age, where people gather to share news, opinions, and personal updates. These platforms enable instant and global communication, making it easier than ever to connect with others. Social media has also democratized content creation, allowing anyone to publish their thoughts, art, and opinions to a potentially vast audience. This has led to a proliferation of voices and perspectives but also to challenges such as misinformation and echo chambers. The algorithms that power social media platforms are designed to maximize engagement, often prioritizing sensational or emotionally charged content, which can contribute to polarization and the spread of false information.

Digital identity, memes, internet subcultures, online privacy, and social media all intersect to create a vibrant and complex cyber culture. Each element influences and is influenced by the others, resulting in a dynamic and constantly evolving digital landscape. The way individuals present themselves online, the rapid spread of cultural elements through memes, the formation of niche communities, the ongoing concerns about privacy, and the central role of social media platforms all contribute to the richness and diversity of cyber culture.

As technology continues to advance and more aspects of life move online, cyber culture will undoubtedly continue to evolve. The rise of new technologies, such as artificial intelligence and the internet of things, will bring new opportunities and challenges, further shaping the digital landscape. The ongoing dialogue around issues such as privacy, authenticity, and the impact of digital interactions on mental health will remain crucial as society navigates the complexities of life in the digital age.

In conclusion, cyber culture encompasses a wide array of practices, behaviors, and norms that define how individuals interact in the digital realm. Digital identity allows for flexible and multifaceted self-representation, while memes serve as rapid and participatory cultural expressions. Internet subcultures provide communities and a sense of belonging, online privacy remains a critical concern, and social media platforms facilitate communication and content sharing on a global scale. Together, these elements create a rich and dynamic cyber culture that continues to shape and be shaped by the ongoing evolution of technology and digital interactions.

21. **Digital Identity**: Online representation of individuals.

In the contemporary digital age, the concept of identity has transcended the physical realm, giving rise to what is now known as digital identity. This online representation of individuals encompasses a broad range of elements that define who we are in the digital world. From usernames and email addresses to social media profiles and biometric data, digital identity plays a crucial role in how we interact, transact, and communicate online.

Digital identity is essentially the compilation of data that uniquely identifies an individual in the digital landscape. It is formed through a combination of personal information, behavioral data, and digital footprints left behind through online activities. This identity is used by various online platforms and services to authenticate users, provide personalized experiences, and ensure security in digital transactions.

One of the most basic components of digital identity is the username. Whether it's an email address, a social media handle, or a login ID, usernames serve as the primary identifier in many online interactions. Coupled with passwords, they form the first line of defense against unauthorized access to personal information. However, as the sophistication of cyber threats increases, the reliance on usernames and passwords alone has proven to be insufficient. This has led to the integration of more advanced authentication methods, such as two-factor authentication (2FA) and biometric verification.

Biometric data, including fingerprints, facial recognition, and voice recognition, has become an integral part of digital identity. These unique biological traits offer a higher level of security compared to traditional methods. For instance, unlocking a smartphone with a fingerprint or accessing a secure facility using facial recognition not only enhances security but also provides convenience to the user. Biometric data is difficult to replicate, making it a robust means of authentication in an increasingly digital world.

Social media profiles are another significant aspect of digital identity. Platforms like Facebook, Twitter, Instagram, and LinkedIn provide users with the opportunity to create and manage their online personas. These profiles often contain a wealth of information, including personal details, interests, connections, and activity history. Social media profiles are not just about personal expression; they have become essential tools for networking, professional branding, and even political activism. The information shared on these platforms contributes to the digital footprint that shapes an individual's online identity.

Digital identity is not limited to personal use. It also plays a vital role in the professional and commercial spheres. For businesses, establishing a digital identity is crucial for building brand reputation and engaging with customers. Corporate websites, online reviews, and social media presence collectively contribute to a company's digital identity. This identity affects consumer perception and can significantly influence business success.

In the financial sector, digital identity verification is paramount to prevent fraud and ensure secure transactions. Financial institutions employ sophisticated systems to verify the identities of their customers, using methods such as digital signatures, blockchain technology, and secure customer databases. This helps in maintaining the integrity of financial transactions and protecting sensitive information from malicious actors.

While digital identity offers numerous benefits, it also presents significant challenges and risks. One of the primary concerns is privacy. The more data that is collected and stored about individuals, the greater the potential for misuse. Data breaches and unauthorized access to personal information can have devastating consequences, ranging from financial loss to identity theft. Protecting digital identity requires robust security measures and adherence to privacy regulations.

Governments and regulatory bodies worldwide have recognized the importance of safeguarding digital identity and have implemented various laws and frameworks to protect individuals' data. The General Data Protection Regulation (GDPR) in the European Union is one such example, emphasizing the need for transparency, consent, and accountability in data handling practices. These regulations aim to give individuals greater control over their personal information and ensure that organizations manage data responsibly.

Another challenge associated with digital identity is the issue of digital exclusion. Not everyone has equal access to digital technologies, and this disparity can create a divide in who can effectively establish and manage their digital identity. Socioeconomic factors, geographic location, and technological literacy all play a role in digital inclusion. Efforts to bridge this gap are essential to ensure that everyone can benefit from the opportunities offered by the digital age.

The concept of digital identity is continually evolving. With advancements in technology, new forms of identity verification and management are emerging. Blockchain technology, for example, offers the potential for decentralized and self-sovereign identity systems, where individuals have greater control over their personal data. In such systems, digital identities are stored on a distributed ledger, making them more secure and less susceptible to tampering.

Artificial intelligence (AI) and machine learning also have significant implications for digital identity. These technologies can analyze vast amounts of data to detect patterns and anomalies, improving the accuracy and reliability of identity verification processes. AI-powered systems can enhance security by identifying suspicious behavior and flagging potential threats in real-time.

As digital identity becomes more integrated into our daily lives, it is essential to consider the ethical implications. Issues such as data ownership, consent, and the potential for surveillance must be addressed to ensure that digital identity systems are used responsibly and ethically. Balancing the benefits of digital identity with the need to protect individual rights and freedoms is a complex but necessary endeavor.

In the context of the global digital economy, digital identity is a key enabler of innovation and growth. It facilitates seamless interactions between individuals, businesses, and governments, driving efficiency and convenience. For instance, digital identity enables online banking, e-commerce, telemedicine, and remote work, transforming how we live and work.

Looking ahead, the future of digital identity is likely to be shaped by several trends. One such trend is the increasing adoption of mobile identity solutions. With the proliferation of smartphones and mobile devices, mobile identity verification is becoming more prevalent. This allows individuals to authenticate their identities and access services on the go, enhancing flexibility and convenience.

Another trend is the rise of digital identity platforms that offer comprehensive identity management solutions. These platforms integrate various authentication methods, provide user-friendly interfaces, and offer robust security features. They aim to simplify the process of managing digital identity while ensuring the highest level of security and privacy.

In conclusion, digital identity is a multifaceted concept that encompasses the various ways in which individuals represent themselves online. It is built from personal information, social media profiles, biometric data, and more, playing a crucial role in both personal and professional contexts. While it offers numerous benefits, including enhanced security and convenience, it also presents challenges related to privacy, security, and digital inclusion. As technology continues to advance, the landscape of digital identity will evolve, bringing new opportunities and challenges. Ensuring that digital identity systems are secure, inclusive, and ethically managed is essential for harnessing the full potential of the digital age.

22. **Memes**: Cultural elements that spread rapidly online.

Memes are a fascinating and pervasive aspect of digital culture, representing cultural elements that spread rapidly online. Originating from the Greek word "mimema," which means "something imitated," the term "meme" was first coined by biologist Richard Dawkins in his 1976 book "The Selfish Gene" to describe an idea, behavior, or style that spreads from person to person within a culture. In the digital age, memes have taken on a new life, evolving into a potent form of online communication that shapes and reflects the zeitgeist.

Digital memes are typically characterized by their format, which often includes an image or video accompanied by text. This format allows for quick and effective transmission of ideas, emotions, and humor. Memes can vary widely in content, from humorous and light-hearted to political and controversial. Their versatility and adaptability make them a powerful tool for commentary, satire, and social engagement.

One of the key factors contributing to the rapid spread of memes is their inherent simplicity and accessibility. Most memes are easy to create and share, requiring minimal technical skills. This democratization of content creation means that anyone with an internet connection can participate in the meme culture, contributing to its rapid proliferation. Platforms like Twitter, Instagram, Reddit, and TikTok serve as fertile ground for the dissemination of memes, enabling them to reach vast audiences in a short period.

Memes often reflect current events and popular culture, acting as a digital barometer of societal trends and attitudes. For example, during significant political events or social movements, memes frequently emerge as a means of expressing support, dissent, or commentary. The 2016 U.S. presidential election saw an explosion of politically charged memes, which were used to mock candidates, highlight key issues, and galvanize supporters. Similarly, during the COVID-19 pandemic, memes about quarantine life, social distancing, and mask-wearing provided a collective outlet for coping with the crisis.

The humor in memes often relies on shared cultural knowledge and inside jokes. This creates a sense of community among those who "get" the meme, fostering a feeling of belonging and shared experience. Memes can also serve as a form of social bonding, with individuals using them to communicate with friends, family, and even strangers. The rapid spread of memes across different cultural and linguistic boundaries highlights their universal appeal and ability to transcend traditional communication barriers.

However, the rapid spread of memes also raises questions about their impact on society. Memes can perpetuate stereotypes, spread misinformation, and contribute to the polarization of public discourse. Because memes are often created and shared quickly, they can lack context and nuance, leading to misunderstandings and misinterpretations. The viral nature of memes means that false or harmful content can spread just as rapidly as beneficial content, posing challenges for content moderation and fact-checking.

The role of memes in shaping public opinion and influencing behavior is a topic of ongoing research and debate. Memes can act as vehicles for propaganda, with political actors and organizations using them to sway public opinion and disseminate ideological messages. The use of memes in political campaigns has become increasingly sophisticated, with targeted meme strategies designed to engage specific demographics and amplify certain narratives. This has raised concerns about the ethical implications of using memes as a tool for manipulation and control.

Despite these challenges, memes also have the potential to foster positive social change. Memes can raise awareness about important issues, mobilize support for causes, and encourage critical thinking. For example, environmental memes have been used to highlight the urgency of climate change, while social justice memes have played a role in movements like Black Lives Matter. The ability of memes to distill complex issues into digestible and shareable content makes them an effective medium for advocacy and education.

The evolution of memes over time is a testament to their adaptability and resilience. Memes often undergo rapid mutation, with new variations emerging as they are shared and remixed by different creators. This process of iteration and adaptation ensures that memes remain relevant and engaging, constantly evolving to reflect the changing cultural landscape. The concept of "meme templates" has emerged, where certain images or formats become standardized frameworks for creating new memes. These templates provide a familiar structure that can be easily customized with new text or context, making meme creation more accessible and consistent.

One of the most notable aspects of meme culture is its embrace of absurdity and irony. Many memes rely on surreal or nonsensical humor, subverting expectations and challenging conventional notions of comedy. This embrace of the absurd can be seen in meme trends like "Deep-fried memes," where images are intentionally distorted and over-saturated to create a bizarre visual effect. The ironic nature of many memes reflects a broader cultural shift towards postmodernism, where traditional boundaries between high and low culture, serious and trivial, are increasingly blurred.

Memes have also given rise to a new form of celebrity and influencer culture. Meme creators and curators can amass large followings and significant influence within online communities. Some meme pages and accounts have become cultural touchstones, with their content shaping online discourse and trends. The rise of meme influencers highlights the changing nature of content creation and consumption in the digital age, where traditional gatekeepers of media and culture are increasingly bypassed.

The commercial potential of memes has not gone unnoticed. Brands and marketers have recognized the power of memes to engage audiences and drive viral marketing campaigns. Memes are often used in advertising to create relatable and shareable content that resonates with consumers. This has led to the phenomenon of "meme marketing," where brands attempt to harness the viral nature of memes to promote their products or services. While this approach can be highly effective, it also carries risks, as attempts to manufacture virality or co-opt meme culture can backfire if perceived as inauthentic or opportunistic.

The intersection of memes and intellectual property is another area of legal and ethical complexity. Memes often involve the use of copyrighted images, videos, and other media, raising questions about fair use and creative ownership. The collaborative and derivative nature of meme creation complicates traditional notions of authorship and copyright, as memes are frequently modified and remixed by multiple creators. This has led to debates about how to balance the protection of intellectual property rights with the need to preserve the open and participatory nature of meme culture.

Looking to the future, the role of memes in digital culture is likely to continue evolving. As technology advances, new forms of meme creation and distribution will emerge, further blurring the lines between content creators and consumers. The integration of artificial intelligence and machine learning in content creation could lead to the development of automated meme generators, capable of producing endless variations on popular themes. Virtual and augmented reality could also open new avenues for meme creation, enabling immersive and interactive experiences that push the boundaries of traditional formats.

In conclusion, memes are a dynamic and influential element of digital culture, representing cultural elements that spread rapidly online. Their simplicity, accessibility, and versatility make them a powerful tool for communication, humor, and social commentary. While memes offer numerous benefits, including fostering community and raising awareness, they also pose challenges related to misinformation, polarization, and intellectual property. As the digital landscape continues to evolve, memes will undoubtedly remain a central and ever-changing facet of how we share, connect, and understand the world around us.

23. **Internet Subcultures**: Communities with shared interests and practices online.

The internet has given rise to a vast array of subcultures, communities with shared interests and practices that thrive in the digital realm. These internet subcultures are diverse, often niche, and deeply connected by their unique passions and collective identities. They represent a modern evolution of traditional subcultures, leveraging the connectivity and anonymity of the internet to foster bonds and create spaces where like-minded individuals can converge, share, and develop their interests.

One of the defining features of internet subcultures is their ability to form around virtually any interest or hobby, no matter how obscure. From fan communities centered around specific TV shows, movies, or books, to hobbyist groups dedicated to crafting, gaming, or technology, the internet has enabled people with even the most niche interests to find one another. Platforms like Reddit, Discord, Tumblr, and specialized forums serve as the primary gathering places for these communities, offering spaces for discussion, collaboration, and the sharing of related content.

The anonymity afforded by the internet is a significant factor in the formation and sustainability of these subcultures. It allows individuals to express themselves freely without fear of judgment from their immediate social circles. This anonymity can foster a sense of belonging and acceptance, particularly for those whose interests might be considered unconventional or misunderstood by mainstream society. For example, the furry fandom, a subculture centered around anthropomorphic animal characters, has flourished online partly because individuals can engage with the community without revealing their identities.

Internet subcultures often develop their own unique languages, symbols, and rituals, further solidifying their group identity. Memes, in-jokes, and specific terminologies become the vernacular through which members communicate. This specialized language not only enhances the sense of community but also acts as a barrier to outsiders, preserving the subculture's distinctiveness. For instance, the language used in the gaming subculture, with terms like "GG" (good game), "noob" (newbie), and "pwn" (dominate), serves as both a means of communication and a marker of membership.

The rapid spread of information on the internet means that these subcultures are dynamic and constantly evolving. Trends, memes, and ideas can disseminate quickly, leading to rapid changes in the subculture's practices and interests. This fluidity is a hallmark of internet subcultures, as they can adapt and respond to new developments in real-time. The speed at which information travels also means that subcultures can quickly gain traction and expand their membership, reaching global audiences almost instantaneously.

A significant aspect of internet subcultures is their potential for both positive and negative impacts on their members and broader society. On the positive side, these communities can provide support, friendship, and a sense of purpose. They often serve as safe spaces for individuals to explore their identities, share their creativity, and find camaraderie. For example, the LGBTQ+ community has found substantial support and visibility online, with various subcultures providing resources, advocacy, and a sense of belonging to individuals who might otherwise feel isolated.

However, the insularity and anonymity of internet subcultures can also give rise to negative behaviors and toxic environments. Some subcultures can become echo chambers, where harmful ideologies and misinformation proliferate unchecked. Online communities dedicated to conspiracy theories, hate speech, or extremist views can radicalize individuals and contribute to real-world harm. The challenge lies in balancing the freedom of expression that the internet provides with the need to mitigate the spread of harmful content.

One notable internet subculture is the hacker community. Hackers are individuals who explore the intricacies of computer systems, often finding vulnerabilities and exploiting them for various purposes. While the mainstream perception of hackers is often negative, equating them with cybercriminals, the hacker subculture is multifaceted and includes many who use their skills for ethical purposes, such as improving security and advocating for digital rights.

Communities like Anonymous, a decentralized group known for its hacktivism, have used their abilities to support political causes, highlighting the complex nature of this subculture.

The rise of streaming platforms and social media has also given birth to new subcultures centered around content creators and influencers. Platforms like YouTube, Twitch, and Instagram have enabled individuals to build massive followings based on their personalities, skills, and interests. These content creators often cultivate dedicated fan communities, where followers engage with their content, support them financially, and participate in communal activities. The phenomenon of "stan culture," where fans exhibit intense loyalty and devotion to their favorite creators, exemplifies how these subcultures can form strong emotional bonds.

Another prominent internet subculture is the world of online gaming. Gamers, united by their passion for video games, form communities that span genres and platforms. These subcultures often revolve around specific games or gaming franchises, with dedicated forums, YouTube channels, and social media groups where players share strategies, fan art, and in-game experiences. Esports, the competitive side of gaming, has grown into a global phenomenon, with professional players and teams attracting millions of viewers and substantial sponsorship deals. The gaming subculture exemplifies how internet-based communities can develop complex ecosystems with their own economies and cultural norms.

Fan fiction and fan art communities are also significant internet subcultures. These groups are composed of fans who create and share their own stories, artwork, and interpretations of existing media. Sites like Archive of Our Own (AO3) and DeviantArt provide platforms for these creators to showcase their work and receive feedback from peers. The fan fiction community, in particular, demonstrates the power of participatory culture, where fans not only consume but also actively contribute to the narratives they love. This creativity fosters a sense of ownership and deeper engagement with the original media.

The internet has also given rise to subcultures centered around various lifestyle choices and philosophies. For instance, the minimalist community advocates for a simpler, more intentional way of living, often sharing tips and inspiration on blogs, YouTube channels, and social media. Similarly, the zero-waste movement, which aims to reduce personal waste production, has found a robust online presence where individuals share strategies, products, and support for living more sustainably. These subcultures highlight how the internet can facilitate the spread of ideas that inspire real-world behavioral changes.

The cryptocurrency and blockchain technology community is another significant internet subculture. Enthusiasts and investors in cryptocurrencies like Bitcoin and Ethereum form tight-knit communities where they discuss market trends, technological advancements, and investment strategies. Forums like Bitcointalk and social media platforms like Twitter are hubs for these discussions. The decentralized and often libertarian ethos of this subculture reflects broader themes of financial independence and skepticism of traditional financial systems. The rapid rise and volatility of cryptocurrencies have made this subculture particularly dynamic and influential.

The DIY (do-it-yourself) and maker communities are also thriving internet subcultures. These groups are composed of individuals who enjoy creating, building, and crafting things by hand. The internet provides a wealth of resources, tutorials, and forums where makers can share their projects, seek advice, and collaborate. Platforms like Instructables and YouTube are treasure troves of DIY content, covering everything from electronics and robotics to woodworking and sewing. The maker subculture embodies a spirit of creativity and self-sufficiency, empowered by the vast knowledge and community support available online.

Internet subcultures also extend into the realm of aesthetics and fashion. Movements like vaporwave, cottagecore, and dark academia have emerged as distinct visual and lifestyle trends, each with its own dedicated online communities. These subcultures often revolve around a shared appreciation for specific visual styles, music genres, and cultural references. Platforms like Tumblr and Instagram play a crucial role in propagating these aesthetics, where users curate and share content that aligns with their subculture's vibe. The internet allows these niche aesthetic movements to gain visibility and influence, shaping broader cultural trends.

While internet subcultures offer many benefits, they also face challenges related to sustainability and inclusivity. The fast-paced nature of online culture means that trends can quickly become outdated, and communities can fragment or fade away. Additionally, issues of accessibility and representation are critical, as not all individuals have equal access to the internet or feel welcome in certain subcultures. Efforts to create more inclusive and diverse online spaces are essential to ensure that everyone can participate and benefit from the rich tapestry of internet subcultures.

In conclusion, internet subcultures represent a dynamic and multifaceted aspect of digital life, characterized by communities with shared interests and practices. These subcultures thrive on the connectivity and anonymity provided by the internet, allowing individuals to find like-minded peers and engage deeply with their passions. While they offer numerous benefits, including support, creativity, and shared identity, they also pose challenges related to misinformation, exclusivity, and ethical concerns. As the digital landscape continues to evolve, internet subcultures will remain a vital and ever-changing component of how we connect, communicate, and create in the online world.

24. **Online Privacy**: Protection of personal information on the internet.

Online privacy is a critical issue in the digital age, concerning the protection of personal information on the internet. As individuals increasingly engage with digital platforms and services, the amount of personal data collected, stored, and processed has grown exponentially. This proliferation of data raises significant concerns about how personal information is safeguarded and the potential risks associated with its misuse.

At its core, online privacy is about ensuring that individuals have control over their personal information and how it is used. This encompasses a wide range of data, including names, addresses, social security numbers, financial details, browsing histories, and even biometric data. Protecting this information is essential to prevent identity theft, financial fraud, and other forms of cybercrime.

One of the fundamental challenges in protecting online privacy is the pervasive nature of data collection. Many online services and platforms collect vast amounts of data about their users, often without explicit consent. This data is used for various purposes, such as targeted advertising, personalization of services, and improving user experiences. However, the collection and use of personal data raise concerns about surveillance, data breaches, and unauthorized access.

The business model of many internet companies relies heavily on data collection and analysis. Social media platforms, search engines, and e-commerce sites often offer free services in exchange for access to user data. This data is then used to build detailed profiles of users, which can be sold to advertisers or other third parties. While this model has led to significant advancements in personalized content and services, it has also created a marketplace for personal data, often without the users' knowledge or explicit consent.

To address these concerns, various regulations and frameworks have been developed to protect online privacy. One of the most prominent is the General Data Protection Regulation (GDPR) in the European Union, which came into effect in 2018. GDPR sets stringent requirements for data protection, giving individuals greater control over their personal information. It mandates that companies obtain explicit consent from users before collecting their data and allows users to request access to, correction of, and deletion of their data. Non-compliance with GDPR can result in hefty fines, emphasizing the importance of data protection.

In the United States, the approach to online privacy has been more fragmented, with various state and federal laws addressing different aspects of data protection. The California Consumer Privacy Act (CCPA), enacted in 2018, is one of the most comprehensive state laws, providing California residents with rights similar to those under GDPR. It allows consumers to know what personal data is being collected, to whom it is being sold, and to request the deletion of their data. Other states have followed suit with their own privacy laws, creating a patchwork of regulations that companies must navigate.

Beyond regulatory measures, technological solutions play a crucial role in protecting online privacy. Encryption is one of the most effective tools for securing data. It involves encoding data so that only authorized parties can access it. End-to-end encryption, used by messaging apps like WhatsApp and Signal, ensures that only the communicating users can read the messages, preventing eavesdropping by third parties, including service providers.

Virtual Private Networks (VPNs) are another tool for enhancing online privacy. VPNs create a secure, encrypted connection between a user's device and the internet, masking the user's IP address and making their online activities more difficult to trace. This is particularly useful for protecting privacy on public Wi-Fi networks, where data can be more easily intercepted.

Despite these tools, achieving comprehensive online privacy remains challenging. Data breaches are a significant threat, with cybercriminals constantly developing new methods to exploit vulnerabilities. High-profile breaches, such as those experienced by Equifax, Target, and Facebook, have exposed the personal information of millions of users, leading to financial losses and identity theft. These incidents highlight the need for robust cybersecurity measures and the importance of regular security audits and updates.

Another aspect of online privacy is the role of cookies and tracking technologies. Cookies are small files stored on a user's device that track their online activities. While they are essential for functionalities like remembering login details and preferences, they can also be used for tracking user behavior across different sites. This has led to the rise of ad blockers and privacy-focused browsers that limit tracking and provide users with greater control over their online footprint.

The rise of the Internet of Things (IoT) has further complicated the landscape of online privacy. IoT devices, such as smart home appliances, wearables, and connected cars, collect vast amounts of data about users' habits and environments. This data can provide valuable insights and conveniences, but it also creates additional vectors for privacy breaches. Ensuring the security and privacy of IoT devices is critical, requiring strong encryption, regular updates, and user awareness.

Social media platforms pose unique challenges to online privacy. Users often share personal information, photos, and updates with their networks, sometimes underestimating the potential reach and permanence of this information. Privacy settings on these platforms can be complex and frequently change, making it difficult for users to manage their data effectively. Additionally, the algorithms used by social media companies can collect and analyze data to serve targeted content and ads, further blurring the lines of user consent.

To mitigate these risks, users need to be proactive about managing their online privacy. This includes using strong, unique passwords for different accounts, enabling two-factor authentication, and regularly reviewing privacy settings on social media and other platforms. Being mindful of the information shared online and understanding the terms and conditions of the services used can also help protect personal data.

Education and awareness are essential components of online privacy. Many users are not fully aware of the extent of data collection and the potential risks associated with it. Public campaigns and educational programs can help individuals understand their rights and the best practices for protecting their data. This is particularly important for vulnerable populations, such as children and the elderly, who may be more susceptible to privacy breaches and cyber threats.

Corporate responsibility is another critical factor in safeguarding online privacy. Companies must prioritize data protection and adopt transparent practices regarding data collection, usage, and sharing. Implementing privacy by design, where privacy considerations are integrated into the development of products and services from the outset, can help build trust with users and ensure compliance with regulatory requirements.

Emerging technologies, such as artificial intelligence (AI) and blockchain, offer new opportunities and challenges for online privacy. AI can enhance security by detecting anomalies and potential threats, but it also raises concerns about data privacy and surveillance. The use of AI in decision-making processes, such as hiring or lending, can lead to biases and privacy infringements if not properly managed.

Blockchain technology, known for its use in cryptocurrencies, provides a decentralized approach to data management. It offers the potential for greater transparency and control over personal information, allowing individuals to manage their digital identities securely. However, the immutability of blockchain records also means that once data is recorded, it cannot be easily altered or deleted, posing unique privacy challenges.

Looking ahead, the future of online privacy will likely involve a combination of regulatory measures, technological advancements, and increased user awareness. Governments, companies, and individuals must work together to create a digital environment where personal information is protected, and privacy is respected.

The ongoing development of international data protection standards could help harmonize privacy regulations and provide a consistent framework for global companies. Collaboration between countries and regulatory bodies can enhance the enforcement of privacy laws and ensure that users' rights are upheld worldwide.

Technological innovation will continue to play a crucial role in enhancing online privacy. Advances in encryption, secure multi-party computation, and privacy-preserving data analytics can help protect personal information while enabling valuable insights and services. Privacy-enhancing technologies, such as differential privacy, which adds noise to data to protect individual identities, can allow for the safe use of data in research and analysis.

Ultimately, the protection of online privacy is a shared responsibility. Individuals must take proactive steps to safeguard their data, while companies and governments must create policies and technologies that prioritize privacy. By working together, we can build a digital future where personal information is protected, and individuals can enjoy the benefits of the internet without compromising their privacy.

25. **Social Media**: Platforms for online communication and content sharing.

Social media platforms have become ubiquitous in the modern digital landscape, serving as pivotal tools for online communication and content sharing. These platforms have revolutionized the way people connect, interact, and disseminate information. From personal updates to global news, social media influences almost every aspect of contemporary life, transforming social interactions, business practices, and even political landscapes.

At the heart of social media is the ability to create and share content. This can range from text-based posts and photos to videos and live streams. Platforms like Facebook, Instagram, Twitter, TikTok, and YouTube provide users with a variety of tools to express themselves and engage with others. Each platform offers unique features tailored to different types of content and audiences, fostering diverse communities and subcultures.

One of the primary functions of social media is to facilitate communication. Users can connect with friends, family, and colleagues, regardless of geographical barriers. This connectivity is particularly significant for maintaining relationships over long distances. Social media also enables the formation of new connections through shared interests and common goals. Online groups and communities allow individuals to interact with like-minded people, fostering a sense of belonging and support.

The evolution of social media has also transformed how people consume and engage with content. Traditional media channels, such as television and print, have been supplemented, and in some cases replaced, by digital content shared on social media. News outlets and journalists use these platforms to disseminate information rapidly and interact with their audiences. This shift has democratized the flow of information, allowing anyone with an internet connection to share their perspective and potentially reach a global audience.

However, the rise of social media has also brought challenges, particularly in the realm of information accuracy. The speed at which content can be shared means that misinformation and fake news can spread rapidly, often outpacing efforts to verify and correct false information. This has significant implications for public opinion and behavior, as seen in events like the spread of misinformation during elections or public health crises. The challenge lies in balancing the open nature of social media with the need for accurate and reliable information.

Another critical aspect of social media is its impact on business and marketing. Companies use these platforms to reach customers, promote products, and build brand loyalty. Social media marketing has become a cornerstone of modern business strategies, leveraging the vast user bases of platforms like Facebook and Instagram to target specific demographics with personalized content. Influencer marketing, where brands collaborate with popular social media personalities, has also become a powerful tool for reaching new audiences and enhancing brand credibility.

The engagement metrics provided by social media platforms offer valuable insights into consumer behavior and preferences. Businesses can analyze likes, shares, comments, and other interactions to gauge the effectiveness of their campaigns and adjust their strategies accordingly. This data-driven approach enables more precise targeting and efficient allocation of marketing resources.

Social media has also changed the dynamics of customer service. Many companies use these platforms to address customer inquiries and complaints, offering a more immediate and interactive form of support. This real-time engagement can enhance customer satisfaction and loyalty, as issues can be resolved quickly and publicly, demonstrating the company's commitment to its customers.

The personal branding aspect of social media is another significant development. Individuals can use platforms like LinkedIn to showcase their professional achievements and network with industry peers. This has transformed job searching and recruitment, making it easier for employers and candidates to connect. Similarly, platforms like Instagram and YouTube allow individuals to build personal brands around their hobbies and interests, potentially turning them into lucrative careers.

The role of social media in activism and social movements cannot be overstated. Platforms like Twitter and Facebook have been instrumental in organizing protests, raising awareness, and mobilizing support for various causes. Hashtags like #BlackLivesMatter and #MeToo have galvanized global movements, highlighting the power of social media to drive social change. These platforms provide a voice to marginalized communities and amplify their messages, fostering a more inclusive public discourse.

Despite its many benefits, social media is not without its downsides. One of the most pressing issues is the impact on mental health. Studies have shown that excessive use of social media can lead to feelings of anxiety, depression, and loneliness. The constant comparison to others, exposure to negative content, and the pressure to maintain a curated online persona can take a toll on mental well-being. Additionally, the addictive nature of social media, driven by the desire for likes and validation, can lead to compulsive behavior and reduced productivity.

Privacy is another significant concern associated with social media. The vast amount of personal information shared on these platforms makes users vulnerable to data breaches and privacy violations. Companies often collect and analyze user data to deliver targeted ads, raising ethical questions about consent and data ownership. High-profile incidents, such as the Cambridge Analytica scandal, have underscored the need for stronger privacy protections and greater transparency in how user data is handled.

The algorithms used by social media platforms to curate content also have profound implications. These algorithms prioritize content based on user preferences and engagement metrics, creating echo chambers where individuals are exposed primarily to information that reinforces their existing beliefs. This can lead to polarization and a fragmented public discourse, as people become isolated within their ideological bubbles. Addressing this issue requires a delicate balance between personalization and exposure to diverse viewpoints.

The regulatory landscape for social media is evolving as governments and organizations grapple with these challenges. Efforts to regulate content, protect user privacy, and ensure fair competition are ongoing, with varying approaches and degrees of success. For example, the European Union's General Data Protection Regulation (GDPR) sets stringent standards for data protection, while the United States has seen a patchwork of state-level regulations addressing different aspects of social media governance.

Looking to the future, the role of social media will likely continue to evolve. Emerging technologies such as virtual reality (VR) and augmented reality (AR) promise to create more immersive social media experiences. These technologies could transform how people interact online, offering new ways to connect and share content. The integration of AI and machine learning will further enhance personalization and engagement, but it also raises questions about the ethical use of these technologies and their impact on privacy.

Another trend to watch is the rise of decentralized social media platforms. These platforms aim to address some of the issues associated with centralized control, such as data privacy and censorship. By leveraging blockchain technology, decentralized platforms can offer greater transparency and user control over data. While still in their early stages, these platforms represent a potential shift in how social media operates, prioritizing user autonomy and privacy.

The role of social media in shaping public opinion and behavior will remain a critical area of focus. As platforms continue to influence how people perceive and interact with the world, the responsibility to manage this influence ethically and transparently will be paramount. Balancing the benefits of connectivity and information sharing with the need for accurate, reliable, and respectful communication is essential for fostering a healthy digital ecosystem.

In conclusion, social media platforms are powerful tools for online communication and content sharing, transforming how people connect, engage, and interact. They offer numerous benefits, from fostering personal relationships and driving business growth to enabling social movements and enhancing personal branding. However, they also present significant challenges, including the spread of misinformation, impacts on mental health, privacy concerns, and the creation of echo chambers. As social media continues to evolve, addressing these challenges through regulation, technological innovation, and ethical practices will be crucial for maximizing the positive impact of these platforms on society.

Computing and Technology

Quantum computing, a revolutionary advancement in the realm of technology, leverages the principles of quantum mechanics to perform computations far beyond the capabilities of classical computers. Unlike classical bits, which can be either 0 or 1, quantum bits (qubits) can exist in multiple states simultaneously due to the phenomenon of superposition. Additionally, quantum entanglement allows qubits that are entangled to instantly affect each other's state, regardless of the distance separating them. These unique properties enable quantum computers to process a vast amount of information concurrently, solving complex problems that are currently intractable for classical computers. Fields such as cryptography, drug discovery, and materials science stand to benefit enormously from the computational power of quantum systems. However, developing stable and scalable quantum computers poses significant technical challenges, including maintaining qubit coherence and error correction. Despite these hurdles, ongoing research and development promise to unlock unprecedented computational potential.

Cloud computing, another transformative technology, refers to the delivery of computing resources over the internet. This model allows individuals and organizations to access and utilize IT services such as storage, databases, servers, and software on a pay-as-you-go basis, without the need to invest in and maintain physical infrastructure. Cloud computing offers several key advantages, including scalability, flexibility, and cost-efficiency. Users can easily scale their resources up or down based on demand, ensuring optimal utilization and cost management. Moreover, cloud services are accessible from anywhere with an internet connection, facilitating remote work and collaboration. Major cloud service providers like Amazon Web Services (AWS), Microsoft Azure, and Google Cloud Platform (GCP) offer a wide array of services, catering to various business needs. However, cloud computing also raises concerns about data security, privacy, and dependency on service providers, necessitating robust security measures and strategic planning.

Edge computing complements cloud computing by bringing data processing closer to the source of data generation, rather than relying solely on centralized data centers. This approach reduces latency, bandwidth usage, and response times, making it ideal for applications requiring real-time data processing, such as autonomous vehicles, industrial automation, and smart cities. In edge computing, data is processed on local devices or edge servers, which can make immediate decisions based on the processed data, while only essential information is sent to the cloud for further analysis or storage. This decentralized model enhances efficiency and reliability, particularly in environments where connectivity is intermittent or bandwidth is limited. However, implementing edge computing involves challenges such as ensuring the security and integrity of distributed data and managing the complexity of edge infrastructure.

The Internet of Things (IoT) represents a network of interconnected physical objects, embedded with sensors, software, and other technologies to collect and exchange data over the internet. IoT enables seamless integration of the physical and digital worlds, transforming everyday objects into smart devices that can monitor and respond to their environment. Applications of IoT span various domains, including smart homes, healthcare, agriculture, transportation, and industrial automation. For example, in a smart home, IoT devices like thermostats, lights, and security systems can be controlled remotely through a smartphone app, enhancing convenience and energy efficiency. In healthcare, wearable devices can monitor patients' vital signs in real time, enabling proactive management of chronic conditions. Despite its vast potential, IoT also presents challenges related to data privacy, security, and interoperability among diverse devices and platforms.

Big Data refers to the massive and complex data sets generated by various sources, including social media, sensors, transactions, and more. The sheer volume, velocity, and variety of big data necessitate advanced analytical techniques and tools to extract valuable insights. Big data analytics involves processes such as data mining, machine learning, and predictive analytics to uncover patterns, trends, and correlations that can inform decision-making and drive innovation. For instance, in the business world, big data analytics can help companies understand customer behavior, optimize operations, and develop targeted marketing strategies. In healthcare, analyzing large datasets can lead to improved diagnostics, personalized treatments, and better patient outcomes. However, managing and analyzing big data require substantial computational resources and expertise, as well as addressing issues related to data quality, privacy, and ethical use.

Digital twins, virtual replicas of physical systems, are another significant innovation in the technological landscape. By creating a digital counterpart of a physical asset, process, or system, digital twins enable real-time monitoring, simulation, and analysis. This technology is particularly valuable in industries such as manufacturing, aerospace, and urban planning. For example, in manufacturing, a digital twin of a production line can simulate different scenarios, predict equipment failures, and optimize maintenance schedules, thereby improving efficiency and reducing downtime. In urban planning, digital twins of cities can help simulate and analyze the impact of infrastructure projects, traffic patterns, and environmental changes. The integration of digital twins with IoT, big data, and artificial intelligence enhances their capability to provide actionable insights and support data-driven decision-making. However, creating and maintaining accurate digital twins require sophisticated modeling techniques, high-quality data, and significant computational power.

The synergy among these technological advancements is reshaping the landscape of computing and technology. Quantum computing, with its unparalleled computational power, promises to solve complex problems that are currently beyond reach, potentially transforming fields such as cryptography, materials science, and drug discovery. Cloud computing democratizes access to IT resources, enabling businesses and individuals to leverage cutting-edge technology without significant upfront investments. Edge computing brings data processing closer to the source, reducing latency and enhancing real-time decision-making, which is crucial for applications such as autonomous vehicles and smart cities.

The Internet of Things connects the physical and digital worlds, enabling smart environments that enhance convenience, efficiency, and safety. Big data analytics unlocks valuable insights from massive datasets, driving innovation and informed decision-making across various sectors. Digital twins provide a powerful tool for real-time monitoring, simulation, and optimization of physical systems, improving efficiency and reducing risks.

As these technologies continue to evolve and converge, they create new opportunities and challenges. Ensuring data security and privacy, managing the complexity of distributed systems, and addressing ethical considerations are critical aspects that need to be carefully navigated. Moreover, the rapid pace of technological advancements necessitates continuous learning and adaptation by individuals, businesses, and policymakers to harness the full potential of these innovations.

In conclusion, the interplay of quantum computing, cloud computing, edge computing, IoT, big data, and digital twins is driving a technological revolution that promises to transform various aspects of our lives. These advancements are not only enhancing efficiency and productivity but also enabling new possibilities and innovations that were previously unimaginable. As we continue to explore and develop these technologies, it is essential to address the associated challenges and ensure that their benefits are accessible and equitable for all.

26. **Quantum Computing**: Advanced computing using quantum-mechanical phenomena.

Quantum computing is an emerging field of technology that utilizes the principles of quantum mechanics to perform computations far more efficiently than classical computers for certain tasks. Unlike classical bits, which can either be in the state 0 or 1, quantum bits, or qubits, exploit the phenomena of superposition and entanglement to process information in ways that classical bits cannot.

At the core of quantum computing is the concept of superposition. In the classical computing world, a bit can be either 0 or 1 at any given time. However, a qubit, due to superposition, can be in a state of 0, 1, or any quantum superposition of these states. This means that a qubit can perform multiple calculations simultaneously. When multiple qubits are entangled, they can represent and process a vast amount of information exponentially greater than the same number of classical bits.

Entanglement is another fundamental property utilized in quantum computing. When qubits become entangled, the state of one qubit becomes dependent on the state of another, regardless of the distance separating them. This unique property allows for the instantaneous transfer of information between entangled qubits, facilitating extremely fast computations.

Quantum computers process information using quantum gates, which manipulate qubits through operations that are fundamentally different from the logic gates used in classical computing. Quantum gates operate on qubits in a reversible manner, meaning that the operations can be undone. This reversibility is a key aspect of quantum algorithms, allowing quantum computers to solve problems in new and efficient ways.

One of the most well-known quantum algorithms is Shor's algorithm, which efficiently factors large numbers into prime numbers. In classical computing, this task is computationally expensive and time-consuming, especially as the size of the numbers increases. However, Shor's algorithm can perform this factorization exponentially faster than the best-known classical algorithms. This capability has significant implications for cryptography, as many encryption schemes rely on the difficulty of factoring large numbers.

Another important quantum algorithm is Grover's algorithm, which provides a quadratic speedup for unstructured search problems. While classical algorithms search through a list of N items in $O(N)$ time, Grover's algorithm can find the desired item in roughly $O(\sqrt{N})$ time. Although this is not as dramatic as the exponential speedup provided by Shor's algorithm, it still represents a significant improvement for many practical applications.

Quantum computing also shows promise in the field of optimization. Many complex optimization problems, such as those encountered in logistics, finance, and machine learning, are challenging for classical computers due to the vast number of possible solutions that must be evaluated. Quantum algorithms, such as the Quantum Approximate Optimization Algorithm (QAOA), aim to find near-optimal solutions more efficiently by exploiting quantum parallelism and entanglement.

One of the major challenges in developing practical quantum computers is maintaining qubit coherence. Qubits are highly susceptible to decoherence, which is the loss of quantum information due to interactions with the external environment. Decoherence can cause errors in quantum computations, making it difficult to achieve reliable results. To address this issue, researchers are developing error correction techniques and fault-tolerant quantum computing architectures that can mitigate the effects of decoherence and other sources of error.

Another challenge is the physical implementation of qubits. Various physical systems can be used to create qubits, including superconducting circuits, trapped ions, and topological qubits. Each of these approaches has its own advantages and challenges. Superconducting qubits, for example, are relatively easy to control and manipulate, but they require extremely low temperatures to operate. Trapped ions offer long coherence times and high-fidelity operations, but they are difficult to scale up to large numbers of qubits. Topological qubits, which are still largely theoretical, promise intrinsic error resistance due to their topological nature, but they are challenging to realize experimentally.

Despite these challenges, significant progress has been made in recent years. Quantum supremacy, the point at which a quantum computer can perform a computation that is infeasible for any classical computer, was achieved by Google's quantum processor, Sycamore, in 2019. Sycamore performed a specific task, sampling the output of a random quantum circuit, in just a few minutes, a feat that would take the most powerful classical supercomputers thousands of years to replicate.

Quantum computing is poised to revolutionize various fields, including chemistry, materials science, and drug discovery. In chemistry, quantum computers can simulate molecular structures and reactions at an unprecedented level of detail, potentially leading to the discovery of new materials and drugs. Classical computers struggle with these simulations due to the exponential complexity of quantum interactions in molecules. Quantum computers, on the other hand, naturally handle these interactions due to their inherent quantum nature.

In finance, quantum computing can optimize portfolios, manage risk, and model complex financial systems more accurately than classical computers. The ability to process large datasets and perform complex calculations quickly could provide significant advantages in predicting market trends and making investment decisions.

Machine learning, another rapidly advancing field, stands to benefit greatly from quantum computing. Quantum machine learning algorithms can process and analyze large datasets more efficiently, leading to faster training times and potentially more accurate models. Techniques such as quantum neural networks and quantum support vector machines are being explored to leverage the unique capabilities of quantum computers for machine learning tasks.

The potential applications of quantum computing extend beyond the scientific and technological realms. In the realm of artificial intelligence (AI), quantum computing could enable more advanced AI systems capable of solving problems that are currently beyond the reach of classical AI. For instance, quantum-enhanced AI could improve natural language processing, enabling more sophisticated and accurate language models.

The field of cybersecurity is also likely to be transformed by quantum computing. While quantum computers pose a threat to current encryption schemes, they also offer the potential for new, quantum-resistant encryption methods. Quantum key distribution (QKD), for example, leverages the principles of quantum mechanics to create secure communication channels that are immune to eavesdropping. In QKD, any attempt to intercept the quantum key alters its state, alerting the communicating parties to the presence of an intruder.

Furthermore, the development of quantum internet, a network that uses quantum signals to transmit information, could revolutionize how we share data securely. Quantum internet would rely on entanglement and quantum teleportation to transfer information instantaneously, offering unprecedented levels of security and speed for data transmission.

The interdisciplinary nature of quantum computing has led to collaborations across various scientific and engineering fields. Physicists, computer scientists, engineers, and mathematicians are working together to solve the complex challenges associated with building practical quantum computers. These collaborations are essential for advancing the theoretical foundations of quantum computing, developing new algorithms, and creating the physical hardware needed to implement these algorithms.

Quantum computing also raises important ethical and societal questions. The potential power of quantum computers to break current encryption schemes poses a significant challenge for data privacy and security. Ensuring that quantum computing technologies are developed and used responsibly will require careful consideration of ethical guidelines and regulations.

As research and development in quantum computing continue to progress, education and workforce development will play a crucial role in preparing the next generation of scientists, engineers, and professionals to work in this field. Universities and research institutions are increasingly offering courses and programs focused on quantum computing, providing students with the knowledge and skills needed to contribute to this rapidly evolving discipline.

In conclusion, quantum computing represents a paradigm shift in the way we process information and solve complex problems. By harnessing the principles of quantum mechanics, quantum computers have the potential to revolutionize a wide range of fields, from cryptography and drug discovery to optimization and artificial intelligence. Despite the significant technical challenges that remain, ongoing research and development are paving the way for practical quantum computers that could transform our world in profound and unpredictable ways. As we continue to explore the possibilities of quantum computing, it is essential to address the associated challenges and ensure that its benefits are realized in a responsible and equitable manner.

27. **Cloud Computing**: Delivery of computing services over the internet.

Cloud computing refers to the delivery of various computing services over the internet, including servers, storage, databases, networking, software, analytics, and intelligence. These services are provided by cloud service providers such as Amazon Web Services (AWS), Microsoft Azure, and Google Cloud Platform (GCP). Cloud computing offers a range of benefits that have revolutionized how businesses and individuals manage and utilize IT resources.

One of the primary advantages of cloud computing is its scalability. In a traditional on-premises computing environment, scaling up resources to meet increased demand can be time-consuming and costly. It often requires significant upfront investment in hardware and infrastructure, followed by ongoing maintenance. Cloud computing, on the other hand, allows users to scale their resources up or down quickly and efficiently based on demand. This flexibility ensures that businesses can handle fluctuations in workload without overcommitting resources, leading to better cost management and resource utilization.

Another key benefit is cost-efficiency. Cloud computing operates on a pay-as-you-go model, meaning that users only pay for the resources they actually use. This model eliminates the need for large capital expenditures on physical hardware and reduces operational costs associated with maintenance and upgrades. Additionally, cloud service providers offer various pricing tiers and discounts for long-term usage, further enhancing cost savings. For startups and small businesses with limited budgets, cloud computing provides access to advanced IT capabilities without the financial burden of maintaining an in-house data center.

Cloud computing also enhances accessibility and collaboration. Because cloud services are accessible via the internet, users can access their applications and data from anywhere with an internet connection. This capability is particularly beneficial in the modern work environment, where remote work and distributed teams are becoming increasingly common. Cloud-based tools and platforms facilitate real-time collaboration, allowing team members to work together seamlessly regardless of their physical location. For example, cloud-based productivity suites like Google Workspace and Microsoft Office 365 enable multiple users to edit documents simultaneously and communicate through integrated chat and video conferencing tools.

The security of data and applications is another critical aspect of cloud computing. Leading cloud service providers invest heavily in security measures to protect their infrastructure and customers' data. These measures include encryption, identity and access management, threat detection, and regular security audits. By leveraging the expertise and resources of cloud providers, businesses can enhance their security posture and reduce the risk of data breaches and cyberattacks. Additionally, cloud providers offer compliance certifications for various industry standards, helping businesses meet regulatory requirements and ensure data protection.

Disaster recovery and business continuity are also significantly improved with cloud computing. Cloud providers typically offer robust backup and recovery solutions that ensure data is regularly backed up and can be restored quickly in the event of a hardware failure, natural disaster, or cyberattack. These solutions often include automated backups, redundancy across multiple geographic regions, and easy-to-use recovery tools. By leveraging cloud-based disaster recovery services, businesses can minimize downtime and data loss, ensuring continuity of operations even in adverse situations.

Cloud computing supports innovation by providing access to cutting-edge technologies and services that might be otherwise out of reach for many organizations. Cloud platforms offer a wide array of tools and services for artificial intelligence, machine learning, data analytics, Internet of Things (IoT), and more. Developers and data scientists can leverage these services to build and deploy sophisticated applications and models without needing to invest in specialized hardware or software. For instance, AWS offers services like SageMaker for machine learning, while Google Cloud provides BigQuery for big data analytics. This access to advanced technology accelerates the development process and fosters innovation across various industries.

The deployment models of cloud computing—public cloud, private cloud, and hybrid cloud—cater to different needs and preferences. The public cloud is a multi-tenant environment where resources are shared among multiple users. It is cost-effective and scalable, making it ideal for businesses with variable workloads and those looking to minimize costs. Private cloud, on the other hand, is a single-tenant environment where resources are dedicated to a single organization. It offers enhanced control and security, making it suitable for businesses with stringent regulatory requirements or sensitive data. Hybrid cloud combines elements of both public and private clouds, allowing businesses to enjoy the benefits of both models. With hybrid cloud, organizations can run sensitive applications in a private cloud while leveraging the scalability and cost-efficiency of the public cloud for less critical workloads.

The concept of Infrastructure as a Service (IaaS) is fundamental to cloud computing. IaaS provides virtualized computing resources over the internet, including virtual machines, storage, and networks. Users can provision and manage these resources through a web-based dashboard or API, allowing for easy scalability and customization. IaaS enables businesses to run applications and workloads without the need for physical hardware, reducing costs and complexity. Major IaaS providers include AWS, Azure, and GCP, each offering a range of services and tools to meet different needs.

Platform as a Service (PaaS) builds on the IaaS model by providing a complete development and deployment environment in the cloud. PaaS includes infrastructure, development tools, middleware, database management systems, and other services required to build and deploy applications. Developers can focus on writing code and developing applications without worrying about managing the underlying infrastructure. PaaS platforms also offer features like automated scaling, load balancing, and continuous integration/continuous deployment (CI/CD) pipelines. Examples of PaaS offerings include Google App Engine, Microsoft Azure App Service, and AWS Elastic Beanstalk.

Software as a Service (SaaS) is another cloud computing model where applications are delivered over the internet on a subscription basis. SaaS eliminates the need for users to install and maintain software on their devices, providing access to applications through a web browser. SaaS applications are managed and updated by the service provider, ensuring that users always have access to the latest features and security updates. Popular examples of SaaS applications include Salesforce for customer relationship management (CRM), Slack for team collaboration, and Zoom for video conferencing. SaaS is particularly advantageous for businesses looking to reduce IT overhead and streamline software management.

Cloud computing has also driven the rise of serverless computing, a model where the cloud provider dynamically manages the infrastructure required to run code. In a serverless environment, developers write and deploy code in the form of functions that are executed in response to events. The cloud provider automatically provisions, scales, and manages the infrastructure, allowing developers to focus solely on their code. Serverless computing offers cost efficiency, as users are billed only for the compute resources used during function execution, rather than for idle infrastructure. AWS Lambda, Azure Functions, and Google Cloud Functions are prominent examples of serverless computing services.

The adoption of cloud computing has transformed various industries, from healthcare and finance to retail and entertainment. In healthcare, cloud computing enables secure storage and sharing of patient records, facilitates telemedicine, and supports advanced analytics for personalized medicine. In finance, cloud platforms provide the scalability and security needed for trading systems, fraud detection, and regulatory compliance. Retailers leverage cloud services for inventory management, customer engagement, and data-driven marketing strategies. In the entertainment industry, cloud computing supports content streaming, gaming, and digital media production, delivering seamless experiences to users worldwide.

The future of cloud computing is likely to be shaped by several emerging trends. Edge computing, which involves processing data closer to its source rather than in centralized data centers, is expected to complement cloud computing by reducing latency and improving real-time decision-making. The integration of cloud computing with artificial intelligence and machine learning will enable more intelligent and automated solutions across various domains. Multi-cloud strategies, where organizations use multiple cloud providers to avoid vendor lock-in and enhance resilience, are becoming increasingly popular. Additionally, advances in quantum computing may eventually be integrated with cloud platforms, offering unprecedented computational power for complex problem-solving.

In conclusion, cloud computing represents a paradigm shift in how computing resources are accessed, managed, and utilized. Its benefits, including scalability, cost-efficiency, accessibility, security, and innovation, have made it a cornerstone of modern IT infrastructure. As cloud technology continues to evolve and integrate with other emerging technologies, it will unlock new possibilities and drive further advancements across industries. Cloud computing is not just a technological advancement but a fundamental enabler of the digital transformation that is reshaping our world.

28. **Edge Computing**: Processing data near its source rather than in a centralized data center.

Edge computing is an innovative computing paradigm that focuses on processing data closer to the data source or end-user rather than relying solely on centralized data centers. This approach is particularly beneficial for applications requiring real-time data processing and low latency. By moving computation and data storage closer to where they are needed, edge computing reduces the distance that data must travel, thus minimizing latency and bandwidth usage, enhancing performance, and improving reliability.

One of the primary drivers of edge computing is the exponential growth of the Internet of Things (IoT). IoT devices generate vast amounts of data, which, if sent to centralized data centers for processing, could overwhelm network bandwidth and introduce significant latency. For instance, in a smart city environment, sensors and cameras continuously collect data on traffic conditions, air quality, and energy usage. Processing this data at the edge allows for faster decision-making and immediate actions, such as adjusting traffic signals to alleviate congestion or controlling street lighting based on real-time conditions.

The benefits of edge computing extend to various other applications and industries. In autonomous vehicles, for example, edge computing is crucial for processing the massive amounts of data generated by sensors and cameras in real time. Autonomous vehicles must make split-second decisions to ensure safety and efficiency, which would be impossible if data had to be sent to a distant data center for processing. By processing data locally, edge computing enables vehicles to quickly respond to changing road conditions, obstacles, and other critical factors.

Similarly, in industrial automation, edge computing plays a vital role in monitoring and controlling machinery and equipment. Manufacturing facilities often use sensors to track the performance and health of machinery, detecting anomalies and predicting maintenance needs. Processing this data at the edge allows for real-time monitoring and immediate response to issues, reducing downtime and maintenance costs. Edge computing can also facilitate advanced analytics and machine learning at the edge, enabling predictive maintenance and optimization of production processes.

Another significant advantage of edge computing is enhanced data privacy and security. By processing data locally rather than sending it to a centralized cloud, sensitive information can be kept closer to its source, reducing the risk of data breaches during transmission. This is particularly important in healthcare, where patient data privacy is paramount. Edge computing enables healthcare providers to analyze and process patient data locally, supporting applications such as remote monitoring and telemedicine while ensuring compliance with data protection regulations.

The gaming industry also benefits from edge computing. Online gaming requires low latency to provide a seamless and responsive experience for players. By processing game data at the edge, close to the players, gaming companies can reduce lag and improve the overall gaming experience. This approach is especially critical for competitive gaming and virtual reality applications, where even slight delays can significantly impact user experience.

In retail, edge computing can enhance customer experiences through personalized services and improved operational efficiency. Retailers can use edge devices to collect and analyze data on customer behavior, inventory levels, and in-store conditions in real time. This data can then be used to optimize store layouts, manage inventory, and deliver personalized promotions to customers based on their preferences and behavior. Edge computing enables these actions to be performed quickly and efficiently, enhancing the shopping experience and driving sales.

Despite its numerous advantages, edge computing also presents certain challenges that need to be addressed. One of the main challenges is the management and orchestration of distributed edge devices and infrastructure. Unlike centralized cloud data centers, edge environments consist of numerous geographically dispersed devices that require effective management and coordination. Ensuring the reliability, security, and performance of these distributed systems can be complex and requires robust edge management solutions.

Another challenge is the integration of edge computing with existing IT infrastructure. Many organizations have already invested heavily in cloud computing and centralized data centers, and integrating edge computing into these existing systems requires careful planning and execution. It involves developing new architectures and frameworks that can seamlessly connect edge and cloud environments, ensuring interoperability and efficient data flow between them.

Security is another critical concern in edge computing. While processing data locally can enhance data privacy, edge devices can also be vulnerable to cyberattacks. These devices often operate in less controlled environments than centralized data centers, making them potential targets for attackers. Implementing robust security measures, such as encryption, secure boot, and regular updates, is essential to protect edge devices and data from threats.

Furthermore, the limited computational resources and power constraints of edge devices can pose challenges for running complex applications and processing large volumes of data. Unlike cloud data centers, which have virtually unlimited resources, edge devices must operate within the constraints of their hardware capabilities. This requires optimizing applications for performance and efficiency, as well as leveraging lightweight and efficient algorithms that can run effectively on edge devices.

To address these challenges, various technologies and solutions are being developed to support edge computing. One such technology is edge orchestration platforms, which provide tools and frameworks for managing and orchestrating edge devices and applications. These platforms enable centralized control and monitoring of distributed edge environments, automating tasks such as deployment, scaling, and updates. Examples of edge orchestration platforms include Microsoft Azure IoT Edge, AWS IoT Greengrass, and Google Cloud IoT Edge.

Another technology supporting edge computing is 5G networks. The high bandwidth and low latency capabilities of 5G make it an ideal enabler for edge computing applications. 5G networks can support massive IoT deployments, providing the connectivity and speed required for real-time data processing and communication. The combination of 5G and edge computing can drive innovation in various industries, from smart cities and autonomous vehicles to industrial automation and healthcare.

Artificial intelligence (AI) and machine learning (ML) are also integral to the success of edge computing. By deploying AI and ML models at the edge, organizations can enable real-time analytics and decision-making. For instance, AI-powered cameras can process video feeds locally to detect anomalies, recognize objects, or monitor safety conditions. Edge AI and ML require efficient models that can run on limited hardware resources, leading to the development of techniques such as model compression and federated learning.

The adoption of edge computing is growing rapidly across different sectors. In the energy industry, for instance, edge computing is used to monitor and manage power grids, enabling real-time control and optimization of energy distribution. In agriculture, edge devices collect data from soil sensors, weather stations, and drones to optimize irrigation, monitor crop health, and improve yield. In transportation, edge computing supports smart traffic management systems, enhancing traffic flow and reducing congestion.

The future of edge computing holds even more potential as technology continues to evolve. The convergence of edge computing with emerging technologies such as AI, IoT, and 5G will drive new applications and use cases that were previously unimaginable. For example, edge computing could enable advanced robotics and automation in industries like manufacturing and logistics, where real-time data processing and decision-making are critical.

As edge computing becomes more prevalent, it is essential to develop standards and best practices to ensure interoperability, security, and reliability. Industry consortia and standardization bodies are working on defining frameworks and guidelines for edge computing, promoting collaboration and innovation. Initiatives such as the Edge Computing Consortium (ECC) and the Industrial Internet Consortium (IIC) are playing a key role in shaping the future of edge computing.

In conclusion, edge computing represents a significant shift in the way data is processed and managed, bringing computation closer to the source of data generation. This approach offers numerous benefits, including reduced latency, improved performance, enhanced data privacy, and real-time decision-making. Edge computing is transforming various industries, from autonomous vehicles and industrial automation to healthcare, gaming, and retail. However, it also presents challenges related to management, integration, security, and resource constraints. As technology advances and new solutions emerge, edge computing will continue to evolve, unlocking new possibilities and driving innovation across different sectors.

29. **Internet of Things (IoT)**: Network of physical objects connected to the internet.

The Internet of Things (IoT) is a transformative concept that refers to the network of physical objects—often referred to as "smart" devices—connected to the internet. These objects can range from everyday household items like refrigerators and thermostats to complex industrial machinery. The core idea behind IoT is to enable these devices to collect, share, and analyze data, thus enhancing efficiency, productivity, and convenience in various domains.

At its most basic level, IoT involves embedding sensors and connectivity in physical devices. These sensors gather data, which is then transmitted over the internet to be processed and analyzed. This connectivity allows devices to communicate with each other and with central systems, facilitating automated decision-making and control. The sensors can monitor various parameters such as temperature, humidity, light, motion, and more, depending on the specific application.

One of the primary benefits of IoT is the ability to create smart environments that can adapt and respond to changing conditions in real-time. In smart homes, for example, IoT devices can automate lighting, heating, and security systems based on user preferences and behaviors. A smart thermostat can learn a household's schedule and adjust the temperature accordingly, saving energy and improving comfort. Smart security cameras can detect unusual activity and send alerts to homeowners, enhancing safety.

In healthcare, IoT has the potential to revolutionize patient care and medical services. Wearable devices like smartwatches and fitness trackers can monitor vital signs such as heart rate, blood pressure, and sleep patterns. This data can be shared with healthcare providers in real-time, enabling continuous monitoring of patients' health and early detection of potential issues. Remote monitoring can be particularly beneficial for managing chronic conditions, allowing patients to receive care without frequent hospital visits.

The industrial sector also benefits significantly from IoT. In manufacturing, IoT devices can monitor equipment performance, detect anomalies, and predict maintenance needs. This capability, known as predictive maintenance, helps prevent equipment failures and reduce downtime, leading to increased efficiency and cost savings. Industrial IoT (IIoT) also enables real-time monitoring and optimization of production processes, improving quality and productivity. For instance, sensors can track the condition of raw materials and finished products, ensuring that manufacturing standards are consistently met.

IoT's impact on agriculture is profound as well. Smart farming techniques utilize IoT devices to monitor soil moisture, temperature, and crop health. Farmers can receive real-time data on their smartphones or computers, allowing them to make informed decisions about irrigation, fertilization, and pest control. This precision agriculture approach helps optimize resource use, increase yields, and reduce environmental impact. For example, smart irrigation systems can water crops based on soil moisture levels, conserving water and improving crop health.

In transportation, IoT is driving the development of smart cities and intelligent transportation systems. Connected vehicles can communicate with each other and with traffic infrastructure, enhancing road safety and reducing congestion. IoT-enabled traffic lights can adjust their timing based on real-time traffic conditions, improving traffic flow. In public transportation, IoT can provide real-time information on bus and train schedules, helping commuters plan their journeys more efficiently.

Retail is another sector where IoT is making significant inroads. Smart shelves equipped with sensors can monitor inventory levels in real-time, triggering automatic reorders when stock is low. Retailers can also use IoT to track customer behavior and preferences, enabling personalized marketing and improving the shopping experience. For instance, beacons can send targeted promotions to customers' smartphones as they walk through a store, increasing engagement and sales.

Despite its many benefits, IoT also presents several challenges that need to be addressed. One of the primary concerns is security. With billions of devices connected to the internet, the attack surface for cybercriminals expands significantly. IoT devices often have limited processing power and memory, making it challenging to implement robust security measures. Ensuring data privacy and protecting against unauthorized access are critical issues that require continuous attention and innovation.

Another challenge is interoperability. The IoT ecosystem comprises a wide variety of devices from different manufacturers, each with its own communication protocols and standards. Ensuring that these devices can seamlessly communicate and work together is essential for realizing the full potential of IoT. Standardization efforts and the development of open protocols are ongoing to address this issue, but achieving universal compatibility remains a complex task.

Scalability is also a concern as the number of connected devices continues to grow exponentially. Managing and analyzing the vast amounts of data generated by IoT devices requires advanced data analytics and storage solutions. Edge computing, which involves processing data closer to its source, is emerging as a solution to reduce latency and bandwidth usage, enhancing the efficiency of IoT systems.

Energy consumption is another consideration, especially for battery-powered IoT devices. Developing energy-efficient hardware and communication protocols is crucial to extending the lifespan of these devices and reducing the need for frequent battery replacements. Advances in low-power wireless communication technologies and energy harvesting techniques are helping address this challenge.

Regulatory and ethical issues also come into play with IoT. As IoT devices collect vast amounts of personal and sensitive data, ensuring compliance with data protection regulations is essential. Additionally, ethical considerations related to data ownership, consent, and usage must be carefully navigated to protect users' rights and privacy.

The future of IoT is promising, with continuous advancements in technology driving new applications and innovations. Artificial intelligence (AI) and machine learning (ML) are increasingly being integrated with IoT to enhance data analysis and decision-making. AI-powered IoT systems can autonomously learn from data, improve over time, and make more accurate predictions and recommendations. For example, smart home systems can use AI to learn occupants' preferences and optimize energy usage, while industrial IoT systems can use ML algorithms to detect and predict equipment failures with greater accuracy.

5G technology is another significant enabler of IoT's future growth. With its high bandwidth, low latency, and ability to support a massive number of devices, 5G will enhance the performance and scalability of IoT applications. Smart cities, autonomous vehicles, and remote healthcare are just a few areas that will benefit from the capabilities of 5G networks.

The convergence of IoT with other emerging technologies like blockchain and augmented reality (AR) also holds great potential. Blockchain can provide secure and transparent transaction records for IoT devices, enhancing trust and security in decentralized IoT networks. AR, combined with IoT, can offer immersive experiences and real-time information overlays, transforming fields such as maintenance, training, and retail.

In conclusion, the Internet of Things is a revolutionary concept that is transforming how we interact with the world around us. By connecting physical objects to the internet, IoT enables the collection, sharing, and analysis of data, driving improvements in efficiency, productivity, and convenience across various domains. From smart homes and healthcare to industrial automation and agriculture, IoT is enhancing our lives in numerous ways. However, challenges related to security, interoperability, scalability, and energy consumption must be addressed to fully realize the potential of IoT. As technology continues to evolve, the integration of AI, 5G, and other emerging technologies will further propel the growth and impact of IoT, leading to a more connected and intelligent world.

30. **Big Data**: Large and complex data sets analyzed computationally.

Big data refers to the large and complex data sets that are analyzed computationally to reveal patterns, trends, and associations, especially relating to human behavior and interactions. The volume, variety, velocity, and veracity of big data differentiate it from traditional data. These attributes make big data both a challenge and an opportunity for various sectors, from business and healthcare to government and beyond.

The sheer volume of big data is one of its defining characteristics. Organizations today generate and collect data at an unprecedented scale. This data comes from numerous sources, including social media, transaction records, sensors, digital images, videos, and more. For example, every minute, users send millions of emails, conduct millions of Google searches, and generate vast amounts of social media content. Managing such massive amounts of data requires advanced storage solutions and scalable infrastructure.

Variety refers to the different types of data available. Big data encompasses structured data, such as database records, and unstructured data, like emails, videos, and social media posts. This variety adds complexity to data processing and analysis. Traditional data processing tools are often ill-equipped to handle the diverse formats and structures of big data. Consequently, new techniques and tools, such as NoSQL databases and Hadoop, have been developed to manage and process diverse data types efficiently.

Velocity is the speed at which data is generated and processed. In today's fast-paced digital world, data is produced in real-time or near real-time. This rapid generation and the need for timely processing pose significant challenges. For instance, financial markets generate massive amounts of data every second, and making timely trading decisions requires processing this data almost instantaneously. Technologies like stream processing and real-time analytics are crucial for handling the velocity of big data.

Veracity refers to the uncertainty and trustworthiness of data. With big data, ensuring data quality is paramount. Data can be noisy, incomplete, or inconsistent, which can impact analysis and decision-making. Techniques for data cleansing, validation, and enrichment are essential to improve the veracity of big data. Organizations must establish robust data governance frameworks to ensure data accuracy, reliability, and compliance with relevant regulations.

The computational analysis of big data enables organizations to extract valuable insights and make data-driven decisions. Advanced analytics techniques, including data mining, machine learning, and artificial intelligence (AI), play a pivotal role in analyzing big data. Data mining involves discovering patterns and relationships in large datasets, while machine learning algorithms can learn from data to make predictions and automate decision-making processes. AI can further enhance the analysis by providing intelligent insights and recommendations based on complex data patterns.

In the business world, big data analytics has transformed various aspects of operations and strategy. Companies use big data to understand customer behavior, preferences, and buying patterns. For example, e-commerce platforms analyze clickstream data to personalize product recommendations, enhancing the customer experience and driving sales. Retailers leverage point-of-sale data and social media trends to optimize inventory management and plan marketing campaigns more effectively.

Big data is also revolutionizing healthcare by enabling more personalized and proactive patient care. Electronic health records, wearable devices, and medical imaging generate vast amounts of health data. Analyzing this data helps identify disease patterns, predict outbreaks, and develop personalized treatment plans. For instance, predictive analytics can identify patients at risk of chronic conditions, allowing for early intervention and improved outcomes. Additionally, big data analytics supports medical research by providing insights into disease mechanisms and treatment efficacy.

In the financial sector, big data is used for fraud detection, risk management, and investment strategies. Financial institutions analyze transaction data, social media sentiment, and market trends to detect fraudulent activities and mitigate risks. Machine learning algorithms can identify anomalies and patterns indicative of fraud, enabling timely intervention. Investment firms use big data to develop trading algorithms, analyze market conditions, and optimize portfolios, leading to better investment decisions.

Government agencies and public sector organizations leverage big data to improve services, enhance public safety, and drive policy decisions. For example, law enforcement agencies use data analytics to predict crime hotspots and allocate resources more effectively. Smart city initiatives use sensor data to manage traffic, reduce energy consumption, and improve urban planning. Analyzing social media and public sentiment helps governments understand public opinion and address citizens' needs more efficiently.

The manufacturing industry benefits from big data through improved operational efficiency and product quality. Sensors and IoT devices on factory floors generate data on equipment performance, production processes, and product quality. Analyzing this data enables predictive maintenance, reducing downtime and maintenance costs. Manufacturers can also optimize production processes, identify bottlenecks, and improve product design based on customer feedback and usage data.

Education is another field where big data is making a significant impact. Educational institutions analyze student performance data, online learning activities, and social interactions to enhance teaching methods and personalize learning experiences. Predictive analytics can identify students at risk of dropping out, allowing for targeted interventions. Additionally, analyzing data from massive open online courses (MOOCs) provides insights into learning patterns and helps improve course content and delivery.

The entertainment industry uses big data to understand audience preferences and create more engaging content. Streaming services analyze viewing habits, search queries, and user ratings to recommend personalized content, increasing viewer satisfaction and retention. Music streaming platforms use data analytics to curate playlists and predict song popularity. Movie studios analyze box office data, social media buzz, and demographic trends to make informed decisions about production and marketing strategies.

Despite the numerous benefits, big data also presents significant challenges and ethical considerations. Data privacy is a major concern, as the collection and analysis of large datasets often involve sensitive personal information. Ensuring that data is collected and used responsibly, with proper consent and compliance with privacy regulations, is essential. Organizations must implement robust data protection measures to safeguard against data breaches and misuse.

The sheer volume and complexity of big data require substantial computational resources and expertise. High-performance computing, distributed computing, and cloud-based solutions are often necessary to process and analyze big data efficiently. However, the costs associated with these resources can be significant, posing a barrier for smaller organizations. Developing scalable and cost-effective solutions for big data processing remains an ongoing challenge.

Additionally, the analysis of big data can sometimes lead to biased or misleading conclusions. Algorithms and models used in data analysis can inherit biases present in the data, leading to unfair or discriminatory outcomes. Ensuring transparency, accountability, and fairness in data analytics is crucial to mitigate these risks. Ethical considerations should be integrated into the design and deployment of big data solutions to promote responsible and equitable use.

The future of big data holds immense potential as technology continues to evolve. Advances in AI and machine learning will further enhance the ability to analyze and interpret complex data. Quantum computing, with its promise of exponentially faster processing speeds, could revolutionize big data analytics by enabling the analysis of even larger and more complex datasets. Edge computing, which involves processing data closer to its source, will reduce latency and bandwidth usage, making real-time data analysis more feasible.

The integration of big data with other emerging technologies, such as the Internet of Things (IoT) and blockchain, will unlock new possibilities. IoT devices will generate even more data, providing richer insights into various aspects of life and business. Blockchain can enhance data security and transparency, ensuring the integrity and trustworthiness of big data analytics.

In conclusion, big data represents a paradigm shift in how organizations and industries leverage data to drive insights and decision-making. The volume, variety, velocity, and veracity of big data present both challenges and opportunities. Advanced analytics techniques, including data mining, machine learning, and AI, enable the extraction of valuable insights from complex datasets. Big data is transforming various sectors, from business and healthcare to government and education, by enhancing efficiency, personalization, and innovation. However, addressing challenges related to data privacy, computational resources, and ethical considerations is essential to fully realize the potential of big data. As technology advances, the future of big data promises even greater possibilities for improving our world through data-driven insights and solutions.

31. **Digital Twins**: Virtual replicas of physical systems for simulation and analysis.

Digital twins are virtual replicas of physical systems that allow for simulation, analysis, and optimization of real-world processes. This technology integrates data from physical systems with advanced modeling and analytics to create a comprehensive digital representation. Digital twins are used across various industries to improve performance, predict failures, optimize operations, and drive innovation. By providing a detailed and dynamic view of physical assets, digital twins enable better decision-making and more efficient management of complex systems.

The concept of digital twins originated from the aerospace industry, where they were initially used to simulate and monitor the performance of aircraft engines. Today, digital twins have expanded into numerous other sectors, including manufacturing, healthcare, energy, urban planning, and transportation. The versatility of digital twins lies in their ability to replicate any physical system, from individual components to entire facilities or cities.

In manufacturing, digital twins play a critical role in the design, production, and maintenance of products. During the design phase, digital twins enable engineers to create and test virtual prototypes, identifying potential issues before physical prototypes are built. This reduces development time and costs, while improving product quality. In production, digital twins monitor the performance of machinery and equipment in real-time, allowing for predictive maintenance and reducing downtime. By analyzing data from sensors and other sources, digital twins can detect anomalies, predict failures, and suggest optimal maintenance schedules. This proactive approach enhances efficiency, extends the lifespan of equipment, and reduces operational costs.

Healthcare is another field where digital twins are making significant strides. By creating digital replicas of patients, healthcare providers can personalize treatment plans and improve patient outcomes. For example, digital twins can simulate the effects of different medications or treatments on a patient's body, helping doctors choose the most effective therapy. In surgical planning, digital twins allow surgeons to practice complex procedures in a virtual environment, enhancing precision and reducing risks. Additionally, digital twins can monitor patients' vital signs and other health metrics in real-time, providing continuous care and early detection of potential issues. This capability is particularly valuable for managing chronic conditions and supporting remote healthcare services.

The energy sector leverages digital twins to optimize the operation and maintenance of power plants, grids, and other infrastructure. By simulating the behavior of energy systems, digital twins help operators balance supply and demand, improve efficiency, and reduce emissions. For instance, in wind farms, digital twins can analyze data from turbines to optimize their performance and predict maintenance needs. In power grids, digital twins enable real-time monitoring and control, enhancing reliability and resilience. As the energy sector transitions to renewable sources, digital twins are instrumental in integrating diverse energy resources and managing their variability.

Urban planning and smart cities benefit from digital twins by enabling more efficient and sustainable development. Digital twins of cities can simulate various scenarios, such as traffic patterns, energy usage, and environmental impact, helping planners make informed decisions. For example, a digital twin of a city's transportation system can analyze the effects of different traffic management strategies, identify bottlenecks, and optimize routes. In building management, digital twins monitor energy consumption, occupancy, and other parameters, supporting energy efficiency and occupant comfort. By providing a holistic view of urban systems, digital twins facilitate the design and operation of smarter, more sustainable cities.

Transportation and logistics are also transforming through the use of digital twins. In the automotive industry, digital twins simulate the performance of vehicles under different conditions, supporting the development of safer and more efficient cars. Autonomous vehicles rely on digital twins to navigate and interact with their environment, improving their accuracy and reliability. In logistics, digital twins optimize supply chain operations by providing real-time visibility into inventory levels, shipment status, and warehouse conditions. This enables companies to respond quickly to disruptions, improve delivery times, and reduce costs.

The construction industry utilizes digital twins to enhance project management and building operations. During construction, digital twins provide a real-time view of progress, allowing project managers to identify and address issues promptly. By integrating data from various sources, such as sensors, drones, and building information modeling (BIM) systems, digital twins create a comprehensive and up-to-date representation of the construction site. This improves coordination, reduces delays, and ensures that projects are completed on time and within budget. After construction, digital twins support the operation and maintenance of buildings by monitoring their performance and identifying areas for improvement. This enhances energy efficiency, occupant comfort, and asset management.

The creation and maintenance of digital twins involve several key technologies, including the Internet of Things (IoT), data analytics, artificial intelligence (AI), and cloud computing. IoT devices, such as sensors and actuators, collect data from physical systems and transmit it to digital twins in real-time. Data analytics processes this data to generate insights and drive decision-making. AI algorithms enhance the capabilities of digital twins by enabling predictive and prescriptive analytics, as well as machine learning-based optimizations. Cloud computing provides the scalable infrastructure needed to store, process, and analyze the vast amounts of data generated by digital twins.

One of the main challenges in implementing digital twins is ensuring data accuracy and reliability. The quality of a digital twin depends on the accuracy of the data it receives from the physical system. Inaccurate or incomplete data can lead to incorrect analyses and decisions. Therefore, robust data collection and validation processes are essential to maintain the integrity of digital twins. Additionally, integrating data from multiple sources and ensuring interoperability between different systems can be complex and requires standardized protocols and interfaces.

Security is another critical concern for digital twins. As they rely on real-time data from physical systems, digital twins are vulnerable to cyberattacks that can compromise their accuracy and functionality. Ensuring the security and privacy of data transmitted between physical systems and digital twins is paramount. Implementing strong encryption, access controls, and cybersecurity measures is essential to protect digital twins from potential threats.

Despite these challenges, the benefits of digital twins are driving their adoption across various industries. By providing a detailed and dynamic view of physical systems, digital twins enable organizations to optimize operations, reduce costs, improve quality, and drive innovation. As technology continues to advance, the capabilities of digital twins will expand, opening up new possibilities for their application.

In the future, the integration of digital twins with emerging technologies such as 5G, blockchain, and edge computing will further enhance their capabilities. 5G networks will provide the high bandwidth and low latency needed for real-time data transmission, supporting more complex and dynamic digital twins. Blockchain technology can enhance the security and transparency of data exchanged between physical systems and digital twins, ensuring data integrity and trustworthiness. Edge computing will enable data processing closer to the physical system, reducing latency and bandwidth usage, and improving the responsiveness of digital twins.

Digital twins also hold great potential for advancing sustainability and environmental protection. By providing detailed insights into resource usage and environmental impact, digital twins can support efforts to reduce carbon emissions, conserve energy, and minimize waste. For example, digital twins of buildings can optimize energy consumption and improve indoor air quality, contributing to greener and healthier living environments. In agriculture, digital twins can support precision farming practices that enhance crop yields while reducing water and pesticide use.

In conclusion, digital twins are virtual replicas of physical systems that enable simulation, analysis, and optimization. By integrating data from physical systems with advanced modeling and analytics, digital twins provide a comprehensive and dynamic view of real-world processes. Their applications span various industries, including manufacturing, healthcare, energy, urban planning, transportation, logistics, and construction. While challenges related to data accuracy, security, and integration exist, the benefits of digital twins are driving their adoption and innovation. As technology continues to evolve, digital twins will play an increasingly important role in optimizing operations, driving innovation, and supporting sustainability across different sectors.

Digital Art and Computer Graphics

Digital art and computer graphics represent a revolution in the way we create, interact with, and appreciate art. This transformation is driven by a range of techniques and tools that expand the boundaries of artistic expression, leveraging the power of computers to produce visually stunning and conceptually profound works.

One of the most exciting developments in this field is **generative art**, which involves creating art through algorithms and computational processes. This approach to art is unique because it allows artists to explore new forms and patterns that would be difficult, if not impossible, to achieve manually. Generative art often involves the use of mathematical functions and data inputs to produce images, animations, or sculptures that can be endlessly varied and complex. The artist essentially sets the rules or parameters, and the computer executes them, generating artwork that can be both surprising and beautiful. This method not only challenges traditional notions of authorship and creativity but also opens up new possibilities for collaboration between humans and machines.

Procedural graphics are closely related to generative art but focus specifically on the algorithmic creation of images. This technique is widely used in video games, simulations, and other applications where vast, detailed worlds need to be created quickly and efficiently. Procedural graphics use rules and algorithms to generate textures, landscapes, and other elements dynamically, ensuring that no two instances are exactly alike. This can involve everything from simple patterns to complex, lifelike environments that evolve and change in response to user interactions. The power of procedural graphics lies in their ability to create highly detailed and intricate visuals without the need for extensive manual effort, making it possible to produce vast amounts of content at a fraction of the time and cost.

Moving from two-dimensional images to three-dimensional forms, **digital sculpting** has emerged as a powerful tool for artists and designers. Unlike traditional sculpting, which involves physically manipulating materials like clay or stone, digital sculpting uses software to create 3D models. This allows for incredible precision and flexibility, enabling artists to work on intricate details and complex shapes with ease. Digital sculpting tools often mimic the experience of working with real-world materials, using techniques like virtual clay modeling, carving, and texturing. These tools have become essential in fields such as animation, video game design, and industrial design, where creating detailed and accurate 3D models is crucial. Moreover, digital sculpting offers the advantage of easy revisions and iterations, allowing artists to experiment and refine their work without the limitations imposed by physical materials.

The advent of **virtual galleries** has transformed the way art is displayed and experienced. These online spaces provide a platform for artists to showcase their work to a global audience without the constraints of physical gallery spaces. Virtual galleries can take many forms, from simple web pages to immersive 3D environments that replicate the experience of walking through a real gallery. They offer a level of accessibility and convenience that traditional galleries cannot match, allowing anyone with an internet connection to view and interact with art. This democratization of art exhibition has opened up new opportunities for emerging artists and provided established artists with new ways to engage with their audience. Virtual galleries can also incorporate multimedia elements, such as audio guides, interactive features, and augmented reality, enhancing the viewer's experience and deepening their understanding of the artwork.

Interactive art takes this a step further by creating works that respond to the viewer's actions. This type of art uses sensors, cameras, and other technologies to detect the presence and movements of viewers, allowing the artwork to change and evolve in real-time. Interactive art can be deeply engaging and immersive, creating a dynamic relationship between the viewer and the artwork. It challenges the passive nature of traditional art viewing, inviting viewers to become active participants in the creative process. Interactive art can be found in a variety of contexts, from museum installations to public spaces and online platforms. It often explores themes of perception, identity, and the relationship between humans and technology, offering unique and thought-provoking experiences.

Together, these techniques and tools represent a new frontier in artistic expression, one where the boundaries between art, technology, and science are increasingly blurred. Generative art, procedural graphics, digital sculpting, virtual galleries, and interactive art each offer unique possibilities for creativity and innovation, expanding the ways in which we can create and experience art.

Generative art, for instance, allows artists to harness the power of algorithms to explore patterns and forms that would be impossible to create manually. By setting the parameters and letting the computer generate the artwork, artists can discover new aesthetic possibilities and push the boundaries of traditional art forms. This approach also raises interesting questions about the nature of creativity and the role of the artist in the digital age.

Procedural graphics, on the other hand, have practical applications that extend beyond the realm of art. In video games and simulations, procedural techniques enable the creation of vast, detailed worlds that can be explored and interacted with in real-time. This not only enhances the visual appeal of these virtual environments but also allows for a level of complexity and variety that would be unfeasible to achieve through manual design alone. Procedural graphics also have the potential to revolutionize industries such as architecture and urban planning, where the ability to quickly generate and visualize complex structures and landscapes can be invaluable.

Digital sculpting offers a level of precision and flexibility that traditional sculpting techniques cannot match. By using software to create 3D models, artists and designers can work on intricate details and complex shapes with ease, making it possible to create highly detailed and accurate representations of their ideas. Digital sculpting tools also allow for easy revisions and iterations, enabling artists to experiment and refine their work without the limitations imposed by physical materials. This has made digital sculpting an essential tool in fields such as animation, video game design, and industrial design, where the ability to create detailed and accurate 3D models is crucial.

Virtual galleries provide a platform for artists to showcase their work to a global audience, breaking down the barriers imposed by physical gallery spaces. These online spaces offer a level of accessibility and convenience that traditional galleries cannot match, allowing anyone with an internet connection to view and interact with art. Virtual galleries can also incorporate multimedia elements, such as audio guides, interactive features, and augmented reality, enhancing the viewer's experience and deepening their understanding of the artwork. This democratization of art exhibition has opened up new opportunities for emerging artists and provided established artists with new ways to engage with their audience.

Interactive art challenges the passive nature of traditional art viewing by creating works that respond to the viewer's actions. By using sensors, cameras, and other technologies to detect the presence and movements of viewers, interactive art can change and evolve in real-time, creating a dynamic relationship between the viewer and the artwork. This type of art can be deeply engaging and immersive, inviting viewers to become active participants in the creative process. Interactive art often explores themes of perception, identity, and the relationship between humans and technology, offering unique and thought-provoking experiences.

In conclusion, digital art and computer graphics represent a new frontier in artistic expression, one where the boundaries between art, technology, and science are increasingly blurred. Generative art, procedural graphics, digital sculpting, virtual galleries, and interactive art each offer unique possibilities for creativity and innovation, expanding the ways in which we can create and experience art. These techniques and tools not only enhance the visual appeal of artwork but also challenge traditional notions of authorship, creativity, and the role of the artist in the digital age. As technology continues to evolve, we can expect to see even more exciting developments in the field of digital art and computer graphics, pushing the boundaries of what is possible and inspiring new forms of artistic expression.

32. **Generative Art**: Art created using algorithms and computational processes.

The artist's vision is translated into a set of instructions that the computer will follow. This phase requires a deep understanding of both the artistic goals and the technical aspects of coding.

Once the algorithm is defined, the artist runs the program to generate the artwork. This can result in a single image, a series of images, or even an animation. Because the process is driven by a combination of rules and random inputs, each execution of the algorithm can produce a different outcome, leading to an almost infinite variety of possible results. This element of randomness is a crucial aspect of generative art, adding a layer of unpredictability and excitement to the creative process.

The output of the algorithm is often not the final artwork. Many generative artists engage in a process of selection and refinement, choosing the most compelling results from a series of generated images and tweaking the parameters to achieve the desired effect. This iterative process allows the artist to maintain a degree of control over the final outcome while still embracing the inherent unpredictability of the generative process.

Generative art can take many forms, from static images and prints to interactive installations and virtual reality experiences. One of the most common forms is the creation of abstract, geometric patterns. Artists like Sol LeWitt and Bridget Riley explored similar ideas in their work, but generative art takes these concepts to new levels of complexity and intricacy. By using algorithms, artists can create patterns that are not only visually stunning but also mathematically precise and infinitely variable.

Another exciting application of generative art is in the field of digital sculpture and 3D modeling. Using algorithms, artists can design complex, organic forms that would be nearly impossible to create by hand. These digital sculptures can be brought to life through 3D printing, allowing for the creation of physical objects that embody the intricacy and dynamism of generative processes. This fusion of digital and physical media opens up new possibilities for artistic expression and experimentation.

Interactive installations are another area where generative art shines. By incorporating sensors and real-time data inputs, artists can create works that respond to the presence and actions of viewers. For example, an installation might change its visual appearance based on the movement of people in the space or react to environmental conditions like temperature or sound. This interactivity creates a dynamic relationship between the artwork and its audience, making each experience unique and personal.

Generative art also has significant implications for the field of music and sound design. Algorithmic composition, a technique where music is generated by a set of rules and parameters, has been explored by composers like Brian Eno and John Cage. These composers use algorithms to create music that is constantly evolving and never exactly the same, producing soundscapes that are both immersive and unpredictable. In the digital age, software like Ableton Live and Max/MSP allows musicians and sound artists to incorporate generative processes into their work, leading to innovative and experimental compositions.

One of the most intriguing aspects of generative art is its ability to mimic natural processes. Algorithms can simulate growth patterns, weather systems, and even evolutionary processes, creating artworks that appear to be alive and constantly changing. These simulations can produce results that are strikingly lifelike, blurring the line between the artificial and the natural. Artists like Casey Reas and Jared Tarbell have explored these ideas in their work, using algorithms to create images and animations that evoke the complexity and beauty of the natural world.

The rise of blockchain technology and non-fungible tokens (NFTs) has also had a significant impact on the generative art scene. NFTs allow artists to create unique, verifiable digital artworks that can be bought and sold on the blockchain. This has opened up new opportunities for generative artists to monetize their work and reach a global audience. Platforms like Art Blocks and Hic et Nunc have become popular venues for showcasing and selling generative art, fostering a vibrant community of artists and collectors.

The use of artificial intelligence (AI) and machine learning in generative art is another exciting development. AI algorithms, such as generative adversarial networks (GANs), can be trained on large datasets of images to generate new, original artworks. These AI-generated works often exhibit a level of creativity and complexity that rivals that of human artists. By collaborating with AI, artists can push the boundaries of their creativity and explore new aesthetic possibilities. However, the use of AI in art also raises important questions about authorship, originality, and the role of the artist in the creative process.

Generative art challenges traditional notions of authorship and creativity in several ways. Since the final artwork is the result of a collaboration between the artist and the algorithm, the question of who is the true creator arises. Is it the artist who designed the algorithm, or the machine that executed it? This ambiguity forces us to reconsider our understanding of creativity and the role of the artist in the digital age. Some argue that the artist retains authorship because they define the parameters and rules that guide the generative process, while others believe that the machine plays a significant creative role by producing the final output.

Moreover, generative art often blurs the line between art and science. The algorithms used to create generative artworks are grounded in mathematical and scientific principles, and the process of designing these algorithms requires a deep understanding of both art and technology. This interdisciplinary nature of generative art fosters collaboration between artists, scientists, and technologists, leading to innovative and boundary-pushing works that challenge our preconceptions about what art can be.

The impact of generative art on contemporary art and culture is profound. It has opened up new avenues for artistic exploration and experimentation, allowing artists to create works that are dynamic, interactive, and constantly evolving. Generative art also democratizes the creative process, making it accessible to anyone with a computer and the desire to learn. By providing tools and platforms for creating generative art, the digital age has empowered a new generation of artists to explore the intersection of art and technology.

In education, generative art is being used as a tool to teach coding and computational thinking. By engaging with generative processes, students can learn the fundamentals of programming in a creative and enjoyable way. This approach not only makes coding more accessible but also encourages students to think critically and creatively about the possibilities of technology.

The future of generative art is filled with exciting possibilities. As technology continues to advance, new tools and techniques will emerge, allowing artists to push the boundaries of their creativity even further. The integration of augmented reality (AR) and virtual reality (VR) will create immersive generative experiences that blend the physical and digital worlds. Additionally, advancements in AI and machine learning will enable even more sophisticated and innovative generative artworks.

Generative art is more than just a novel way to create visual experiences; it is a transformative force that challenges our understanding of creativity, authorship, and the role of technology in the arts. By embracing the power of algorithms and computational processes, generative artists are pioneering a new frontier in art, one that is dynamic, unpredictable, and infinitely variable. This movement not only expands the possibilities of artistic expression but also invites us to reconsider our relationship with technology and its potential to enhance and transform the creative process.

33. **Procedural Graphics**: Creating images algorithmically rather than manually.

Procedural graphics represent a groundbreaking approach in the field of digital art and design, leveraging algorithms and computational processes to generate images automatically. This method contrasts sharply with traditional techniques that rely on manual creation, offering a powerful, flexible, and efficient way to produce complex visuals. By using mathematical functions, procedural graphics can create a wide array of textures, patterns, and even entire landscapes that are highly detailed and consistent, yet also unique and dynamic.

The essence of procedural graphics lies in its reliance on algorithms. An algorithm, in this context, is a precise set of instructions that the computer follows to create an image. These instructions can range from simple mathematical equations to intricate programs that simulate natural phenomena. The beauty of this approach is that it allows for the generation of images that can be easily modified and scaled, providing an extraordinary level of control and variability. This is particularly useful in fields such as video game design, animation, and virtual reality, where vast amounts of content need to be created efficiently.

One of the primary advantages of procedural graphics is the ability to create highly detailed and realistic textures without the need for extensive manual effort. Traditional texture creation can be a labor-intensive process, requiring artists to painstakingly paint or photograph surfaces and then edit them to fit seamlessly into a digital environment. In contrast, procedural textures are generated using mathematical models, which can produce patterns that mimic the appearance of natural materials like wood, stone, or fabric. These models can include parameters for different attributes, such as color, roughness, and reflectivity, allowing for endless variations and adjustments.

A classic example of procedural texture generation is Perlin noise, developed by Ken Perlin in 1983. Perlin noise is a type of gradient noise that produces natural-looking random patterns. It has become a fundamental tool in computer graphics, used to create everything from clouds and smoke to terrain and water surfaces. By combining Perlin noise with other mathematical functions, artists and developers can generate highly realistic and varied textures that enhance the visual fidelity of digital environments.

Procedural generation extends beyond textures to include entire landscapes and environments. In video game development, for instance, procedural algorithms can be used to create vast, immersive worlds that would be impossible to build manually. Games like "Minecraft," "No Man's Sky," and "Terraria" utilize procedural generation to create expansive, dynamic worlds that players can explore. These algorithms take into account various factors such as topography, climate, and vegetation, ensuring that the generated environments are both diverse and believable.

The creation of procedural landscapes typically involves several layers of algorithms working together. At the base level, terrain generation algorithms define the shape and features of the land, using techniques such as fractals, noise functions, and heightmaps. Additional layers can then add details like rivers, forests, and mountains, with each layer interacting with the others to produce a cohesive and realistic world. The result is a rich, detailed environment that feels organic and lifelike, providing an immersive experience for the user.

Another significant application of procedural graphics is in the field of animation and special effects. Procedural techniques can be used to simulate complex physical phenomena, such as fire, smoke, water, and explosions. These effects are challenging to animate manually due to their intricate and dynamic nature. By using procedural algorithms, animators can create realistic simulations that respond to physical forces and interactions. For example, fluid simulation algorithms can model the behavior of liquids, capturing the way they flow, splash, and interact with objects. These simulations are essential for creating convincing special effects in movies, video games, and virtual reality experiences.

The flexibility of procedural graphics also makes them ideal for generating content that needs to be scalable and adaptable. In architectural visualization, for instance, procedural techniques can be used to create detailed building facades, urban environments, and interior designs. By defining a set of rules and parameters, architects and designers can quickly generate multiple variations of a design, adjusting elements like materials, lighting, and layout with ease. This not only speeds up the design process but also allows for greater experimentation and creativity.

One of the most powerful aspects of procedural graphics is their ability to create content that is not only visually appealing but also functionally adaptive. In procedural modeling, objects are defined by a set of rules and parameters that determine their shape and structure. This approach allows for the creation of complex, intricate models that can be easily modified and customized. For example, a procedural tree model can be adjusted to produce trees of different sizes, shapes, and species, all while maintaining a consistent level of detail and realism. This adaptability is particularly useful in applications like virtual reality and simulation, where a high degree of variability and interactivity is required.

The use of procedural graphics also extends to generative design, an innovative approach that combines computational algorithms with design principles to create optimized solutions. In generative design, the designer sets the goals and constraints, and the algorithm explores numerous possibilities to find the most effective design. This method has been used in various fields, including architecture, industrial design, and engineering, to create structures and products that are both functional and aesthetically pleasing. For example, generative design has been used to create lightweight, strong components for aerospace and automotive applications, as well as innovative architectural forms that respond to environmental conditions.

Despite its many advantages, procedural graphics also present certain challenges and limitations. One of the primary challenges is the complexity of creating and fine-tuning the algorithms. Designing effective procedural algorithms requires a deep understanding of both mathematics and programming, as well as a creative vision for the desired outcome. Additionally, procedural techniques can sometimes produce results that lack the subtlety and nuance of manually created art. Achieving a balance between algorithmic generation and artistic control is crucial for producing high-quality procedural graphics.

Another challenge is the computational cost associated with procedural generation. Complex algorithms and simulations can be resource-intensive, requiring significant processing power and memory. This can be a limiting factor in real-time applications, such as video games and virtual reality, where performance and responsiveness are critical. Optimizing procedural algorithms to run efficiently on available hardware is an ongoing area of research and development.

Despite these challenges, the future of procedural graphics is bright, with ongoing advancements in technology and methodology continuing to push the boundaries of what is possible. The integration of artificial intelligence and machine learning into procedural techniques is an exciting development that promises to enhance the capabilities and potential of this approach. By leveraging AI, procedural systems can learn and adapt, producing even more sophisticated and realistic results. This convergence of AI and procedural graphics is likely to lead to new levels of creativity and innovation in digital art and design.

In education, procedural graphics offer valuable opportunities for learning and experimentation. By engaging with procedural techniques, students can develop a deeper understanding of mathematical concepts and computational thinking, while also exploring their creative potential. Educational tools and platforms that support procedural graphics, such as Processing and Unity, provide accessible entry points for students to start creating their own algorithmic art and designs.

The impact of procedural graphics on various industries is profound and far-reaching. In entertainment, procedural techniques have revolutionized the way digital content is created, enabling the production of vast, detailed worlds and realistic special effects. In design and architecture, procedural methods offer new possibilities for innovation and optimization, leading to more efficient and sustainable solutions. In education, procedural graphics provide a powerful tool for teaching and learning, fostering a new generation of artists and designers who are proficient in both creativity and technology.

As we look to the future, the potential of procedural graphics continues to expand, driven by advancements in technology and an ever-growing interest in the intersection of art and science. The ability to create complex, detailed, and adaptive visuals through algorithms is transforming the landscape of digital art and design, opening up new possibilities for creativity and exploration. Whether in the creation of immersive virtual environments, the simulation of natural phenomena, or the optimization of architectural designs, procedural graphics are poised to play a pivotal role in the future of visual expression and innovation.

34. **Digital Sculpting**: Using software to create 3D models.

Digital sculpting is a revolutionary technique in the world of 3D modeling and design, offering artists and designers an unparalleled level of control and detail. This method uses specialized software to manipulate digital objects in a way that mimics traditional sculpting techniques. With the advent of powerful computers and advanced software, digital sculpting has become an essential tool in industries ranging from film and video games to product design and medical visualization.

At its core, digital sculpting involves the manipulation of a digital mesh, which is a network of vertices, edges, and faces that form the surface of a 3D object. The artist can push, pull, smooth, pinch, and otherwise modify this mesh using a variety of tools that simulate the physical actions of sculpting clay. Unlike traditional polygonal modeling, which involves creating and manipulating geometric shapes to build a model, digital sculpting allows for a more organic and intuitive approach. This makes it particularly well-suited for creating highly detailed and complex forms, such as characters, creatures, and intricate surface details.

One of the most significant advantages of digital sculpting is its flexibility and ease of use. Traditional sculpting requires physical materials like clay or stone, which can be messy and difficult to work with. Additionally, any mistakes made in the sculpting process can be hard to correct without damaging the material. In contrast, digital sculpting allows for easy undoing of actions, making it simple to experiment and iterate on designs. Artists can quickly try out different ideas and refine their models without the fear of making irreversible errors.

The process of digital sculpting typically begins with a basic mesh, often referred to as a base mesh or a primitive. This base mesh can be a simple shape like a sphere or a cube, or it can be a more complex structure that provides a rough outline of the final model. The artist then uses sculpting tools to add detail and refine the form. These tools can be customized to achieve different effects, such as adding fine textures, creating sharp edges, or smoothing out surfaces. The ability to work with varying levels of detail, from broad strokes to intricate surface patterns, is one of the key strengths of digital sculpting.

Software such as ZBrush, Mudbox, and Blender are among the most popular tools for digital sculpting. Each of these programs offers a range of features and capabilities tailored to different aspects of the sculpting process. ZBrush, for example, is known for its powerful brushes and high-resolution detailing capabilities, making it a favorite among character and creature artists. Mudbox, on the other hand, integrates well with other Autodesk products and is often used in conjunction with traditional 3D modeling workflows. Blender, a free and open-source option, provides a comprehensive suite of tools for both sculpting and general 3D modeling, making it accessible to a wide range of users.

One of the critical features of digital sculpting software is the ability to work with multiple levels of detail through a process known as subdivision. Subdivision allows the artist to increase the density of the mesh, adding more vertices and faces to work with. This enables the creation of fine details that would be impossible with a low-resolution mesh. Artists can switch between different levels of detail, making broad changes to the overall shape at lower resolutions and adding intricate details at higher resolutions. This multi-resolution workflow is essential for creating complex models that require both large-scale shaping and fine surface detailing.

Another powerful aspect of digital sculpting is the use of alphas and textures to add detail to the model. Alphas are grayscale images that can be used as stamps or brushes to apply detailed patterns and textures to the surface of the model. This technique is particularly useful for creating organic textures like skin, scales, or fabric, as well as intricate mechanical details. By using alphas, artists can achieve a high level of realism and complexity without manually sculpting every detail.

In addition to static models, digital sculpting is also used in the creation of animated characters and creatures. Once a model is sculpted, it can be rigged with a skeleton and animation controls, allowing it to be posed and animated. The detailed geometry created through sculpting can be preserved during animation, ensuring that the final result retains the intricate details and realistic appearance of the original model. This capability is essential in industries like film and video games, where highly detailed and expressive characters are crucial for storytelling and immersion.

Digital sculpting is not limited to organic forms; it is also used extensively in the creation of hard surface models, such as machinery, vehicles, and architectural elements. While traditional polygonal modeling is often preferred for these types of objects due to its precision and control, digital sculpting can be used to add wear and tear, surface imperfections, and other details that enhance realism. By combining sculpting with traditional modeling techniques, artists can achieve a balance between precise control and organic detail.

The impact of digital sculpting extends beyond the entertainment industry. In product design, digital sculpting allows designers to create and visualize complex forms and surfaces that would be challenging to prototype using traditional methods. This capability is particularly valuable in industries like automotive and consumer electronics, where aesthetic and ergonomic considerations are paramount. By using digital sculpting, designers can iterate on concepts quickly, exploring different shapes and surface treatments before committing to physical prototypes.

In the field of medical visualization, digital sculpting is used to create detailed anatomical models for educational and diagnostic purposes. These models can be based on medical imaging data, such as MRI or CT scans, and can provide a highly accurate representation of human anatomy. Digital sculpting allows for the creation of customized models that can be used for surgical planning, patient education, and the development of medical devices. This application of digital sculpting demonstrates its potential to improve outcomes in healthcare by providing more accurate and detailed visualizations.

Digital sculpting also plays a role in the growing field of virtual reality (VR) and augmented reality (AR). In VR and AR applications, detailed and realistic 3D models are essential for creating immersive experiences. Digital sculpting provides the tools necessary to create these models, ensuring that virtual environments are both visually stunning and believable. As VR and AR technologies continue to advance, the demand for high-quality digital content will only increase, making digital sculpting an indispensable skill for artists and designers working in these fields.

One of the most exciting developments in digital sculpting is the integration of artificial intelligence (AI) and machine learning. These technologies have the potential to enhance the sculpting process by providing intelligent tools that can assist with tasks like detail generation, symmetry, and error correction. AI-driven sculpting tools can analyze the model in real-time, suggesting improvements and automating repetitive tasks. This integration has the potential to make digital sculpting more accessible to a broader audience, reducing the learning curve and allowing artists to focus on their creative vision.

The community around digital sculpting is vibrant and constantly evolving. Online platforms like ArtStation, ZBrushCentral, and Polycount provide spaces for artists to share their work, exchange tips and techniques, and collaborate on projects. These communities are invaluable resources for both beginners and experienced artists, offering a wealth of knowledge and inspiration. The rise of online tutorials, courses, and workshops has also made it easier than ever to learn digital sculpting, with countless resources available to help artists develop their skills.

Despite its many advantages, digital sculpting is not without its challenges. The high level of detail and complexity achievable with digital sculpting can result in large file sizes and performance issues, particularly when working with real-time applications like video games and VR. Optimizing sculpted models for performance while maintaining visual fidelity is a critical skill that requires a deep understanding of both the artistic and technical aspects of 3D modeling. Additionally, the learning curve for digital sculpting software can be steep, requiring a significant investment of time and effort to master the tools and techniques.

Looking to the future, digital sculpting is poised to continue evolving, driven by advancements in technology and the growing demand for high-quality 3D content. Innovations in hardware, such as more powerful processors and advanced graphics cards, will enable even more detailed and complex models. Software developments will continue to enhance the capabilities of digital sculpting tools, providing artists with new features and workflows that streamline the creative process.

Digital sculpting represents a fusion of art and technology that has transformed the way we create and visualize 3D models. Its flexibility, detail, and efficiency make it an indispensable tool in a wide range of industries, from entertainment and product design to healthcare and virtual reality. As technology continues to advance, the potential of digital sculpting will only expand, offering new possibilities for creativity and innovation. Whether used to create fantastical creatures, realistic human characters, or intricate mechanical designs, digital sculpting empowers artists to bring their visions to life in stunning detail and with unparalleled precision.

35. **Virtual Galleries**: Online spaces for displaying digital art.

Virtual galleries represent a significant evolution in the world of art exhibition, leveraging the power of the internet to create spaces where digital art can be displayed and appreciated by a global audience. These online platforms offer numerous advantages over traditional brick-and-mortar galleries, including accessibility, interactivity, and the ability to showcase a diverse range of artistic styles and mediums. As technology continues to advance, virtual galleries are becoming increasingly sophisticated, providing artists and viewers with immersive and engaging experiences that transcend physical limitations.

The concept of virtual galleries is rooted in the democratization of art. Traditional galleries often have geographic and economic barriers that can limit who can participate in the art world, whether as an artist or a viewer. Virtual galleries, however, are accessible to anyone with an internet connection, allowing artists from around the world to share their work with a global audience. This increased accessibility is particularly important for emerging artists who may not have the resources or connections to exhibit their work in established galleries. By providing a platform for these artists, virtual galleries help to promote diversity and inclusivity in the art world.

One of the primary benefits of virtual galleries is the ability to display a wide variety of digital art forms. Digital art encompasses a broad range of mediums, including digital painting, 3D modeling, animation, and interactive installations. Traditional galleries may struggle to accommodate these diverse forms due to space and technical constraints, but virtual galleries can easily showcase them in a way that highlights their unique qualities. For example, an animation can be displayed as a looping video, allowing viewers to experience it as intended, while an interactive piece can be programmed to respond to user input, creating a dynamic and engaging experience.

The design and functionality of virtual galleries can vary widely, from simple websites that display images of artwork to fully immersive 3D environments that replicate the experience of walking through a physical gallery. The most basic virtual galleries consist of webpages with images of artworks, often accompanied by descriptions and artist statements. These platforms are straightforward to navigate and provide a convenient way for viewers to browse and learn about the art. However, they may lack the immersive qualities that can make viewing art in person so compelling.

More advanced virtual galleries utilize 3D modeling and virtual reality (VR) technologies to create interactive spaces that mimic the experience of a physical gallery. Users can navigate through these virtual environments using their mouse and keyboard, or with VR headsets for a more immersive experience. These platforms can replicate the layout and ambiance of a traditional gallery, complete with virtual walls, lighting, and even ambient sounds. This approach allows viewers to experience the scale and spatial relationships of the artworks, which can be an important aspect of their impact.

One of the key features of virtual galleries is the ability to integrate multimedia elements that enhance the viewer's experience. In addition to displaying images and videos of the artwork, virtual galleries can include audio descriptions, artist interviews, and behind-the-scenes footage of the creative process. These elements provide valuable context and insight into the artworks, helping viewers to understand and appreciate them on a deeper level. Additionally, virtual galleries can include interactive features, such as comment sections and live chat functions, that encourage dialogue and engagement between artists and viewers.

The rise of blockchain technology and non-fungible tokens (NFTs) has also had a significant impact on virtual galleries. NFTs allow digital artworks to be authenticated and sold as unique, collectible items, providing artists with a new way to monetize their work. Virtual galleries that support NFTs can offer a secure and transparent marketplace for digital art, where artists can showcase and sell their pieces directly to collectors. Platforms like SuperRare, Foundation, and OpenSea have become popular venues for NFT-based art exhibitions, fostering a vibrant community of digital artists and collectors.

The interactivity and accessibility of virtual galleries make them particularly well-suited for educational purposes. Art educators can use virtual galleries to create curated exhibitions that align with their teaching objectives, providing students with opportunities to engage with a wide range of artworks and artistic styles. Virtual galleries can also include interactive elements, such as quizzes and discussion prompts, that encourage students to think critically about the art and its context. This approach can help to make art education more engaging and accessible, especially for students who may not have access to physical galleries or museums.

Another significant advantage of virtual galleries is their ability to reach a global audience. Unlike traditional galleries, which are limited by their physical location, virtual galleries can be accessed by anyone with an internet connection, regardless of where they are in the world. This global reach allows artists to share their work with a much larger and more diverse audience, increasing their visibility and expanding their potential market. For viewers, virtual galleries provide an opportunity to discover and explore art from different cultures and perspectives, fostering greater understanding and appreciation of the global art community.

Virtual galleries also offer practical benefits in terms of cost and logistics. Running a physical gallery can be expensive, with costs for rent, utilities, staffing, and maintenance. Virtual galleries, on the other hand, require significantly lower overhead, making them a more affordable option for both artists and curators. Additionally, virtual exhibitions can be organized and launched much more quickly than physical ones, as there is no need to transport and install the artworks. This efficiency allows for more frequent and diverse exhibitions, keeping the content fresh and engaging for viewers.

The flexibility of virtual galleries also allows for innovative exhibition formats that would be difficult or impossible to achieve in a physical space. For example, virtual galleries can host collaborative exhibitions where multiple artists contribute to a shared virtual environment, creating a dynamic and interactive experience. They can also include elements like time-based changes, where the exhibition evolves over time, or gamified components that encourage viewers to explore and interact with the art in new ways. These innovative approaches can make virtual galleries exciting and engaging spaces for both artists and viewers.

Despite their many advantages, virtual galleries also present certain challenges. One of the primary challenges is the need for digital literacy and access to technology. While internet access is widespread, there are still many people who lack the necessary devices or skills to fully engage with virtual galleries. Ensuring that these platforms are user-friendly and accessible to a wide audience is crucial for their success. Additionally, the experience of viewing art on a screen can be quite different from seeing it in person. Factors like screen resolution, color accuracy, and the scale of the display can all impact how the artwork is perceived. Virtual galleries must carefully consider these factors to ensure that the art is presented in a way that does it justice.

Another challenge is the potential for digital fatigue. With so much of our lives now taking place online, from work and education to socializing and entertainment, there is a risk that virtual galleries may struggle to capture and retain viewers' attention. To address this, virtual galleries need to offer unique and compelling experiences that differentiate them from other online content. This might include incorporating interactive elements, offering exclusive content, or creating immersive environments that provide a sense of presence and engagement.

As technology continues to advance, the future of virtual galleries looks promising. Developments in VR and augmented reality (AR) are likely to play a significant role in shaping the next generation of virtual art spaces. VR can provide an even more immersive and interactive experience, allowing viewers to feel as though they are truly present in the gallery. AR, on the other hand, can blend the virtual and physical worlds, enabling viewers to experience digital art in their own environment. These technologies have the potential to revolutionize the way we experience and interact with art, creating new possibilities for creativity and engagement.

Virtual galleries are also likely to benefit from advancements in artificial intelligence (AI) and machine learning. AI can be used to create personalized experiences for viewers, curating exhibitions based on their interests and preferences. Machine learning algorithms can analyze viewer behavior and feedback to continuously improve the design and functionality of the gallery. These technologies can help to make virtual galleries more engaging, user-friendly, and effective at connecting artists with their audience.

In conclusion, virtual galleries represent a significant shift in the way we create, display, and experience art. By leveraging the power of the internet and digital technologies, they offer numerous advantages over traditional galleries, including accessibility, flexibility, and the ability to showcase a wide range of digital art forms. As technology continues to evolve, virtual galleries are likely to become even more sophisticated and immersive, providing artists and viewers with new opportunities for creativity and engagement. Despite the challenges, the potential of virtual galleries to democratize the art world and reach a global audience makes them an exciting and valuable addition to the art ecosystem.

36. **Interactive Art**: Art that responds to the viewer's actions.

Interactive art is a dynamic and engaging form of artistic expression that transforms passive viewers into active participants. Unlike traditional art forms, where the audience observes from a distance, interactive art invites viewers to engage with the piece, often influencing its form, behavior, or message. This genre blurs the lines between the artist and the audience, creating a collaborative experience where the final outcome depends on the viewer's actions.

The roots of interactive art can be traced back to the 1960s and 1970s with the advent of kinetic art and installation art, where artists began experimenting with viewer participation. Early pioneers such as Allan Kaprow and Nam June Paik explored these concepts through happenings and video installations, setting the stage for the evolution of interactive art. As technology advanced, the scope and complexity of interactive art expanded, incorporating digital media, sensors, and software to create sophisticated and immersive experiences.

One of the key features of interactive art is its reliance on technology to mediate the interaction between the artwork and the audience. This often involves the use of sensors, cameras, and computers to detect and respond to the viewer's actions. For example, an interactive installation might use motion sensors to detect the presence and movement of viewers, altering its visual or auditory output accordingly. This creates a responsive environment where the artwork changes in real-time based on the behavior of the audience, making each interaction unique.

A well-known example of interactive art is Rafael Lozano-Hemmer's "Pulse Room" (2006). In this installation, a grid of incandescent light bulbs hangs from the ceiling, each bulb connected to a sensor that measures the viewer's heartbeat. When a participant places their hand on the sensor, their heartbeat is translated into flashes of light, creating a visual representation of their pulse. As more viewers interact with the piece, the room fills with the rhythmic pulsing of lights, creating a communal experience that highlights the shared human experience of the heartbeat.

Interactive art can take many forms, from installations and sculptures to digital media and performance art. One of the most common formats is the interactive installation, where viewers can physically engage with the artwork. These installations often create immersive environments that envelop the participant, encouraging exploration and discovery. For instance, teamLab, a Japanese art collective, is renowned for its interactive digital installations that blend art, technology, and nature. Their works, such as "Borderless" and "Planets," use projection mapping, sensors, and digital screens to create ever-changing landscapes that respond to the presence and movement of viewers, allowing them to become part of the artwork.

Digital and online interactive art has also gained prominence, particularly with the rise of the internet and social media. These works often invite global participation, allowing people from around the world to contribute to the artwork in real-time. An example is Aaron Koblin's "The Johnny Cash Project" (2010), which invited participants to create individual frames for a music video of Johnny Cash's song "Ain't No Grave." Each frame was drawn by a different participant using an online drawing tool, resulting in a collectively created animation that is constantly evolving as new contributions are added.

The interactivity in art can also be driven by data and algorithms. In data-driven interactive art, the artwork responds to data inputs, which can be anything from environmental data, like weather patterns, to social media activity. Such works can reveal patterns and connections that might not be immediately apparent, transforming abstract data into tangible and engaging experiences. An example is "Wind Map" by Fernanda Viégas and Martin Wattenberg, an interactive visualization that shows the wind patterns across the United States in real-time. By interacting with the map, viewers can explore different regions and see how the wind currents change, creating a deeper understanding of meteorological phenomena.

Interactive art often seeks to provoke thought and reflection, challenging viewers to consider their role in the experience. This can involve social and political themes, using interactivity to engage audiences in a dialogue about important issues. For instance, "The Climate Ribbon" project, created by Eve Mosher and others, is an interactive installation that invites participants to write their hopes and fears about climate change on ribbons. These ribbons are then tied to a large structure, creating a visual representation of collective concern and commitment to addressing climate change.

Performance art also offers rich opportunities for interactivity, with artists incorporating audience participation directly into their performances. Marina Abramović's "The Artist Is Present" (2010) at the Museum of Modern Art in New York is a notable example. During this performance, Abramović sat silently at a table, inviting viewers to sit across from her and engage in a silent exchange. The simplicity of the setup belied the profound impact it had on participants, many of whom reported intense emotional experiences. The performance highlighted the power of presence and the deep connections that can be formed through direct, unmediated interaction.

The rise of augmented reality (AR) and virtual reality (VR) technologies has opened new frontiers for interactive art. These technologies create immersive environments that can respond to the viewer's movements and actions in real-time, offering unprecedented levels of interactivity. AR and VR artworks can transport viewers to entirely new worlds, where they can interact with virtual objects and environments in ways that were previously impossible. For example, the artist Olafur Eliasson has used AR to create "Wunderkammer," an app that allows users to place and interact with virtual objects in their real-world environment, blending the physical and digital realms.

The educational potential of interactive art is also significant. By engaging viewers in active participation, interactive artworks can create memorable and impactful learning experiences. Museums and educational institutions increasingly incorporate interactive installations to make learning more engaging and accessible. These installations can range from interactive exhibits that explain scientific concepts to art pieces that encourage creative exploration. By involving the viewer in the learning process, interactive art can foster a deeper understanding and appreciation of the subject matter.

Interactive art is not without its challenges. Creating works that effectively engage and respond to viewers requires a deep understanding of both artistic principles and technological capabilities. Artists must carefully consider how their work will interact with participants and anticipate a range of possible interactions. Technical challenges, such as ensuring reliable sensor performance and real-time responsiveness, can also be significant. Additionally, there is the challenge of accessibility, as not all viewers may be comfortable or familiar with the technologies used in interactive art.

Despite these challenges, the potential of interactive art to create powerful and transformative experiences is immense. By breaking down the barriers between the artist and the audience, interactive art fosters a sense of connection and collaboration that is unique in the art world. It encourages viewers to become co-creators, contributing their actions and perspectives to the final outcome. This collaborative aspect can create a strong sense of community and shared experience, making interactive art a powerful tool for social and cultural engagement.

Looking to the future, the field of interactive art is likely to continue evolving, driven by advances in technology and changing societal needs. The integration of artificial intelligence (AI) and machine learning offers exciting possibilities for creating more sophisticated and responsive artworks. AI can enable artworks to learn and adapt to viewer interactions over time, creating experiences that are personalized and evolving. Additionally, the increasing prevalence of wearable technology and smart devices opens up new avenues for interaction, allowing artworks to respond to a wider range of inputs and creating more immersive and intuitive experiences.

Interactive art also has the potential to play a significant role in addressing global challenges. By engaging viewers in meaningful and thought-provoking interactions, interactive art can raise awareness and inspire action on issues such as climate change, social justice, and mental health. Artists can use interactivity to create powerful narratives and experiences that highlight these issues, encouraging viewers to reflect on their own role and responsibility. In this way, interactive art can be a catalyst for change, using creativity and technology to address the most pressing challenges of our time.

In conclusion, interactive art represents a dynamic and evolving form of artistic expression that transforms the relationship between the artwork and the viewer. By inviting active participation, interactive art creates collaborative and immersive experiences that are unique and engaging. As technology continues to advance, the potential for interactive art to create powerful and transformative experiences will only grow. Whether through digital installations, performance art, or data-driven visualizations, interactive art offers new ways to engage, inspire, and connect with audiences, making it a vital and exciting area of contemporary art.

Communications and Media

In the rapidly evolving landscape of the 21st century, communications and media have undergone profound transformations, reshaping how information is created, shared, and consumed. Digital literacy has become an essential skill, enabling individuals to navigate and utilize various digital tools and media effectively. This proficiency extends beyond mere technical ability to encompass critical thinking and the capacity to evaluate digital content's credibility and relevance.

Digital literacy empowers individuals to engage with the digital world confidently. It involves understanding how to use digital devices and platforms, creating and sharing content, and protecting one's privacy and security online. This skill set is crucial in an era where digital media pervades nearly every aspect of life, from education and work to social interactions and entertainment. Being digitally literate means being able to decipher the vast amounts of information encountered daily, distinguishing between reliable sources and misinformation.

The concept of media convergence is central to the ongoing transformation in communications and media. Media convergence refers to the merging of traditional and digital media platforms, creating a seamless flow of content across multiple formats. This phenomenon has blurred the lines between different types of media, such as television, radio, print, and online platforms. The result is an integrated media environment where content is readily accessible across various devices and channels.

Media convergence has revolutionized how content is produced and consumed. It has enabled the creation of multimedia stories that combine text, audio, video, and interactive elements, offering richer and more engaging experiences for audiences. For instance, news organizations now deliver stories through articles, podcasts, video reports, and social media updates, catering to diverse audience preferences. This convergence also allows for more personalized and on-demand content consumption, where users can access what they want, when they want it.

A notable development in the realm of media convergence is the rise of virtual influencers. These AI-generated characters, designed to interact with users on social media, have gained significant popularity and influence. Unlike human influencers, virtual influencers are entirely digital creations, often managed by marketing teams or tech companies. They engage with followers, promote products, and even participate in brand collaborations, much like their human counterparts.

The appeal of virtual influencers lies in their ability to be meticulously crafted and controlled. They can maintain a consistent persona, free from the unpredictability of human behavior. This predictability makes them attractive to brands seeking to manage their image and reach target audiences effectively. Moreover, virtual influencers can be designed to embody diverse appearances, backgrounds, and personalities, allowing for a wide range of representations and relatability.

Streaming services have also played a pivotal role in the transformation of media consumption. These platforms, which deliver digital content in real-time over the internet, have revolutionized how people access and enjoy entertainment. Services like Netflix, Amazon Prime Video, Disney+, and Spotify have become household names, offering vast libraries of movies, TV shows, music, and more. The convenience of streaming services lies in their on-demand nature, allowing users to watch or listen to content whenever and wherever they choose.

Streaming services have disrupted traditional media industries, particularly television and cinema. The ability to binge-watch entire seasons of TV shows or access a wide array of movies without leaving home has reshaped viewing habits. Additionally, streaming platforms have provided a platform for diverse and niche content that might not have found a place in mainstream media. This democratization of content has given rise to new voices and perspectives, enriching the cultural landscape.

Digital journalism represents another significant shift in the media landscape. As news consumption increasingly moves online, traditional print journalism has had to adapt to survive in the digital age. Digital journalism encompasses a wide range of practices, from online newspapers and magazines to blogs, social media updates, and independent news websites. This form of journalism leverages the immediacy and interactivity of digital platforms to deliver news and information to global audiences in real time.

The transition to digital journalism has brought both opportunities and challenges. On the positive side, it has democratized the creation and dissemination of news, allowing more voices to be heard. Social media and blogging platforms have enabled citizen journalists and independent reporters to share their perspectives and stories, often bypassing traditional gatekeepers. Digital journalism also allows for more interactive and multimedia-rich storytelling, engaging readers through videos, infographics, and interactive features.

However, the digital age has also introduced challenges for journalism. The rise of misinformation and fake news, facilitated by the ease of sharing content online, has undermined trust in media. Journalists and news organizations must now navigate an environment where credibility and accuracy are paramount, yet increasingly difficult to maintain. Additionally, the shift to digital has disrupted traditional revenue models for journalism, with many publications struggling to monetize online content effectively.

In response to these challenges, many news organizations have adopted new strategies to engage audiences and ensure sustainability. Subscription models, membership programs, and crowdfunding have emerged as alternative revenue streams. Some organizations have also embraced data journalism, using data analysis and visualization to uncover and report on complex stories. This approach not only enhances the depth and accuracy of reporting but also attracts readers interested in detailed and evidence-based journalism.

The intersection of digital literacy, media convergence, virtual influencers, streaming services, and digital journalism highlights the dynamic and interconnected nature of modern communications and media. These elements collectively shape how information is produced, shared, and consumed, influencing societal trends and individual behaviors. As technology continues to evolve, so too will the landscape of media, presenting both opportunities and challenges for creators, consumers, and regulators alike.

To navigate this ever-changing environment, fostering digital literacy remains crucial. Educating individuals, particularly younger generations, about the responsible use of digital tools and media can help mitigate the spread of misinformation and promote informed and engaged citizenship. Encouraging critical thinking skills and media literacy can empower people to discern credible sources and make thoughtful decisions in the digital realm.

Moreover, the rise of virtual influencers and streaming services underscores the need for ethical considerations in media production and consumption. As AI-generated characters become more prevalent, questions about authenticity, transparency, and the potential impact on human influencers and the broader media ecosystem arise. Similarly, the dominance of streaming services raises concerns about data privacy, content diversity, and the implications for traditional media industries.

In the realm of digital journalism, maintaining high standards of accuracy and integrity is paramount. Journalists and news organizations must adapt to new technologies and audience behaviors while upholding the principles of ethical journalism. This includes verifying information, providing context, and avoiding sensationalism. Collaboration between traditional journalists and new media practitioners can also enrich the quality of journalism, combining the strengths of both approaches.

Looking ahead, the continued convergence of media forms and platforms will likely lead to even more integrated and immersive media experiences. The development of augmented reality (AR) and virtual reality (VR) technologies promises to create new possibilities for storytelling and content consumption. These technologies can transport users to virtual worlds, offering unprecedented levels of interactivity and engagement.

As media and communications evolve, so too will the ways in which societies understand and interact with the world. The blending of traditional and digital media, coupled with the rise of new forms of content creation and consumption, underscores the importance of adaptability and lifelong learning. Staying informed about technological advancements and their implications will be key to navigating the future media landscape effectively.

In conclusion, the ongoing transformation of communications and media is characterized by the interplay of digital literacy, media convergence, virtual influencers, streaming services, and digital journalism. Each of these elements contributes to the dynamic and multifaceted nature of modern media, shaping how information is created, shared, and consumed. As technology continues to advance, fostering digital literacy and ethical media practices will be essential to ensuring a vibrant, informed, and engaged society.

37. **Digital Literacy**: The ability to use and understand digital tools and media.

Digital literacy is an essential skill in the 21st century, encompassing the ability to use and understand digital tools and media. As society becomes increasingly interconnected through technology, digital literacy has emerged as a fundamental competence required for personal, professional, and educational success. It goes beyond mere technical know-how to include critical thinking, ethical considerations, and the ability to evaluate and create digital content effectively.

At its core, digital literacy involves the ability to operate digital devices and navigate digital environments. This includes using computers, smartphones, tablets, and other electronic devices that provide access to the internet and various applications. Familiarity with operating systems, software applications, and digital communication tools is also a crucial aspect of digital literacy. This foundational knowledge allows individuals to perform everyday tasks such as sending emails, browsing the web, using social media, and managing files.

However, digital literacy is not limited to basic operational skills. It extends to understanding how digital tools and media function, and the implications of their use. This understanding encompasses knowledge of how data is created, shared, and stored, as well as the potential privacy and security risks associated with digital interactions. Being digitally literate means being aware of the importance of protecting personal information and using tools such as passwords, encryption, and secure connections to safeguard online activities.

One of the critical components of digital literacy is the ability to critically evaluate digital content. The internet is a vast repository of information, but not all of it is accurate or trustworthy. Digital literacy involves the capacity to assess the credibility of online sources, discern between reliable and unreliable information, and identify potential biases or misinformation. This skill is increasingly important in an era where fake news, deepfakes, and misinformation can spread rapidly through social media and other digital platforms.

Critical evaluation also includes understanding the broader context in which digital content is created and consumed. This means recognizing the economic, political, and social factors that influence media production and distribution. For instance, being aware of how algorithms curate content on social media platforms can help users understand why they see certain posts and advertisements and how their online behavior influences the information they receive.

Creating digital content is another vital aspect of digital literacy. This involves using various digital tools to produce and share information, whether through writing, images, video, or other multimedia formats. Proficiency in content creation requires not only technical skills but also an understanding of digital communication principles. Effective digital content is clear, engaging, and appropriate for its intended audience. It also adheres to ethical standards, respecting copyright laws and avoiding plagiarism.

Digital literacy also encompasses the ability to participate actively and responsibly in digital communities. This includes understanding the norms and etiquette of online interactions, such as respecting others' opinions, avoiding harmful behaviors like cyberbullying, and contributing positively to discussions. Digital literacy involves being an informed and respectful digital citizen, aware of one's rights and responsibilities in the online world.

The importance of digital literacy extends to education, where it plays a crucial role in enhancing learning experiences and outcomes. In today's educational landscape, digital tools and resources are integral to teaching and learning processes. Students use digital devices to access educational materials, collaborate with peers, and complete assignments. Teachers leverage technology to deliver interactive lessons, assess student progress, and provide personalized feedback. Digital literacy empowers students to navigate these digital learning environments effectively, enhancing their academic success and preparing them for future careers.

Moreover, digital literacy is essential for professional development and career advancement. In many industries, digital skills are a prerequisite for employment. Jobs in fields such as information technology, marketing, healthcare, finance, and more require proficiency with digital tools and platforms. Even in roles that are not explicitly tech-focused, digital literacy can enhance productivity and efficiency. For example, understanding how to use project management software, data analysis tools, or digital communication platforms can improve workflow and collaboration in the workplace.

The digital economy also demands a continuous commitment to learning and adapting to new technologies. As technology evolves, so too must the skills required to use it effectively. This means that digital literacy is not a static skill set but an ongoing process of education and development. Lifelong learning is a critical aspect of digital literacy, as individuals must stay informed about technological advancements and be willing to update their skills regularly.

In addition to personal and professional benefits, digital literacy has broader societal implications. It enables individuals to engage with digital government services, access healthcare information, participate in civic activities, and stay connected with family and friends. Digital literacy can also empower marginalized communities, providing access to information and opportunities that might otherwise be out of reach. For instance, digital literacy programs can help bridge the digital divide, ensuring that all members of society have the skills needed to participate fully in the digital world.

Addressing the digital divide is a significant challenge that requires coordinated efforts from governments, educational institutions, and private organizations. The digital divide refers to the gap between individuals who have access to digital technologies and those who do not. This divide can be influenced by factors such as socioeconomic status, geographic location, age, and education level. Digital literacy initiatives aimed at reducing this divide focus on providing access to technology, training individuals in digital skills, and promoting inclusive digital policies.

Effective digital literacy education involves a combination of formal and informal learning opportunities. Schools and universities play a vital role in integrating digital literacy into their curricula, ensuring that students develop the necessary skills from an early age. Additionally, community programs, online courses, and workplace training can provide valuable resources for individuals seeking to improve their digital literacy. Collaboration between educators, policymakers, and industry leaders is essential to create comprehensive digital literacy programs that address the diverse needs of the population.

Another critical aspect of digital literacy is the ethical use of digital tools and media. This includes understanding the impact of one's online actions on others and the broader digital ecosystem. Ethical digital literacy involves promoting positive behaviors, such as respecting intellectual property, protecting privacy, and fostering inclusive online communities. It also means being aware of the potential negative consequences of digital activities, such as cyberbullying, identity theft, and the spread of misinformation.

Educators and parents play a crucial role in fostering ethical digital literacy in children and young adults. By modeling responsible digital behavior and providing guidance on navigating the digital world, they can help young people develop a strong ethical foundation. Discussions about digital ethics should be an integral part of digital literacy education, addressing topics such as online privacy, digital footprints, and the importance of respectful online communication.

In conclusion, digital literacy is a multifaceted and dynamic skill set that encompasses the ability to use and understand digital tools and media. It involves technical proficiency, critical thinking, ethical considerations, and the ability to create and evaluate digital content. Digital literacy is essential for personal, professional, and educational success, enabling individuals to navigate the digital world confidently and responsibly. As technology continues to evolve, fostering digital literacy through education, lifelong learning, and ethical practices will be crucial to ensuring that all members of society can participate fully in the digital age. Addressing the digital divide and promoting inclusive digital literacy initiatives are essential steps towards achieving digital equity and empowering individuals to thrive in an increasingly interconnected world.

38. **Media Convergence**: Blending of different media forms and platforms.

Media convergence is a transformative phenomenon in the landscape of communication and information dissemination, characterized by the blending of different media forms and platforms. This process has reshaped how content is produced, distributed, and consumed, leading to a more integrated and dynamic media environment. Media convergence encompasses various dimensions, including technological, industrial, cultural, and social aspects, each playing a crucial role in the evolution of modern media.

At the heart of media convergence is the technological dimension, which involves the integration of various digital technologies that enable the seamless flow of content across multiple platforms. The advent of the internet and digital technologies has facilitated the convergence of previously distinct media forms such as print, radio, television, and the web. This technological integration allows content to be created once and distributed across multiple platforms, reaching audiences through diverse channels such as websites, social media, mobile apps, and streaming services. For example, a news story can be reported on a television broadcast, published as an article on a news website, shared on social media, and discussed in a podcast, all stemming from the same core content.

The industrial dimension of media convergence refers to the restructuring of media industries to accommodate and capitalize on the opportunities presented by technological advancements. Media companies are increasingly adopting multi-platform strategies, investing in digital technologies, and forming partnerships and mergers to enhance their capabilities. This shift has led to the creation of conglomerates that own a variety of media outlets, allowing for cross-promotion and resource sharing across different platforms. For instance, a media conglomerate might own a television network, a film studio, a publishing house, and several online properties, enabling it to distribute content widely and synergistically.

One significant impact of industrial convergence is the rise of integrated media companies that produce and distribute content across multiple platforms. These companies leverage their diverse assets to create a unified brand presence and offer audiences a consistent experience, regardless of the medium they use. For example, Disney's acquisition of various entertainment properties and platforms allows it to deliver content through movies, television shows, theme parks, merchandise, and online streaming services like Disney+. This integrated approach enhances the company's ability to engage audiences and monetize content across different channels.

The cultural dimension of media convergence explores how the blending of media forms influences cultural production and consumption. Media convergence has democratized content creation, allowing individuals and small organizations to produce and distribute content more easily. This shift has given rise to new forms of storytelling and artistic expression, as creators experiment with blending different media formats to engage audiences in innovative ways. For example, transmedia storytelling involves telling a single narrative or story experience across multiple platforms and formats, each contributing uniquely to the overall narrative. A film might be complemented by an interactive website, a series of social media posts, and a video game, each providing different pieces of the story.

Additionally, cultural convergence has fostered greater audience participation and interactivity. Audiences are no longer passive consumers of content; they actively engage with media by commenting, sharing, remixing, and creating their own content. This participatory culture is exemplified by fan communities that produce fan fiction, fan art, and other user-generated content based on popular media franchises. Social media platforms, in particular, have facilitated this cultural convergence by providing spaces for fans to connect, collaborate, and share their creations.

The social dimension of media convergence examines how the blending of media forms affects social interactions and relationships. Social media platforms have become central to how people communicate, share information, and form communities. These platforms integrate various media formats, including text, images, video, and live streaming, allowing users to interact with content and with each other in multifaceted ways. For example, a user might watch a live-streamed event, comment on it in real time, share clips on social media, and discuss it in an online forum, all within a single digital ecosystem.

Moreover, media convergence has influenced the nature of news consumption and public discourse. Traditional news outlets have adapted to the digital age by incorporating multimedia elements into their reporting and distributing content across multiple platforms. News organizations use social media to reach wider audiences, engage with readers, and gather real-time feedback. This convergence has also led to the rise of citizen journalism, where ordinary individuals report news and share information using digital tools. While this democratization of news has expanded the diversity of voices and perspectives, it has also raised concerns about the accuracy and reliability of information in the digital age.

The blending of media forms and platforms has also transformed advertising and marketing strategies. Advertisers now use integrated campaigns that leverage various media channels to reach target audiences more effectively. For instance, a brand might launch a marketing campaign that includes television commercials, social media ads, sponsored content on websites, influencer partnerships, and interactive experiences. This multi-platform approach allows brands to create cohesive and immersive experiences that resonate with consumers across different touchpoints.

Media convergence has also led to the development of new business models and revenue streams. Subscription-based services, such as streaming platforms like Netflix and Spotify, have become increasingly popular, offering users access to vast libraries of content for a monthly fee. These services often combine various media forms, providing not only films and TV shows but also music, podcasts, and original content. Additionally, freemium models, where basic access is free but premium features require payment, have gained traction in industries such as gaming and software.

However, media convergence also presents several challenges and concerns. One significant issue is the consolidation of media ownership, which can lead to a concentration of power in the hands of a few large corporations. This concentration can limit diversity in content and perspectives, as media conglomerates prioritize commercially viable content that appeals to broad audiences. Moreover, the blending of media platforms raises concerns about data privacy and security, as companies collect and analyze vast amounts of user data to tailor content and advertising.

Another challenge is the digital divide, which refers to the gap between those who have access to digital technologies and those who do not. Media convergence relies on digital infrastructure, and individuals without access to high-speed internet, modern devices, or digital literacy skills may be excluded from the benefits of converged media. Addressing this divide requires investment in digital infrastructure, education, and policies that promote equitable access to technology.

In conclusion, media convergence represents a significant shift in the media landscape, characterized by the blending of different media forms and platforms. This convergence is driven by technological advancements, industrial restructuring, cultural innovation, and social interactions. It has transformed how content is created, distributed, and consumed, leading to more integrated and dynamic media experiences. While media convergence offers numerous opportunities for creativity, engagement, and business innovation, it also presents challenges related to media ownership, data privacy, and digital inclusion. As media convergence continues to evolve, it will be essential to address these challenges and ensure that the benefits of converged media are accessible to all members of society.

39. **Virtual Influencers**: AI-generated characters influencing social media.

Virtual influencers, or AI-generated characters, are becoming increasingly influential on social media platforms. These digital personas are crafted using advanced computer graphics and artificial intelligence technologies, allowing them to interact with real users in ways that are strikingly similar to human influencers. The rise of virtual influencers marks a significant shift in the landscape of digital marketing and social media engagement, with far-reaching implications for brands, consumers, and the broader cultural context.

At the core of virtual influencers is the blend of artistry and technology. These characters are created using sophisticated 3D modeling software and AI algorithms, which enable them to exhibit lifelike appearances and behaviors. The realism of virtual influencers is often so convincing that it can be challenging to distinguish them from human influencers at first glance. Their creators can meticulously design every aspect of their appearance, from facial features and expressions to clothing and accessories, ensuring they align perfectly with desired brand aesthetics or audience preferences.

One of the key advantages of virtual influencers is their ability to maintain a consistent persona. Unlike human influencers, who may have off days or personal issues that affect their performance, virtual influencers can be perfectly controlled to always present an ideal image. This consistency is particularly appealing to brands seeking reliable representatives for their products and services. Virtual influencers do not age, fall ill, or engage in scandals, which makes them a more predictable and manageable asset in the marketing world.

The rise of virtual influencers can be attributed to several factors, including the growing importance of social media in marketing strategies and the increasing capabilities of AI and graphic technologies. Social media platforms have become critical channels for reaching and engaging with consumers, particularly younger demographics who spend a significant amount of time online. Virtual influencers offer a novel and intriguing way to capture these audiences' attention, leveraging the power of visual appeal and digital interaction.

In addition to their visual and interactive capabilities, virtual influencers can be programmed to embody specific values, interests, and personalities that resonate with target audiences. For example, a virtual influencer designed to promote sustainable fashion can consistently share content related to eco-friendly products, environmental advocacy, and ethical consumerism. This targeted approach allows brands to craft highly specialized marketing campaigns that align with their core messages and audience values.

The popularity of virtual influencers is evident in their substantial followings on social media platforms like Instagram, TikTok, and YouTube. These characters often amass millions of followers, with engagement rates that rival or even surpass those of human influencers. One notable example is Lil Miquela, a virtual influencer created by the company Brud. Since her debut in 2016, Lil Miquela has garnered millions of followers on Instagram, collaborated with high-profile brands like Calvin Klein and Prada, and even released music tracks. Her success demonstrates the significant impact virtual influencers can have in the digital space.

Brands are increasingly recognizing the potential of virtual influencers to drive engagement and sales. Collaborations between brands and virtual influencers can take various forms, including sponsored posts, product placements, and branded content. These partnerships often leverage the unique characteristics of virtual influencers to create memorable and visually stunning campaigns. For instance, a beauty brand might collaborate with a virtual influencer to showcase new makeup products through hyper-realistic tutorials and glamorous photoshoots.

The use of virtual influencers is not limited to consumer goods; they are also being employed in industries such as entertainment, fashion, and travel. In the entertainment industry, virtual influencers can promote movies, TV shows, and music albums through creative and engaging content. Fashion brands can use virtual influencers to model clothing and accessories, participate in virtual fashion shows, and offer styling tips. In the travel industry, virtual influencers can "visit" and promote destinations, hotels, and experiences, providing visually captivating content without the logistical challenges of real-world travel.

While virtual influencers offer numerous advantages, their rise also raises several ethical and practical questions. One major concern is the issue of transparency. Consumers may not always realize that they are interacting with a virtual character rather than a real person. This lack of transparency can lead to questions about authenticity and trust. To address this, some creators and brands are making efforts to be clear about the artificial nature of virtual influencers, ensuring that followers are aware they are engaging with digital personas.

Another ethical consideration is the potential impact on human influencers and the broader job market. As virtual influencers become more popular, there may be concerns about job displacement for human influencers and other professionals in related fields, such as modeling and photography. However, it is also possible that virtual influencers and human influencers can coexist and complement each other, offering diverse approaches to digital marketing and content creation.

The use of virtual influencers also prompts discussions about creativity and originality. While virtual influencers can be designed to exhibit unique and captivating personalities, their behavior and content are ultimately controlled by their creators. This raises questions about the authenticity of the connections they build with their audiences. Some critics argue that the interactions and relationships formed with virtual influencers may lack the genuine emotional depth that can be achieved with human influencers.

Despite these concerns, the trend towards virtual influencers shows no signs of slowing down. As AI and graphic technologies continue to advance, the realism and capabilities of virtual influencers are likely to improve further. This evolution will open up new possibilities for storytelling, brand engagement, and audience interaction. For example, future virtual influencers might be able to respond to comments and messages in real time, participate in live events, and even adapt their content based on audience feedback and preferences.

In addition to their roles in marketing and entertainment, virtual influencers could also serve as educational tools and role models. For instance, virtual characters could be designed to promote positive behaviors, such as healthy living, environmental conservation, and social justice. These influencers could collaborate with educational institutions, non-profits, and government agencies to raise awareness about important issues and encourage positive social change.

Furthermore, virtual influencers could play a role in shaping cultural narratives and representations. Because they can be designed to embody any appearance or identity, virtual influencers have the potential to diversify media representation and challenge traditional beauty standards. This flexibility allows for the creation of characters that reflect a wide range of ethnicities, body types, genders, and backgrounds, contributing to more inclusive and representative media.

The business model of virtual influencers also offers intriguing possibilities for monetization and revenue generation. Virtual influencers can generate income through sponsored content, brand partnerships, and merchandise sales. Additionally, they can explore new revenue streams such as virtual events, exclusive content, and digital collectibles, including non-fungible tokens (NFTs). These diverse monetization opportunities highlight the economic potential of virtual influencers in the digital economy.

Looking ahead, the development of virtual influencers may also intersect with other emerging technologies, such as virtual reality (VR) and augmented reality (AR). These technologies could enhance the interactivity and immersion of virtual influencers, allowing users to engage with them in more immersive and lifelike ways. For example, users might interact with virtual influencers in VR environments, participate in AR-enhanced experiences, or even "meet" virtual influencers through holographic projections.

In conclusion, virtual influencers represent a fascinating and rapidly evolving phenomenon in the realm of social media and digital marketing. These AI-generated characters offer numerous advantages, including consistent personas, targeted engagement, and creative flexibility. Their popularity and influence continue to grow, driven by advancements in technology and the increasing importance of social media in marketing strategies. While their rise raises important ethical and practical questions, virtual influencers have the potential to transform how brands connect with audiences, shape cultural narratives, and explore new business models. As the technology behind virtual influencers advances, their impact on the digital landscape will likely deepen, opening up new possibilities for innovation and engagement in the years to come.

40. **Streaming Services**: Platforms delivering digital content in real-time.

Streaming services have revolutionized the way we consume digital content, transforming the landscape of entertainment, education, and communication. These platforms deliver content in real-time, providing immediate access to a vast array of media, including movies, TV shows, music, live broadcasts, and more. The evolution of streaming services can be traced back to the early days of the internet, but their impact has become most pronounced in the past decade, significantly altering consumer habits and industry dynamics.

One of the most significant advantages of streaming services is the convenience they offer. Unlike traditional media formats that require physical storage or scheduled broadcasts, streaming allows users to access content instantly from any device connected to the internet. This flexibility has been a game-changer for many, enabling viewers to watch their favorite shows or listen to music on-demand, whether at home, on the go, or during a commute. The ability to pause, rewind, and resume content at any time further enhances the user experience, making streaming an attractive option for busy lifestyles.

The rise of streaming services has also led to a democratization of content creation and distribution. Platforms like YouTube, Twitch, and TikTok have given rise to a new generation of content creators who can reach global audiences without the need for traditional media gatekeepers. This has resulted in a diverse array of content, ranging from professional productions to user-generated videos, catering to niche interests and communities. Independent filmmakers, musicians, and artists now have the opportunity to showcase their work to a worldwide audience, potentially achieving fame and success without the backing of major studios or record labels.

Subscription-based streaming services such as Netflix, Hulu, and Disney+ have set the standard for high-quality, on-demand content. These platforms have invested heavily in original programming, producing critically acclaimed series, films, and documentaries that rival traditional television networks and movie studios. The success of shows like "Stranger Things," "The Mandalorian," and "The Crown" highlights the potential of streaming services to deliver compelling, exclusive content that attracts and retains subscribers. This shift has prompted major media companies to launch their own streaming platforms, leading to increased competition and more choices for consumers.

In addition to video streaming, music streaming services like Spotify, Apple Music, and Amazon Music have transformed the music industry. These platforms provide access to millions of songs and albums, allowing users to create personalized playlists and discover new artists through algorithm-driven recommendations. The convenience of streaming music has contributed to the decline of physical media sales and digital downloads, as consumers increasingly prefer the ease of accessing a vast music library from their smartphones or other devices. For artists, streaming services offer a new revenue stream, albeit one that has sparked debates over fair compensation and the financial viability of streaming as a primary income source.

Live streaming has also gained significant traction, particularly in the realms of gaming, sports, and events. Platforms like Twitch and YouTube Live enable gamers to broadcast their gameplay to audiences in real-time, fostering interactive communities and giving rise to professional streamers who can earn money through subscriptions, donations, and sponsorships. Sports leagues and events have embraced live streaming to reach global audiences, offering fans the ability to watch games and events live from anywhere in the world. This trend has been accelerated by the COVID-19 pandemic, which forced many events to go virtual and highlighted the importance of live streaming in maintaining audience engagement.

The educational sector has also benefited from the advent of streaming services. Online learning platforms like Coursera, Khan Academy, and edX provide access to a wide range of courses and lectures from prestigious institutions, democratizing education and making it more accessible to learners worldwide. Live streaming technology has enabled virtual classrooms, allowing students and teachers to interact in real-time despite geographical barriers. This has been particularly valuable during the pandemic, as schools and universities had to pivot to remote learning to ensure the continuity of education.

Despite the many benefits of streaming services, there are challenges and concerns that need to be addressed. One major issue is the digital divide, as access to high-speed internet is not universal. Rural and underserved communities may struggle to access streaming content, exacerbating existing inequalities. Additionally, the increasing number of subscription-based services can lead to "subscription fatigue," where consumers are overwhelmed by the costs and complexity of managing multiple subscriptions. This has led to calls for more affordable and accessible options, such as ad-supported streaming models.

Privacy and data security are also significant concerns in the streaming industry. Streaming platforms collect vast amounts of data on user behavior and preferences, raising questions about how this data is used and protected. Instances of data breaches and unauthorized access to personal information have highlighted the need for stringent security measures and transparent data practices. Users must be aware of the privacy policies of the services they use and take steps to protect their personal information.

The environmental impact of streaming services is another area of concern. The infrastructure required to support streaming, including data centers and network operations, consumes significant amounts of energy. As the demand for streaming continues to grow, so does the carbon footprint associated with it. Industry leaders are exploring ways to make streaming more sustainable, such as investing in renewable energy sources and optimizing data center efficiency. Consumers can also play a role by being mindful of their streaming habits and supporting platforms that prioritize sustainability.

In terms of future trends, the streaming industry is poised for continued growth and innovation. The integration of artificial intelligence and machine learning is enhancing content recommendations and personalizing the user experience. Virtual reality (VR) and augmented reality (AR) are emerging as new frontiers for streaming, offering immersive experiences that go beyond traditional media formats. As 5G technology becomes more widespread, the quality and speed of streaming will improve, enabling more seamless and high-definition content delivery.

The proliferation of streaming services has also sparked discussions about the future of traditional media. Cable and satellite TV providers are experiencing a decline in subscribers as more people "cut the cord" in favor of streaming options. This shift is prompting traditional media companies to adapt by offering their content through streaming platforms and exploring new business models. The convergence of traditional and digital media is likely to continue, resulting in a more integrated and dynamic entertainment ecosystem.

In conclusion, streaming services have fundamentally changed the way we access and consume digital content. The convenience, variety, and immediacy of streaming have made it a preferred choice for millions of users worldwide. While the industry faces challenges related to accessibility, privacy, and sustainability, ongoing innovation and adaptation are driving its evolution. As streaming becomes increasingly integral to our daily lives, its impact on entertainment, education, and communication will continue to grow, shaping the future of media consumption.

41. **Digital Journalism**: News and information disseminated online.

Digital journalism represents a transformative shift in how news and information are disseminated, consumed, and interacted with by audiences worldwide. The advent of the internet and the proliferation of digital devices have fundamentally altered the landscape of journalism, presenting both opportunities and challenges for traditional news organizations and new media entrants alike.

At its core, digital journalism involves the use of online platforms to distribute news content. This encompasses a wide range of formats, including articles, videos, podcasts, infographics, and interactive multimedia. Unlike traditional print or broadcast journalism, digital journalism leverages the internet's immediacy and reach, enabling news to be published and accessed in real time by a global audience. This has led to a more dynamic and fast-paced news cycle, where stories can evolve and be updated continuously as new information emerges.

One of the most significant advantages of digital journalism is the democratization of news production and distribution. The barriers to entry for publishing news content have been significantly lowered, allowing independent journalists, bloggers, and citizen reporters to reach wide audiences without the need for large-scale infrastructure or substantial financial backing. This has resulted in a more diverse media landscape, where a variety of voices and perspectives can be heard. Social media platforms like Twitter, Facebook, and Instagram play a crucial role in this ecosystem, serving as both distribution channels and sources of news themselves.

Digital journalism has also enhanced the interactivity of news consumption. Readers are no longer passive recipients of information; they can engage with content through comments, shares, likes, and other forms of interaction. This two-way communication fosters a sense of community and dialogue around news stories, allowing journalists to receive immediate feedback and gauge public opinion. Additionally, the use of multimedia elements such as videos, audio clips, and interactive graphics can enrich the storytelling experience, making complex issues more accessible and engaging for audiences.

The shift to digital has also necessitated changes in how news organizations operate. Traditional media outlets have had to adapt to the new digital environment by developing online editions, investing in digital tools, and rethinking their business models. Many have embraced a "digital-first" approach, prioritizing online content and using print or broadcast as secondary channels. This transition has not been without its challenges, as legacy media companies grapple with declining print circulation and advertising revenues. However, it has also opened up new revenue streams, such as digital subscriptions, sponsored content, and native advertising.

One of the hallmarks of digital journalism is its emphasis on data and analytics. News organizations now have access to a wealth of information about how readers interact with their content, allowing them to make data-driven decisions about what stories to cover and how to present them. Analytics tools can track metrics such as page views, time spent on articles, social media engagement, and more, providing valuable insights into audience preferences and behavior. This data-driven approach can enhance the effectiveness of news coverage and help organizations better serve their readers.

Despite these advancements, digital journalism faces several significant challenges. One of the most pressing issues is the proliferation of misinformation and "fake news." The ease with which content can be published online has led to an explosion of unreliable and misleading information, which can spread rapidly through social media and other digital channels. This has serious implications for public discourse and trust in the media. Combatting misinformation requires a multi-faceted approach, including robust fact-checking processes, media literacy education, and collaboration between news organizations and tech platforms to identify and mitigate false information.

Another challenge is the economic sustainability of digital journalism. While the internet has lowered the cost of distribution, it has also disrupted traditional revenue models. The decline of print advertising and the rise of digital ad blockers have made it difficult for many news organizations to generate sufficient revenue from advertising alone.

Paywalls and subscription models offer a potential solution, but they require a critical mass of paying subscribers to be viable. Many organizations are experimenting with hybrid models, combining free and premium content to attract and retain readers.

The rise of algorithm-driven news distribution is another critical issue. Platforms like Facebook and Google use complex algorithms to determine which content is shown to users, based on their behavior and preferences. While this can enhance the relevance of the news users see, it also raises concerns about filter bubbles and echo chambers, where individuals are only exposed to information that reinforces their existing beliefs. This can contribute to polarization and a fragmented public sphere. Ensuring a diverse and balanced news diet requires transparency and accountability from tech companies, as well as efforts by news organizations to reach and engage a broad audience.

The impact of digital journalism on the role of the journalist is also profound. The skills required for modern journalism now extend beyond traditional reporting and writing to include digital literacy, multimedia production, and social media proficiency. Journalists must be adept at using digital tools to gather and verify information, as well as at engaging with audiences online. This has led to the emergence of new forms of journalism, such as data journalism, which involves analyzing and visualizing data to tell stories, and mobile journalism, which relies on smartphones and other mobile devices to report from the field.

Despite these challenges, digital journalism has also led to significant innovations in storytelling. Long-form articles and investigative reports can be complemented with interactive elements that provide deeper insights and context. For example, multimedia features can include video interviews, animated graphics, and interactive maps that allow readers to explore the story in a more immersive way. This enhances the reader's understanding and engagement, making complex topics more accessible.

Digital journalism has also fostered greater transparency and accountability in reporting. The internet provides an open platform for scrutiny and critique, where readers can question, challenge, and fact-check the information presented to them. This has pushed journalists to adhere to higher standards of accuracy and integrity, knowing that errors or biases can be quickly exposed. Additionally, the practice of linking to primary sources and supporting documents has become more common, allowing readers to verify the information themselves.

The global reach of digital journalism cannot be overstated. News organizations can now report on events from anywhere in the world and distribute their content to a global audience instantly. This has the potential to foster a greater understanding of international issues and bring attention to stories that might otherwise be overlooked. However, it also requires journalists to be mindful of cultural differences and sensitivities when reporting for a diverse audience.

In conclusion, digital journalism represents a fundamental shift in the way news is produced, distributed, and consumed. It offers unprecedented opportunities for innovation, interactivity, and audience engagement, while also presenting significant challenges related to misinformation, economic sustainability, and the role of algorithms. As the digital landscape continues to evolve, so too will the practices and principles of journalism, shaping the future of how we understand and interact with the world around us.

Futurism and Speculative Concepts

Futurism often delves into speculative concepts that challenge our understanding of technology and its potential impacts on humanity. One of the most debated and intriguing ideas is the Singularity, a hypothetical future point at which artificial intelligence (AI) surpasses human intelligence. This concept, popularized by futurist Ray Kurzweil, envisions a transformative era where machines not only perform tasks more efficiently than humans but also develop capabilities far beyond human comprehension. The implications of such a development are profound and multifaceted, sparking both excitement and concern among scientists, ethicists, and the general public.

As we inch closer to the potential realization of the Singularity, the discourse around Transhumanism becomes increasingly relevant. Transhumanism advocates for the enhancement of human capabilities through advanced technologies. This movement seeks to transcend the limitations of our biological bodies, proposing the integration of cybernetic implants, genetic modifications, and other technological augmentations. The goal is to improve physical and cognitive abilities, extend lifespan, and ultimately redefine what it means to be human. Proponents argue that these advancements could lead to a utopian future where disease, aging, and even death are eradicated. However, critics caution against the ethical and societal implications, including issues of equity, consent, and the potential loss of human essence.

Biotechnology is at the forefront of these transhumanist aspirations. It involves using living systems and organisms to develop products and technologies that can enhance our lives. Innovations in biotechnology have already led to significant breakthroughs in medicine, agriculture, and environmental management. For example, gene editing techniques like CRISPR-Cas9 allow for precise modifications to DNA, opening possibilities for curing genetic diseases, creating drought-resistant crops, and even de-extincting species. As biotechnology continues to advance, it holds the promise of not only addressing current challenges but also unlocking new potentials for human evolution and ecological sustainability.

Parallel to biotechnology is the field of Nanotechnology, which involves manipulating matter at an atomic or molecular scale. This technology has the potential to revolutionize various industries by enabling the creation of materials with unprecedented properties. In medicine, nanotechnology could lead to the development of targeted drug delivery systems that directly attack cancer cells without harming healthy tissue. In electronics, it promises more efficient and smaller devices with greater capabilities. The potential applications are vast, ranging from environmental cleanup through nanomaterials that can remove pollutants to the creation of incredibly strong and lightweight materials for construction and transportation.

Cybernetics, the study of systems—both biological and mechanical—for control and communication, is another cornerstone of futuristic speculation. This interdisciplinary field combines elements of engineering, biology, mathematics, and computer science to understand and design systems that can self-regulate and adapt. The principles of cybernetics are already evident in modern technologies such as prosthetics that can be controlled by neural signals and smart home systems that learn and adapt to users' preferences. As cybernetic systems become more sophisticated, they raise questions about the integration of humans and machines, the potential for enhanced human-machine interfaces, and the broader implications for society.

The convergence of these fields—AI, transhumanism, biotechnology, nanotechnology, and cybernetics—paints a picture of a future where the boundaries between the biological and the technological blur. This convergence could lead to a post-human era, characterized by beings that are a hybrid of organic and synthetic components, capable of feats unimaginable to present-day humans. The transformative potential of these technologies offers solutions to many of humanity's current problems but also presents new ethical dilemmas and risks.

One significant concern is the potential for unequal access to these advanced technologies, which could exacerbate existing social inequalities. If enhancements and longevity treatments are only available to the wealthy, it could lead to a new form of class division based on biological enhancements. Additionally, the potential for misuse of these technologies cannot be ignored. Genetic editing, for example, could be used for eugenics purposes, and advanced AI systems could be weaponized or used for surveillance in ways that undermine privacy and human rights.

Moreover, the integration of technology into our bodies and minds raises philosophical questions about identity and consciousness. If we can enhance our cognitive abilities or even upload our consciousness into a digital form, what does it mean to be an individual? How do we define personhood and humanity in a world where our thoughts and experiences can be manipulated or transferred between different mediums? These questions challenge our fundamental understanding of self and society, prompting a reevaluation of our ethical frameworks and cultural norms.

Another dimension to consider is the environmental impact of these advanced technologies. While nanotechnology and biotechnology offer solutions to many environmental problems, they also present new risks.

42. **Singularity**: Hypothetical point when AI surpasses human intelligence.

The concept of the Singularity refers to a hypothetical point in time when artificial intelligence (AI) surpasses human intelligence. This moment, often called the technological singularity, represents a significant and unprecedented transformation in human history. The implications of such an event are profound, as it suggests that machines will not only match human cognitive abilities but will also rapidly exceed them. The idea of the Singularity has captivated the imaginations of scientists, futurists, and thinkers for decades, prompting both excitement and concern about the future of humanity.

The notion of the Singularity is rooted in the exponential growth of technology, particularly in the fields of computing and artificial intelligence. The term itself was popularized by mathematician and science fiction writer Vernor Vinge, who suggested in the 1980s that the creation of superintelligent AI would mark the end of the human era as we know it. According to Vinge and other proponents of the Singularity, this event would lead to an intelligence explosion, where AI systems improve themselves at an accelerating pace, resulting in a level of intelligence far beyond human comprehension.

One of the key factors driving the concept of the Singularity is Moore's Law, which observes that the number of transistors on a microchip doubles approximately every two years, leading to a corresponding increase in computational power. While Moore's Law specifically pertains to hardware, the underlying principle of exponential growth can be applied more broadly to advancements in AI and machine learning. As AI systems become more sophisticated and capable, the rate of progress in these fields accelerates, bringing us closer to the Singularity.

The potential consequences of reaching the Singularity are both exhilarating and terrifying. On one hand, superintelligent AI could solve some of humanity's most pressing problems, such as disease, poverty, and climate change. With unparalleled processing power and cognitive abilities, these machines could analyze vast amounts of data, identify patterns, and develop solutions that are beyond the reach of human intellect. This could usher in a new era of prosperity, health, and well-being for all of humanity.

However, the Singularity also poses significant risks and ethical dilemmas. One of the primary concerns is the possibility of losing control over superintelligent AI. Once machines surpass human intelligence, they may develop goals and motivations that are not aligned with human values or interests. Ensuring that AI systems remain aligned with our values and act in ways that are beneficial to humanity is a daunting challenge, known as the alignment problem. If we fail to address this issue, the consequences could be catastrophic, potentially leading to the extinction of the human race.

Another major concern is the impact of superintelligent AI on employment and the economy. As machines become more capable of performing tasks that were once the domain of humans, there is a risk of widespread job displacement and economic upheaval. While some argue that new jobs will be created to replace those that are lost, others fear that the pace of technological change will outstrip our ability to adapt, leading to increased inequality and social unrest. Ensuring a fair and equitable distribution of the benefits of AI will be crucial in mitigating these risks.

The ethical implications of the Singularity extend beyond practical concerns to fundamental questions about the nature of intelligence and consciousness. If machines achieve superintelligence, it raises the question of whether they should be granted rights and protections similar to those afforded to humans. The distinction between human and machine may become increasingly blurred, challenging our understanding of what it means to be a conscious, sentient being. This could lead to profound shifts in our moral and legal frameworks, as we grapple with the ethical status of superintelligent entities.

Despite the potential risks and challenges, the pursuit of the Singularity continues to drive innovation and research in AI. Numerous organizations and researchers are working to advance the field, motivated by the promise of creating machines that can outperform human intelligence. Some of the most notable efforts include projects like

OpenAI, which aims to develop safe and beneficial artificial general intelligence (AGI), and initiatives like the Future of Humanity Institute, which studies the long-term impact of technological advancements on society.

As we move closer to the Singularity, it is essential to engage in thoughtful and informed discussions about the potential implications and ethical considerations of this transformative event. Policymakers, scientists, and the general public must work together to ensure that the development of superintelligent AI is guided by principles that prioritize human well-being and safety. This includes establishing regulatory frameworks, investing in research on AI safety and alignment, and fostering a culture of transparency and accountability in the development of AI technologies.

One of the critical aspects of preparing for the Singularity is addressing the alignment problem. Ensuring that superintelligent AI systems act in ways that are consistent with human values and interests requires a deep understanding of both human cognition and machine learning. Researchers are exploring various approaches to this challenge, including value alignment, which involves encoding ethical principles into AI systems, and inverse reinforcement learning, where machines learn human values by observing human behavior. While these efforts are still in their early stages, they represent important steps toward creating AI that can coexist with humanity in a safe and beneficial manner.

Another important consideration is the potential impact of the Singularity on global power dynamics. The development of superintelligent AI could confer significant strategic advantages to the countries or organizations that possess it, potentially leading to new forms of geopolitical competition and conflict. To mitigate these risks, it will be important to promote international cooperation and collaboration in AI research and development. Establishing norms and agreements around the use of AI, similar to those in place for nuclear weapons, could help prevent an arms race and ensure that the benefits of AI are shared equitably among all nations.

The Singularity also has implications for our understanding of human identity and the future of our species. As machines become more intelligent and capable, we may need to reconsider what it means to be human in a world where our cognitive abilities are no longer unique. This could lead to new forms of human enhancement, such as brain-computer interfaces and other technologies that augment our mental and physical capabilities. While these advancements hold great promise, they also raise ethical and philosophical questions about the nature of personhood and the potential for inequality between enhanced and non-enhanced individuals.

In the face of these profound changes, it is crucial to cultivate a sense of humility and caution as we approach the Singularity. While the potential benefits of superintelligent AI are immense, the risks are equally significant. Navigating this transition will require careful planning, robust ethical frameworks, and a commitment to ensuring that the development of AI serves the greater good of humanity. By approaching the Singularity with a balanced perspective, we can harness the transformative power of AI while safeguarding our values and future.

In conclusion, the Singularity represents a pivotal moment in the trajectory of human civilization, marking the point at which artificial intelligence surpasses human intelligence. While the potential benefits of this transformation are extraordinary, the risks and ethical challenges are equally profound. As we move closer to this hypothetical future, it is essential to engage in thoughtful and informed discussions about the implications of superintelligent AI and to take proactive steps to ensure that its development aligns with human values and interests. By doing so, we can navigate the Singularity in a way that maximizes its benefits while minimizing its risks, ultimately shaping a future that is both technologically advanced and ethically grounded.

43. **Transhumanism**: Enhancing human capabilities through technology.

Transhumanism is a philosophical and scientific movement dedicated to enhancing human capabilities through advanced technology. At its core, transhumanism seeks to transcend the limitations of the human condition by using technology to augment physical, cognitive, and emotional capacities. This movement envisions a future where humans can overcome aging, disease, and perhaps even death, achieving unprecedented levels of health, intelligence, and well-being.

The roots of transhumanism can be traced back to the Enlightenment, a period that championed reason, science, and progress. Early thinkers like Francis Bacon and René Descartes laid the groundwork for the idea that humanity could harness technology to improve the human condition. However, it wasn't until the 20th century that the term "transhumanism" began to take shape. British biologist Julian Huxley coined the term in the 1950s, suggesting that humanity could evolve beyond its current physical and mental limitations through the application of science and technology.

One of the fundamental tenets of transhumanism is the belief in the malleability of the human body and mind. Transhumanists argue that, just as technology has transformed society, it can also transform individuals on a biological level. This perspective is reflected in various fields of research and innovation, including biotechnology, artificial intelligence, neuroscience, and nanotechnology. Each of these disciplines offers tools and techniques that could potentially enhance human abilities in profound ways.

Biotechnology, for example, holds the promise of genetic engineering, which could allow us to modify our DNA to eliminate genetic diseases, enhance physical traits, and even extend our lifespan. Techniques like CRISPR-Cas9 have already demonstrated the potential to edit genes with remarkable precision, opening up possibilities for preventing hereditary conditions and improving overall health. Beyond genetic modification, biotechnology also encompasses regenerative medicine, which aims to repair or replace damaged tissues and organs. Stem cell therapy and tissue engineering are at the forefront of this field, offering the potential to heal injuries and cure diseases that were once thought incurable.

Artificial intelligence (AI) is another pillar of transhumanist thought, with the potential to augment human intelligence and cognitive capabilities. AI technologies, such as machine learning and neural networks, can process vast amounts of data at speeds far beyond human capacity, providing insights and solutions to complex problems. In the context of transhumanism, AI could be integrated with the human brain through brain-computer interfaces (BCIs), enabling direct communication between the mind and machines. BCIs could enhance memory, learning, and problem-solving abilities, effectively merging human and artificial intelligence to create a new form of cognitive augmentation.

Neuroscience, the study of the nervous system and the brain, plays a crucial role in understanding and enhancing human cognition and behavior. Advances in this field have led to the development of neuroprosthetics, devices that can restore lost sensory or motor functions by interfacing with the nervous system. Cochlear implants, which provide a sense of sound to individuals with hearing loss, are a well-known example of neuroprosthetics in action. Looking ahead, researchers are exploring ways to enhance normal brain function, potentially improving memory, attention, and emotional regulation through targeted interventions.

Nanotechnology, the manipulation of matter on an atomic or molecular scale, offers another avenue for enhancing human capabilities. Nanomedicine, the application of nanotechnology to medical treatments, holds the promise of more precise drug delivery systems, advanced diagnostic tools, and innovative therapies. For example, nanoparticles can be designed to target specific cells in the body, delivering medication directly to diseased tissues while minimizing side effects. Nanotechnology also has the potential to enhance physical abilities, such as strength and endurance, by creating materials and devices that integrate seamlessly with the human body.

The pursuit of transhumanist goals raises a host of ethical and philosophical questions. One of the primary concerns is the potential for inequality. If access to enhancement technologies is limited to the wealthy or privileged, it could exacerbate existing social and economic disparities, creating a society divided between the "enhanced" and the "unenhanced." Ensuring equitable access to these technologies will be crucial in preventing such a divide and promoting a more inclusive vision of human enhancement.

Another ethical consideration is the question of consent and autonomy. As enhancement technologies become more advanced and pervasive, individuals must have the freedom to choose whether or not to undergo such procedures. This raises questions about informed consent, particularly in cases where the long-term effects of enhancements are not fully understood. Additionally, societal pressures or norms could influence individuals' decisions, potentially compromising their autonomy.

The concept of identity is also challenged by transhumanism. As humans incorporate more technological enhancements, the line between human and machine becomes increasingly blurred. This raises questions about what it means to be human and how we define personhood. Philosophers and ethicists are grappling with these questions, considering scenarios where individuals might possess both biological and artificial components that contribute to their identity.

Despite these challenges, transhumanism offers a vision of the future that is both inspiring and transformative. By embracing the potential of technology to enhance human capabilities, we can aspire to a world where individuals are healthier, more intelligent, and better equipped to address the challenges of the modern world. This vision aligns with the broader goals of human progress, seeking to improve the quality of life and expand the boundaries of human potential.

One of the most ambitious goals of transhumanism is the pursuit of radical life extension. By addressing the biological mechanisms of aging, scientists hope to significantly extend the human lifespan, allowing individuals to live longer, healthier lives. Research into the biology of aging has identified several pathways that contribute to the aging process, such as cellular senescence, telomere shortening, and oxidative stress. Interventions targeting these pathways, including senolytic drugs, telomerase activators, and antioxidant therapies, are being explored as potential means of slowing or reversing the effects of aging.

In addition to extending lifespan, transhumanists also envision a future where human consciousness can be preserved and transferred. The concept of mind uploading, or transferring an individual's consciousness to a digital substrate, is a central idea in many transhumanist circles. This would involve creating a detailed map of the brain's neural connections and replicating its functions in a computer or other digital medium. While this concept remains speculative and faces significant technical and philosophical hurdles, it represents a radical rethinking of the possibilities for human existence.

Transhumanism also explores the potential for enhancing human emotions and experiences. By understanding the neurological basis of emotions, researchers hope to develop technologies that can modulate mood, reduce suffering, and enhance well-being. Neurostimulation techniques, such as transcranial magnetic stimulation (TMS) and deep brain stimulation (DBS), are already being used to treat conditions like depression and chronic pain. In the future, these and other technologies could be refined to provide more precise and effective ways of enhancing emotional states and overall quality of life.

The potential for enhancing human capabilities through technology extends beyond the individual to society as a whole. Transhumanists envision a future where collective intelligence and cooperation are enhanced through advanced communication and collaboration tools. Technologies like the internet and social media have already transformed the way we share information and connect with others. Future innovations, such as augmented reality (AR) and virtual reality (VR), could create immersive environments that facilitate collaboration and problem-solving on a global scale.

Transhumanism also intersects with other futuristic concepts, such as space exploration and colonization. As humans look beyond Earth to establish colonies on other planets, the ability to enhance physical and cognitive capabilities could be crucial for adapting to the harsh conditions of space. Enhanced humans may be better equipped to withstand the physical and psychological challenges of long-duration space travel, as well as the rigors of living in extraterrestrial environments. This vision aligns with the broader transhumanist goal of expanding the horizons of human potential and exploring new frontiers.

As we move forward into an era of unprecedented technological advancement, the principles and goals of transhumanism will continue to shape the discourse around human enhancement. The potential benefits of these technologies are immense, offering the possibility of healthier, more fulfilling lives. However, realizing this potential will require careful consideration of the ethical, social, and philosophical implications. By engaging in thoughtful and inclusive discussions, we can navigate the complexities of transhumanism and work towards a future that maximizes the benefits of human enhancement while minimizing the risks.

In conclusion, transhumanism represents a bold vision for the future of humanity, one that embraces the potential of technology to enhance human capabilities and transcend the limitations of the human condition. From biotechnology and artificial intelligence to neuroscience and nanotechnology, the tools for achieving these goals are rapidly advancing. While the pursuit of transhumanist ideals raises significant ethical and philosophical questions, it also offers the promise of a future where humans can achieve unprecedented levels of health, intelligence, and well-being. By approaching these challenges with a commitment to equity, autonomy, and thoughtful deliberation, we can work towards a future that benefits all of humanity and expands the boundaries of what it means to be human.

44. **Biotechnology**: Using living systems and organisms in technology.

Biotechnology is a field that merges biology and technology, leveraging living systems and organisms to develop products and processes that improve human life and the environment. This interdisciplinary field encompasses a wide range of applications, from medical and agricultural advancements to environmental and industrial innovations. The fundamental principle of biotechnology is the use of cellular and biomolecular processes to develop technologies and products that help in improving the quality of life and the health of the planet.

One of the most significant areas of biotechnology is its application in medicine. Medical biotechnology has revolutionized healthcare by enabling the development of novel treatments and diagnostics. A prime example is the production of recombinant insulin. Before the advent of biotechnology, insulin for diabetic patients was extracted from the pancreases of pigs and cows, which was a complex and inefficient process. With the advent of recombinant DNA technology, human insulin genes can be inserted into bacteria, which then produce insulin that is identical to that naturally produced by humans. This has made insulin production more efficient, less expensive, and more reliable.

Another groundbreaking medical application of biotechnology is the development of monoclonal antibodies. These are antibodies that are made by identical immune cells that are clones of a unique parent cell. Monoclonal antibodies are designed to target specific cells or proteins in the body, making them highly effective in treating diseases like cancer and autoimmune disorders. The ability to create these targeted therapies has significantly improved the outcomes for patients with conditions that were previously difficult to treat.

Gene therapy is another promising area within medical biotechnology. This technique involves altering the genes inside a patient's cells to treat or prevent disease. Gene therapy can be used to replace a mutated gene that causes disease with a healthy copy of the gene, inactivate a mutated gene that is functioning improperly, or introduce a new gene into the body to help fight a disease. Recent advancements in gene-editing technologies like CRISPR-Cas9 have made gene therapy more precise and efficient, offering hope for curing genetic disorders that were once thought incurable.

Biotechnology also plays a crucial role in the development of vaccines. Traditional vaccines are made using weakened or inactivated forms of viruses or bacteria. However, biotechnological advancements have led to the creation of new types of vaccines, such as mRNA vaccines. These vaccines use messenger RNA to instruct cells to produce a protein that triggers an immune response. The rapid development and deployment of mRNA vaccines during the COVID-19 pandemic is a testament to the power of biotechnology in addressing global health challenges.

In agriculture, biotechnology has been instrumental in enhancing crop yields, improving resistance to pests and diseases, and reducing the environmental impact of farming. Genetically modified organisms (GMOs) are a prominent example of agricultural biotechnology. By inserting genes from one organism into another, scientists can create crops that are more resilient to adverse conditions and have higher nutritional value. For instance, Bt corn is a type of genetically modified corn that produces a protein from the bacterium Bacillus thuringiensis, which is toxic to certain pests but safe for human consumption. This reduces the need for chemical pesticides, which can have harmful environmental and health effects.

Biotechnology also enables the development of crops that can withstand environmental stresses such as drought, salinity, and extreme temperatures. For example, researchers have developed drought-tolerant maize varieties that can thrive in regions with limited water availability. These innovations are particularly important in the context of climate change, which poses significant challenges to global food security. By improving the resilience of crops to changing environmental conditions, biotechnology can help ensure a stable food supply for the growing global population.

In addition to improving crop traits, biotechnology has been used to develop biofortified crops that address nutritional deficiencies. Golden Rice is a well-known example of this. It has been genetically engineered to produce beta-carotene, a precursor of vitamin A. This innovation aims to combat vitamin A deficiency, which is a major cause of blindness and mortality in children in developing countries. By enhancing the nutritional content of staple crops, biotechnology can play a crucial role in improving public health.

Environmental biotechnology focuses on using biological processes to address environmental problems. One of the key applications in this field is bioremediation, which involves using microorganisms to clean up contaminated environments. For example, certain bacteria and fungi can break down pollutants such as oil spills, heavy metals, and pesticides, transforming them into less harmful substances. This natural process can be harnessed to restore polluted sites, making bioremediation a cost-effective and environmentally friendly alternative to traditional cleanup methods.

Another important area of environmental biotechnology is the development of biofuels. Biofuels are derived from biological materials such as plants, algae, and waste products. Unlike fossil fuels, biofuels are renewable and can help reduce greenhouse gas emissions. Ethanol and biodiesel are the most common types of biofuels, and they can be produced from crops like corn, sugarcane, and soybeans. Advances in biotechnology have led to the development of more efficient methods for producing biofuels, such as the use of genetically engineered microorganisms that can convert biomass into fuel more effectively.

Industrial biotechnology, also known as white biotechnology, applies biotechnological methods to industrial processes. This field aims to create more sustainable and efficient manufacturing processes by using enzymes, microorganisms, and plants. Enzymes, for example, are used in the production of bio-based chemicals, detergents, and textiles. They can catalyze reactions under mild conditions, reducing the need for harsh chemicals and high temperatures, which in turn reduces energy consumption and waste production.

One of the promising developments in industrial biotechnology is the production of bioplastics. Traditional plastics are made from petroleum, a non-renewable resource, and they contribute significantly to environmental pollution. Bioplastics, on the other hand, are made from renewable biological sources such as corn starch, sugarcane, and cellulose. They are biodegradable, which means they can be broken down by microorganisms into harmless substances, reducing their environmental impact. Advances in biotechnology are making it possible to produce bioplastics that have similar properties to conventional plastics, making them a viable alternative for various applications.

The field of synthetic biology is an emerging area within biotechnology that combines biology and engineering principles to design and construct new biological parts, devices, and systems. Synthetic biology has the potential to create organisms with novel functions that do not exist in nature. For example, researchers are developing synthetic organisms that can produce biofuels, pharmaceuticals, and specialty chemicals more efficiently than natural organisms. This field also holds promise for creating new materials with unique properties, such as self-healing concrete and bio-based sensors.

The advancements in biotechnology raise important ethical, social, and regulatory considerations. The manipulation of living organisms and genetic material poses ethical questions about the extent to which humans should interfere with natural processes. Issues such as the safety and long-term effects of genetically modified organisms, the potential for unintended consequences, and the ethical implications of gene editing in humans need to be carefully considered. Regulatory frameworks must be established to ensure that biotechnological innovations are developed and deployed safely and responsibly.

Public perception and acceptance of biotechnology also play a crucial role in its development and application. Effective communication and education about the benefits and risks of biotechnology are essential to build public trust and support. Engaging with diverse stakeholders, including scientists, policymakers, industry leaders, and the general public, can help address concerns and foster a collaborative approach to biotechnological advancements.

In conclusion, biotechnology represents a powerful and transformative field that leverages living systems and organisms to develop innovative solutions across medicine, agriculture, environment, and industry. The advancements in biotechnology have the potential to improve human health, enhance food security, mitigate environmental challenges, and create sustainable industrial processes. As we continue to explore the possibilities of biotechnology, it is essential to navigate the ethical, social, and regulatory challenges with care and responsibility. By doing so, we can harness the full potential of biotechnology to address some of the most pressing issues facing humanity and create a better future for all.

45. **Nanotechnology**: Manipulating matter on an atomic or molecular scale.

Nanotechnology is a field of science and engineering dedicated to the study and manipulation of matter at the atomic and molecular scale, typically between 1 and 100 nanometers. This scale is where the fundamental properties of materials are determined, and by understanding and controlling these properties, nanotechnology aims to create new materials and devices with unprecedented capabilities and applications. The implications of nanotechnology span across various fields, including medicine, electronics, energy, and environmental science, promising revolutionary advancements in each.

One of the most exciting applications of nanotechnology is in the field of medicine, where it has the potential to revolutionize the way diseases are diagnosed, treated, and prevented. One key area is drug delivery. Traditional drug delivery methods can be inefficient and imprecise, often affecting healthy tissues as well as diseased ones. Nanotechnology enables the creation of nanoparticles that can deliver drugs directly to targeted cells, significantly improving the efficacy and reducing side effects. These nanoparticles can be engineered to recognize and bind to specific types of cells, ensuring that the drug is released exactly where it is needed.

For example, in cancer treatment, nanoparticles can be designed to target cancer cells specifically, sparing healthy cells and thus reducing the harmful side effects of chemotherapy. Additionally, these nanoparticles can be equipped with imaging agents that help doctors visualize the distribution and effectiveness of the treatment in real-time. This targeted approach not only improves the effectiveness of the treatment but also enhances the quality of life for patients by minimizing adverse effects.

Beyond drug delivery, nanotechnology also holds promise in diagnostics. Nanoscale sensors can detect the presence of disease markers with unprecedented sensitivity and specificity. These sensors can be used in a variety of diagnostic tools, such as lab-on-a-chip devices, which integrate multiple laboratory functions on a single chip only a few square centimeters in size. These devices can perform complex analyses quickly and with minimal sample volumes, making diagnostics faster, cheaper, and more accessible.

Another significant application of nanotechnology is in the field of electronics. As electronic devices become smaller and more powerful, the need for miniaturization and improved performance at the nanoscale becomes increasingly critical. Nanotechnology enables the development of components such as transistors, capacitors, and memory devices at the molecular level, leading to faster, smaller, and more energy-efficient electronics. One notable example is the development of carbon nanotubes, which are cylindrical nanostructures with exceptional electrical conductivity and mechanical strength. Carbon nanotubes can be used to create transistors that are much smaller and faster than those made with traditional silicon technology, potentially leading to a new generation of ultra-fast, ultra-small electronic devices.

In addition to improving existing technologies, nanotechnology opens the door to entirely new types of devices. Quantum dots, for example, are nanoscale semiconductor particles that have unique optical and electronic properties due to their size. These properties make quantum dots ideal for applications such as high-resolution displays, solar cells, and quantum computing. In displays, quantum dots can produce more vivid colors and higher brightness than conventional technologies. In solar cells, they can be used to create more efficient photovoltaic materials that convert sunlight into electricity. In quantum computing, quantum dots can function as qubits, the basic units of information, offering the potential for computers that are exponentially more powerful than today's supercomputers.

Energy is another sector where nanotechnology has the potential to make a substantial impact. As the demand for clean and renewable energy sources grows, nanotechnology offers innovative solutions for energy production, storage, and efficiency. In solar energy, nanotechnology can enhance the efficiency of photovoltaic cells. For instance, incorporating nanostructured materials can increase the surface area for light absorption and improve the conversion efficiency of solar panels. This makes solar energy more viable and cost-effective as a sustainable energy source.

Nanotechnology also plays a crucial role in improving energy storage systems. Traditional batteries have limitations in terms of energy density, charging speed, and lifespan. Nanomaterials can be used to develop batteries with higher energy densities, faster charging times, and longer lifespans. For example, incorporating nanoparticles into the electrodes of lithium-ion batteries can increase their capacity and stability, making them more efficient for use in electric vehicles and portable electronics. Additionally, nanotechnology enables the development of supercapacitors, which can store and release energy much more rapidly than conventional batteries, providing a complementary solution for energy storage needs.

Environmental science is another area where nanotechnology can offer transformative solutions. One of the most pressing environmental challenges is pollution, and nanotechnology provides innovative approaches to both detecting and addressing contaminants. Nanosensors can detect pollutants at very low concentrations, providing early warning systems for environmental monitoring. These sensors can be deployed in water, air, and soil to monitor the presence of harmful substances in real-time, enabling prompt action to mitigate environmental damage.

Nanotechnology also offers solutions for pollution remediation. Nanoparticles can be designed to bind to specific contaminants and either neutralize them or facilitate their removal from the environment. For example, nanomaterials can be used to clean up oil spills by adsorbing oil molecules and breaking them down into less harmful substances. Similarly, nanoparticles can be used to remove heavy metals and other toxins from water, making it safe for consumption and reducing the impact on ecosystems.

Another environmental application of nanotechnology is in the development of sustainable materials. Traditional manufacturing processes often rely on non-renewable resources and produce significant waste. Nanotechnology enables the creation of materials with improved properties and reduced environmental impact. For instance, nanocomposites can combine different materials at the nanoscale to produce stronger, lighter, and more durable products, reducing the need for raw materials and extending the lifespan of the products. Additionally, nanotechnology can be used to develop biodegradable materials and more efficient recycling processes, contributing to a circular economy.

The field of nanotechnology also raises important ethical, societal, and regulatory considerations. The manipulation of matter at such a small scale poses unique risks and challenges that must be carefully managed. One of the primary concerns is the potential impact of nanoparticles on human health and the environment. Due to their small size, nanoparticles can enter the human body through inhalation, ingestion, or skin contact, and their interactions with biological systems are not yet fully understood. Ensuring the safe use of nanotechnology requires rigorous testing and evaluation of the potential risks associated with exposure to nanoparticles.

Additionally, the environmental impact of nanomaterials needs to be considered throughout their lifecycle, from production to disposal. Nanotechnology can contribute to sustainability by providing solutions for energy efficiency and pollution remediation, but the production and disposal of nanomaterials must be managed responsibly to prevent unintended environmental consequences.

The regulatory landscape for nanotechnology is still evolving, and it is essential to develop comprehensive frameworks that address the unique challenges posed by this field. Policymakers, scientists, and industry leaders must work together to establish standards and guidelines for the safe development and use of nanotechnology. Public engagement and education are also crucial to ensure that the benefits of nanotechnology are understood and accepted by society while addressing any concerns or misconceptions.

In conclusion, nanotechnology represents a groundbreaking field that has the potential to transform multiple aspects of human life and the environment. By manipulating matter at the atomic and molecular scale, nanotechnology enables the development of innovative solutions in medicine, electronics, energy, and environmental science. The applications of nanotechnology are vast and varied, offering the promise of improved health outcomes, more efficient energy systems, advanced electronic devices, and a cleaner environment. However, the advancement of nanotechnology also necessitates careful consideration of ethical, societal, and regulatory issues to ensure its safe and responsible use. As we continue to explore the possibilities of nanotechnology, it is essential to balance innovation with safety, maximizing the benefits while minimizing potential risks. Through collaborative efforts and responsible stewardship, nanotechnology can contribute to a more sustainable and prosperous future for all.

46. **Cybernetics**: Study of systems, including biological and mechanical, for control and communication.

Cybernetics is a multidisciplinary field that examines systems, both biological and mechanical, to understand and improve their control and communication processes. It encompasses a broad spectrum of studies, from the regulation of biological organisms and ecosystems to the operation and management of machines and computers. Originating in the mid-20th century, cybernetics has evolved to become a cornerstone of modern science and technology, influencing diverse fields such as robotics, artificial intelligence, systems theory, and neuroscience.

The term "cybernetics" was coined by Norbert Wiener in the 1940s, deriving from the Greek word "kybernētēs," meaning "steersman" or "governor." Wiener defined cybernetics as the scientific study of control and communication in animals and machines. This definition underscores the field's focus on how systems use information to regulate their behavior and maintain stability, adapt to changes, and achieve specific goals.

At its core, cybernetics is concerned with feedback mechanisms. Feedback is the process by which a system monitors its own output and uses this information to make adjustments. This concept is crucial for maintaining homeostasis in biological organisms and for the stable operation of mechanical and electronic systems. For example, in biology, homeostasis is the ability of an organism to regulate its internal environment to maintain a stable, constant condition, such as body temperature or pH levels. This regulation often involves feedback loops, where sensors detect changes in the internal environment and trigger responses that restore balance.

In mechanical and electronic systems, feedback is equally important. Consider a thermostat used to regulate the temperature of a room. The thermostat measures the current temperature and compares it to a desired set point. If the temperature deviates from the set point, the thermostat activates heating or cooling mechanisms to bring the temperature back to the desired level. This is a simple example of a negative feedback loop, where the system's response counteracts the deviation to maintain stability.

Cybernetics extends these principles to more complex systems, including social and economic systems. For instance, in economics, feedback mechanisms can be observed in market dynamics, where supply and demand influence prices, which in turn affect production and consumption patterns. Understanding these feedback loops can help in designing policies and interventions that promote economic stability and growth.

One of the significant contributions of cybernetics is the concept of the "black box." In cybernetics, a black box is a system whose internal workings are not known or are too complex to be understood, but whose inputs and outputs can be observed and analyzed. By studying the relationships between inputs and outputs, cyberneticists can infer the behavior of the system and develop models to predict and control its performance. This approach is particularly useful in fields where the complexity of systems makes detailed understanding impractical, such as in neuroscience or social sciences.

In neuroscience, for example, the brain can be considered a black box. While the detailed workings of neural circuits are still being unraveled, cybernetic principles can be applied to understand how the brain processes information and controls behavior. Neurocybernetics explores how neural networks function, how they adapt through learning, and how they maintain stability in the face of changing inputs. Insights from this field have led to advances in artificial intelligence, where neural network models inspired by the brain are used to solve complex problems in pattern recognition, decision making, and more.

Cybernetics also plays a crucial role in the development of robotics and autonomous systems. Robots are designed to interact with their environment, process information from sensors, and make decisions based on that information. These tasks require sophisticated control systems that can adapt to changing conditions and perform complex behaviors. Cybernetic principles guide the design of these control systems, ensuring that robots can operate reliably and effectively in diverse environments.

One of the key challenges in robotics is achieving robust and adaptive behavior. This requires integrating feedback from multiple sensors, making sense of this information, and responding appropriately. For example, an autonomous vehicle must constantly monitor its surroundings using cameras, radar, and other sensors, interpret this data to identify obstacles and navigate safely, and adjust its speed and direction to avoid collisions. Cybernetic approaches help in designing control algorithms that enable such adaptive and intelligent behavior.

The interplay between biological and mechanical systems is particularly evident in the field of bionics, where cybernetics principles are applied to develop prosthetic devices and other assistive technologies. Bionic limbs, for example, use sensors to detect the user's muscle movements and translate these signals into actions, allowing individuals to perform tasks with a high degree of precision and natural motion. Advances in cybernetics have led to the development of more sophisticated prosthetics that can provide sensory feedback to the user, enhancing their ability to interact with their environment.

In addition to physical systems, cybernetics also explores the control and communication processes in social and organizational systems. Social cybernetics examines how groups, organizations, and societies use information to regulate behavior, maintain stability, and achieve collective goals. This involves studying feedback mechanisms in communication, decision making, and governance. For example, in an organization, feedback from employees and customers can be used to improve processes, products, and services, leading to greater efficiency and satisfaction.

The principles of cybernetics are also applied in the field of systems theory, which seeks to understand the behavior of complex systems through the interactions of their components. Systems theory provides a framework for analyzing how systems are structured, how they evolve over time, and how they respond to internal and external influences. This holistic approach is particularly valuable in addressing complex, interdisciplinary problems, such as environmental sustainability, public health, and global security.

Cybernetics has also had a profound influence on the development of information theory and communication systems. Information theory, pioneered by Claude Shannon, quantifies the amount of information in a message and the capacity of communication channels. This theoretical framework is essential for designing efficient communication systems, from data compression algorithms to error-correcting codes. Cybernetic principles are applied to ensure that communication systems can reliably transmit information, even in the presence of noise and other disruptions.

The advent of the digital age has further expanded the scope of cybernetics. The proliferation of computers, networks, and digital devices has created new opportunities for studying and controlling complex systems. Cyber-physical systems, which integrate computation, networking, and physical processes, exemplify the convergence of cybernetics and digital technology. These systems are used in a wide range of applications, from smart grids and autonomous vehicles to industrial automation and healthcare.

In smart grids, for example, cybernetic principles are applied to optimize the generation, distribution, and consumption of electricity. Sensors and communication networks provide real-time data on energy usage, which can be used to balance supply and demand, reduce waste, and integrate renewable energy sources. Similarly, in healthcare, cyber-physical systems enable remote monitoring and management of patients, improving the delivery of care and enhancing patient outcomes.

Despite its broad applications, cybernetics also faces challenges and criticisms. One challenge is the complexity of modeling and controlling highly interconnected and dynamic systems. While cybernetic principles provide powerful tools for understanding these systems, developing accurate models and effective control strategies remains a formidable task. Additionally, there are ethical and societal implications of cybernetic technologies, particularly in areas such as surveillance, privacy, and autonomy. Balancing the benefits and risks of cybernetics requires careful consideration and responsible governance.

In conclusion, cybernetics is a foundational field that bridges biology, engineering, and information science to study and enhance control and communication in complex systems. Its principles have led to significant advancements in medicine, robotics, neuroscience, social sciences, and digital technology. By understanding and applying feedback mechanisms, black box modeling, and systems theory, cyberneticists continue to push the boundaries of what is possible, contributing to a deeper understanding of both natural and artificial systems. As the field evolves, it will undoubtedly play a crucial role in addressing the challenges and opportunities of the 21st century, shaping the future of technology and society.

Additional Concepts

The study of technology and its integration into society involves a myriad of theories and concepts, each providing unique insights into how technology shapes and is shaped by cultural, social, and individual forces. Among these theories, four stand out for their profound implications: Deconstruction, Postmodernism, Simulation Theory, and Digital Ecosystems. These concepts offer diverse lenses through which we can understand the complex interplay between technology and human experience.

Deconstruction originates from the field of literary criticism and philosophy, primarily associated with the work of Jacques Derrida. It involves analyzing texts and media to uncover underlying assumptions, contradictions, and biases. When applied to technology, deconstruction encourages us to look beyond the surface of technological artifacts and systems to understand their deeper implications. For instance, a smartphone is not just a device for communication; it is embedded with cultural assumptions about connectivity, privacy, and social interaction. By deconstructing the design and use of smartphones, we can reveal how they perpetuate certain ideologies and power structures. This critical approach allows us to question the neutrality of technology and recognize its role in shaping societal norms and behaviors.

Postmodernism, emerging in the late 20th century, challenges the idea of grand narratives and embraces fragmented, diverse perspectives. In the context of technology, postmodernism questions the dominant narratives of progress and innovation that often accompany technological advancements. Instead of viewing technology as a linear progression towards a better future, postmodernism highlights the multiplicity of experiences and meanings that technology can generate. This perspective is particularly relevant in today's digital age, where diverse voices and identities are expressed through various online platforms. Postmodernism encourages us to appreciate the plurality of technological experiences and resist the temptation to impose a singular, homogenizing vision of technological progress. It also calls attention to the ways in which technology can both liberate and constrain, offering new opportunities for expression while also reinforcing existing inequalities.

Simulation Theory posits that our reality could be an artificial simulation, akin to a sophisticated computer program. This idea, popularized by philosophers like Nick Bostrom, has gained traction in both academic and popular discourse. The theory challenges our understanding of reality and raises profound questions about the nature of existence and consciousness. If we consider the possibility that our reality is a simulation, it prompts us to rethink the role of technology in constructing and mediating our experiences. Virtual reality, artificial intelligence, and other advanced technologies can be seen as precursors to the creation of simulated worlds. The implications of simulation theory extend beyond philosophical speculation; they influence how we perceive technological advancements and their potential to create immersive, artificial environments. This theory also invites us to explore the ethical dimensions of creating and inhabiting simulated realities, questioning the responsibilities of those who build and maintain such systems.

Digital Ecosystems refer to the interconnected digital environments and platforms that constitute the contemporary technological landscape. These ecosystems are characterized by complex networks of devices, applications, and services that interact with each other and with users. Understanding digital ecosystems requires recognizing the interdependencies and feedback loops that shape their development and functionality. For example, social media platforms, online marketplaces, and cloud computing services are all part of larger digital ecosystems that influence user behavior, data flows, and economic activities. By examining these ecosystems, we can gain insights into the dynamics of technological change and the factors that drive innovation and competition. Digital ecosystems also highlight the importance of interoperability and standardization, as seamless integration between different components is crucial for their effective operation. Moreover, the concept of digital ecosystems underscores the role of users as active participants who contribute to and shape these environments through their interactions and choices.

The interplay between these four concepts—deconstruction, postmodernism, simulation theory, and digital ecosystems—provides a rich framework for exploring the complexities of technology in contemporary society. Each concept offers a distinct perspective, yet they are interconnected in their emphasis on questioning assumptions, embracing diversity, and understanding the multifaceted nature of technological phenomena.

Deconstruction's focus on uncovering hidden assumptions can be applied to the analysis of digital ecosystems, revealing the power dynamics and cultural biases embedded in their design and operation. For instance, the algorithms that govern social media platforms often reflect and reinforce societal inequalities, such as racial and gender biases. By deconstructing these algorithms, we can identify the ways in which they perpetuate discrimination and work towards more equitable technological solutions. Similarly, postmodernism's rejection of grand narratives aligns with the decentralized and fragmented nature of digital ecosystems, where multiple voices and perspectives coexist and interact. This alignment encourages us to appreciate the diversity of experiences within digital environments and resist the imposition of a singular, dominant narrative.

Simulation theory, with its provocative hypothesis about the nature of reality, intersects with both deconstruction and postmodernism by challenging our fundamental assumptions about existence and experience. The possibility that our reality is a simulation forces us to reconsider the boundaries between the real and the artificial, the natural and the technological. This reconsideration is particularly relevant in the context of digital ecosystems, where virtual interactions and digital representations increasingly blur these boundaries. The exploration of simulated realities also raises ethical questions about the creation and manipulation of digital environments, echoing the concerns of deconstruction about the power and responsibility of those who design and control technological systems.

Digital ecosystems, as interconnected networks of digital environments, provide a concrete manifestation of the theoretical concepts discussed. They exemplify the complexity and interdependence of modern technology, illustrating the need for a nuanced understanding of technological phenomena. By examining digital ecosystems through the lenses of deconstruction, postmodernism, and simulation theory, we can develop a more comprehensive and critical perspective on the role of technology in shaping human experience.

In summary, the integration of deconstruction, postmodernism, simulation theory, and digital ecosystems into our understanding of technology offers valuable insights into the multifaceted nature of technological phenomena. These concepts encourage us to question assumptions, embrace diversity, and explore the ethical and philosophical dimensions of technological advancements. By applying these theoretical frameworks, we can better navigate the complexities of the digital age and work towards more inclusive, equitable, and meaningful technological futures.

47. **Deconstruction**: Analyzing cultural texts and media to reveal assumptions and contradictions.

Deconstruction is a critical approach that emerged in the late 20th century, primarily through the work of the French philosopher Jacques Derrida. It focuses on analyzing cultural texts and media to uncover hidden assumptions and contradictions, challenging traditional notions of meaning and interpretation. This method has profound implications for a wide range of disciplines, including literature, philosophy, art, and cultural studies, offering a way to question and destabilize established norms and conventions.

At its core, deconstruction involves a meticulous and often skeptical examination of texts. It seeks to reveal the ways in which meaning is not fixed or stable but is instead constructed through a complex interplay of language, context, and interpretation. This approach challenges the idea that texts have a single, authoritative meaning that can be definitively understood. Instead, deconstruction posits that texts are inherently unstable and open to multiple interpretations.

One of the key concepts in deconstruction is "différance," a term coined by Derrida that plays on the dual meanings of "to differ" and "to defer." Différance suggests that meaning is always deferred, never fully present or complete. This concept highlights the fluidity of language and the impossibility of pinning down a single, fixed meaning. Every attempt to define or interpret a text is inevitably influenced by the context in which it is read and the perspectives of the reader, leading to an endless play of meanings.

Deconstruction also emphasizes the importance of binary oppositions in the construction of meaning. Traditional Western thought often relies on binary pairs, such as presence/absence, speech/writing, and male/female, to structure understanding. Deconstruction seeks to expose the inherent hierarchies and power dynamics within these oppositions. It reveals how one term in each pair is typically privileged over the other, and it works to destabilize these hierarchies by showing how each term depends on its opposite for meaning. For example, the concept of "presence" is defined in contrast to "absence," and vice versa. By deconstructing these oppositions, we can see how they are mutually dependent and how their apparent stability is actually an illusion.

A practical application of deconstruction can be seen in the analysis of literary texts. Traditional literary criticism often seeks to uncover the "true" meaning of a work by examining the author's intentions, historical context, or thematic elements. Deconstruction, however, approaches texts with a focus on their internal contradictions and ambiguities. For instance, a deconstructive reading of a novel might highlight how the narrative's structure undermines its apparent themes, or how characters embody conflicting values that challenge a straightforward interpretation. This type of analysis can reveal the complexities and multiplicities of meaning that conventional readings might overlook.

Deconstruction is not limited to literary texts; it can be applied to any form of cultural production, including visual art, film, and media. In the realm of visual art, deconstruction can involve examining the ways in which artistic works challenge traditional notions of representation and meaning. For example, the work of contemporary artists often plays with the boundaries between reality and representation, using techniques such as appropriation, pastiche, and parody to question the authenticity and originality of art. By deconstructing these works, we can see how they engage with and subvert established artistic conventions.

In film and media studies, deconstruction can be used to analyze how films and other media products construct meaning and convey ideological messages. This involves looking at the formal elements of a film, such as narrative structure, cinematography, and editing, as well as the broader cultural and social contexts in which the film was produced and received. A deconstructive analysis might reveal how a film perpetuates or challenges dominant cultural narratives, such as those related to gender, race, and class. For example, a deconstructive reading of a Hollywood blockbuster might uncover the ways in which it reinforces traditional gender roles or perpetuates stereotypes, despite its surface-level messages of empowerment or diversity.

One of the significant contributions of deconstruction to cultural criticism is its emphasis on the role of the reader or viewer in creating meaning. Traditional approaches often assume that meaning resides within the text itself, waiting to be discovered by a skilled interpreter. Deconstruction, however, argues that meaning is produced through the interaction between the text and the reader. This shift in focus highlights the active role of interpretation and the ways in which different readers bring their own perspectives and experiences to bear on their understanding of a text. This approach democratizes the process of interpretation, suggesting that there is no single "correct" reading of a text but rather a multitude of possible interpretations.

Deconstruction also has important implications for understanding the relationship between language and reality. Traditional views often assume a straightforward correspondence between words and the things they represent. Deconstruction challenges this assumption by showing how language is a system of signs that derive their meaning from their differences from other signs, rather than from any direct connection to the world. This insight destabilizes the notion of objective reality and suggests that our understanding of the world is always mediated by language and interpretation. This perspective can be particularly powerful in critiquing ideologies and power structures, as it reveals how language can be used to construct and maintain particular views of reality.

In addition to its analytical applications, deconstruction has a performative aspect. Derrida often employed playful and provocative writing styles to illustrate his philosophical points, using techniques such as wordplay, paradox, and irony to unsettle conventional ways of thinking. This performative dimension of deconstruction underscores its commitment to challenging established norms and opening up new possibilities for thought and expression. It suggests that deconstruction is not just a method for analyzing texts but also a way of engaging with the world that embraces ambiguity, complexity, and change.

Critics of deconstruction often argue that it leads to relativism and nihilism, suggesting that if all meanings are unstable and open to interpretation, then there can be no basis for truth or ethical judgment. However, proponents of deconstruction argue that it does not deny the possibility of meaning or truth but rather calls attention to the complexities and contingencies of meaning-making. By revealing the limitations and contradictions of traditional ways of thinking, deconstruction opens up new avenues for critical reflection and ethical engagement. It encourages us to be more aware of the assumptions and biases that shape our interpretations and to remain open to alternative perspectives and possibilities.

Deconstruction has had a profound impact on a wide range of disciplines, influencing not only literary and cultural studies but also fields such as law, architecture, and political theory. In legal studies, for example, deconstruction has been used to critique the idea of objective legal interpretation and to highlight the ways in which legal texts are shaped by social and political contexts. In architecture, deconstructivist architects such as Peter Eisenman and Zaha Hadid have drawn on deconstructive principles to challenge traditional notions of form and function, creating buildings that embrace fragmentation, asymmetry, and complexity.

In political theory, deconstruction has been employed to critique the foundational assumptions of modern political thought, such as the concepts of sovereignty, identity, and democracy. By deconstructing these concepts, theorists such as Derrida and Judith Butler have revealed the exclusions and contradictions that underpin traditional political categories and have opened up new possibilities for thinking about politics and ethics in more inclusive and flexible ways.

In conclusion, deconstruction is a powerful and provocative approach to analyzing cultural texts and media. By revealing the hidden assumptions and contradictions within texts, it challenges traditional notions of meaning and interpretation and opens up new possibilities for critical reflection and engagement. Deconstruction's emphasis on the fluidity and contingency of meaning encourages us to question established norms and to remain open to alternative perspectives. Its impact extends across a wide range of disciplines, demonstrating its relevance and applicability to various fields of study. As a method and a way of thinking, deconstruction invites us to embrace complexity, ambiguity, and change in our understanding of the world.

48. **Postmodernism**: Critique of grand narratives and embrace of fragmented, diverse perspectives.

Postmodernism is a broad and complex intellectual movement that emerged in the mid-to-late 20th century as a response to the perceived limitations and assumptions of modernist thought. One of the central tenets of postmodernism is its critique of grand narratives—overarching, universal explanations or stories that claim to provide comprehensive and definitive accounts of reality. Instead, postmodernism embraces fragmented, diverse perspectives, acknowledging the multiplicity and complexity of human experience.

The term "grand narratives," also known as "metanarratives," was popularized by the French philosopher Jean-François Lyotard in his influential book "The Postmodern Condition: A Report on Knowledge" (1979). Lyotard argued that modernity was characterized by its reliance on grand narratives to legitimize knowledge, progress, and social order. Examples of such grand narratives include the Enlightenment belief in reason and scientific progress, the Marxist vision of historical materialism leading to a classless society, and the capitalist narrative of continuous economic growth and development. These grand narratives promised universal truths and solutions to societal problems, but postmodernists contend that they often failed to deliver on these promises and tended to marginalize or silence alternative viewpoints.

Postmodernism, therefore, seeks to expose and challenge the limitations of grand narratives. It questions their assumptions, critiques their claims to universality, and highlights the ways in which they can be exclusionary and oppressive. For postmodernists, grand narratives are seen as tools of power that impose a particular vision of reality while suppressing diversity and difference. By deconstructing these narratives, postmodernism aims to create space for a plurality of voices and perspectives, recognizing the value of localized, contingent, and context-specific forms of knowledge.

One of the key features of postmodernism is its embrace of fragmentation. In contrast to the modernist quest for coherence, unity, and order, postmodernism celebrates the breakdown of traditional structures and the proliferation of diverse, sometimes contradictory, viewpoints. This fragmentation can be seen in various aspects of culture, from literature and art to architecture and media. In literature, for instance, postmodern works often eschew linear narratives and coherent plots in favor of fragmented, non-linear, and metafictional forms. Authors such as Thomas Pynchon, Don DeLillo, and Italo Calvino employ techniques like pastiche, intertextuality, and self-referentiality to highlight the constructed nature of texts and to resist the imposition of a single, authoritative meaning.

Similarly, in the visual arts, postmodernism is marked by a rejection of the idea of artistic originality and the embrace of eclecticism, appropriation, and parody. Artists like Cindy Sherman, Jean-Michel Basquiat, and Jeff Koons draw on a wide range of styles, images, and cultural references, blurring the boundaries between high and low art, the authentic and the reproduced. This multiplicity of influences and the playful mixing of genres and styles reflect postmodernism's challenge to the notion of a singular, unified artistic vision.

In architecture, postmodernism emerged as a reaction against the functionalism and austerity of modernist design. Architects such as Robert Venturi, Denise Scott Brown, and Michael Graves advocated for a more inclusive and playful approach to building design, incorporating historical references, ornamentation, and a mix of materials and styles. This postmodern architectural style is characterized by its diversity and complexity, rejecting the uniformity and purity of modernist principles in favor of a more pluralistic and context-sensitive approach.

Postmodernism's embrace of diverse perspectives is also evident in its approach to identity and subjectivity. While modernist thought often emphasized the idea of a coherent, stable self, postmodernism views identity as fluid, fragmented, and constructed through language, culture, and power relations. This perspective has been particularly influential in fields such as gender studies, queer theory, and postcolonial studies. Scholars like Judith Butler, Homi K. Bhabha, and Gayatri Chakravorty Spivak have drawn on postmodern ideas to challenge essentialist notions of identity and to highlight the ways in which identities are performed, negotiated, and contested.

Judith Butler's concept of gender performativity, for example, argues that gender is not a fixed attribute but rather a set of repeated actions and behaviors that produce the illusion of a stable identity. This idea disrupts traditional binary understandings of gender and opens up possibilities for more fluid and diverse expressions of identity. Similarly, postcolonial theorists have used postmodern insights to critique colonial discourses and to foreground the hybrid, diasporic, and contested nature of postcolonial identities. By emphasizing the constructed and contingent nature of identity, postmodernism encourages a more inclusive and dynamic understanding of the self and others.

In addition to its impact on cultural and identity studies, postmodernism has also influenced our understanding of knowledge and epistemology. Postmodernists argue that knowledge is not objective or universal but is always situated, partial, and influenced by power relations. This perspective challenges the modernist faith in scientific rationality and objective truth, highlighting instead the ways in which knowledge is produced, contested, and legitimized within specific historical and cultural contexts. Michel Foucault's work on power/knowledge, for example, explores how discourses and institutions shape what is considered true or false, normal or abnormal, and how these categories are used to regulate and control behavior.

Postmodernism's critique of grand narratives and its embrace of fragmented, diverse perspectives have significant implications for politics and ethics. By questioning the legitimacy of universal claims and emphasizing the importance of local, context-specific knowledge, postmodernism promotes a more pluralistic and democratic approach to social and political issues. It encourages us to listen to marginalized voices, to recognize the validity of different experiences and perspectives, and to resist the imposition of a single, dominant worldview.

However, postmodernism has also been criticized for its potential to lead to relativism and nihilism. Critics argue that by rejecting the possibility of universal truths and objective standards, postmodernism undermines the basis for ethical and political action. If all perspectives are equally valid, they ask, how can we make judgments or take action to address social injustices and inequalities?

In response to these criticisms, some postmodern thinkers have sought to develop approaches that combine the insights of postmodernism with a commitment to social justice and ethical responsibility. For instance, Jean Baudrillard's concept of simulacra and hyperreality highlights the ways in which contemporary culture is dominated by images and representations that have become detached from any grounding in reality. While this analysis can seem pessimistic, it also opens up possibilities for resistance and critique by exposing the artificiality and manipulation of media and consumer culture.

Similarly, postmodern feminist theorists have used deconstructive methods to challenge patriarchal structures and to advocate for more inclusive and egalitarian social arrangements. By revealing the contradictions and exclusions within traditional narratives of gender, race, and class, these theorists aim to create space for alternative ways of thinking and being that can lead to more just and equitable societies.

In conclusion, postmodernism's critique of grand narratives and its embrace of fragmented, diverse perspectives have profoundly reshaped our understanding of culture, identity, knowledge, and politics. By challenging the assumptions and limitations of modernist thought, postmodernism opens up new possibilities for critical reflection and engagement. It encourages us to question dominant narratives, to recognize the multiplicity of experiences and viewpoints, and to create more inclusive and pluralistic forms of understanding and social organization. Despite the challenges and criticisms it faces, postmodernism remains a vital and influential framework for analyzing and addressing the complexities of contemporary life.

49. **Simulation Theory**: The hypothesis that reality could be an artificial simulation.

Simulation Theory is a compelling and thought-provoking hypothesis that posits the possibility that our reality might be an artificial simulation, akin to an extremely sophisticated computer program. This idea has captivated the imaginations of philosophers, scientists, and technologists, leading to a wide range of discussions and debates about the nature of existence, consciousness, and the boundaries between the real and the virtual.

The roots of Simulation Theory can be traced back to philosophical inquiries into the nature of reality and perception. Plato's Allegory of the Cave, for instance, suggests that what we perceive as reality may be merely shadows on a wall, a mere illusion compared to a deeper truth. Similarly, René Descartes' famous thought experiment about an evil demon deceiving him into believing in a false reality can be seen as a precursor to modern simulation arguments. However, it is in the contemporary digital age, with its advancements in computer technology and virtual reality, that Simulation Theory has gained significant traction.

One of the most influential contemporary proponents of Simulation Theory is the philosopher Nick Bostrom. In his 2003 paper "Are You Living in a Computer Simulation?", Bostrom presents a trilemma, suggesting that one of the following propositions must be true: (1) almost all civilizations at our level of technological development go extinct before reaching a "posthuman" stage; (2) posthuman civilizations are not interested in running ancestor simulations; or (3) we are almost certainly living in a computer simulation. Bostrom argues that if future civilizations develop the capability to run detailed simulations of their ancestors and are interested in doing so, the number of simulated realities could vastly outnumber the one base reality, making it statistically likely that we are living in one of those simulations.

The hypothesis raises profound questions about the nature of reality and our place within it. If we are living in a simulation, it suggests that our understanding of the physical world is fundamentally flawed. The laws of physics, the passage of time, and even our own consciousness could all be products of a sophisticated program designed by an advanced civilization. This notion challenges our concepts of objectivity and truth, suggesting that what we perceive as the external world is merely a constructed environment, subject to manipulation and control by unknown entities.

The technological advancements of recent decades have further fueled speculation about Simulation Theory. The rapid progress in computing power, artificial intelligence, and virtual reality has demonstrated the potential to create increasingly immersive and realistic virtual environments. Video games, in particular, have shown how complex and detailed simulated worlds can become, leading some to wonder whether our own reality might be a more advanced version of such creations. The development of AI characters that can learn and adapt within these environments also raises questions about the nature of consciousness and whether it could emerge within a simulated context.

Moreover, certain anomalies and unexplained phenomena in our universe have been interpreted by some as potential evidence for Simulation Theory. For example, the fine-tuning of the fundamental constants of physics, which seem precisely calibrated to allow for the existence of life, has led some to speculate that these values might have been set intentionally by the creators of our simulation. Similarly, the discovery of patterns or glitches in the fabric of reality, such as the peculiarities of quantum mechanics, could be seen as artifacts of the underlying computational framework.

However, Simulation Theory is not without its critics and challenges. One major objection is the so-called "infinite regress" problem: if our reality is a simulation, then the reality of the beings who created our simulation could also be a simulation, and so on ad infinitum. This raises the question of whether there is any ultimate base reality or if the concept of reality itself becomes meaningless. Additionally, some argue that the sheer computational resources required to simulate an entire universe, including all its intricate details and conscious beings, would be so vast as to be practically impossible, even for an advanced civilization.

Another significant criticism is the lack of empirical evidence. While Simulation Theory is a fascinating and provocative idea, it remains speculative and difficult to test. Unlike scientific theories that make falsifiable predictions,

Simulation Theory operates on a level that may be beyond our current capacity to investigate. Some argue that it is akin to a modern form of metaphysical speculation, captivating but ultimately unprovable.

Despite these challenges, the philosophical implications of Simulation Theory continue to intrigue thinkers across various fields. One of the most profound implications is its impact on our understanding of consciousness and identity. If we are indeed living in a simulation, it raises questions about the nature of our own minds. Are our thoughts, emotions, and experiences real, or are they mere simulations as well? This line of inquiry touches on deep philosophical questions about the mind-body problem and the nature of subjective experience.

Furthermore, Simulation Theory has ethical and existential implications. If our reality is a simulation, what does that mean for our moral and ethical frameworks? Are the simulated beings within our world deserving of moral consideration, and if so, how should we treat them? Additionally, the possibility that our actions and experiences might be monitored or controlled by an external intelligence could lead to a sense of existential unease or even paranoia.

Some have suggested that embracing Simulation Theory could lead to a form of existential liberation. If we recognize that our reality is a simulation, it might prompt us to question the constraints and limitations we perceive and explore new possibilities for existence and action. This perspective aligns with certain strains of existentialist thought, which emphasize the importance of creating meaning and purpose in a world that may be inherently indifferent or absurd.

Simulation Theory also intersects with religious and spiritual ideas. The notion of an external intelligence creating and overseeing our reality bears similarities to certain theistic conceptions of a deity. Some have drawn parallels between Simulation Theory and the concept of divine creation, suggesting that the creators of our simulation could be seen as god-like beings. This perspective invites a reconsideration of traditional religious beliefs in light of contemporary technological and philosophical developments.

In popular culture, Simulation Theory has found expression in various forms of media, from literature and film to video games and television. The 1999 film "The Matrix," directed by the Wachowskis, is perhaps the most iconic depiction of a simulated reality, exploring themes of control, resistance, and the nature of existence. Other works, such as Philip K. Dick's novels and the television series "Westworld," similarly delve into the implications of artificial realities and the boundaries between the real and the virtual.

Ultimately, Simulation Theory invites us to question the nature of reality and our place within it. Whether or not we are living in a simulation, the hypothesis challenges us to reconsider our assumptions and to explore the profound mysteries of existence. It encourages a sense of curiosity and wonder about the universe and our own minds, prompting us to look beyond the surface of everyday experience and to delve into deeper philosophical and existential questions.

While the idea that we might be living in a simulation remains speculative and controversial, it serves as a powerful reminder of the limits of human knowledge and the boundless potential of human imagination. It pushes us to confront the mysteries of consciousness, the nature of reality, and the possibilities of technological advancement. In doing so, Simulation Theory continues to captivate and inspire thinkers across disciplines, offering a rich and challenging framework for exploring some of the most profound questions of our time.

50. **Digital Ecosystems**: Interconnected digital environments and platforms.

Digital ecosystems are the interconnected digital environments and platforms that form a complex, dynamic, and interdependent web of technology. These ecosystems encompass a vast array of devices, applications, services, and networks that facilitate seamless communication, interaction, and integration among users and systems. Understanding digital ecosystems involves recognizing their structure, functionality, and the impact they have on various aspects of modern life, including business, communication, education, and social interaction.

At the core of digital ecosystems are the technologies that enable connectivity and interoperability. The internet is the backbone of these ecosystems, providing the infrastructure that allows different components to communicate and work together. Cloud computing, which offers scalable and flexible resources over the internet, is another crucial element. It enables the storage, processing, and management of data and applications across distributed networks. This flexibility and scalability are essential for supporting the diverse and ever-expanding needs of digital ecosystems.

One of the defining characteristics of digital ecosystems is their interconnectedness. Unlike traditional isolated systems, digital ecosystems are designed to work together, creating a synergistic effect where the whole is greater than the sum of its parts. For example, a smartphone is not just a standalone device; it is part of a larger ecosystem that includes mobile operating systems, applications (apps), cloud services, and other smart devices like wearables and smart home appliances. These interconnected components enhance the functionality and user experience, allowing users to perform a wide range of activities seamlessly.

Applications, or apps, play a pivotal role in digital ecosystems. They provide the interface through which users interact with the ecosystem. Apps can range from simple utilities to complex software systems, and they often rely on cloud services for data storage and processing. The app ecosystems created by companies like Apple and Google illustrate the power of interconnected digital environments. The Apple App Store and Google Play Store serve as centralized platforms where developers can distribute their apps, and users can download them. These platforms ensure that apps adhere to certain standards of quality and security, fostering a reliable and consistent user experience.

Social media platforms are another vital component of digital ecosystems. Platforms like Facebook, Twitter, Instagram, and LinkedIn are not just social networks but integral parts of the digital ecosystem. They connect billions of users worldwide, allowing for instant communication, content sharing, and social interaction. These platforms also integrate with other services and apps, enhancing their functionality. For instance, users can log into various websites using their social media credentials, share content from apps directly to their social media profiles, and even use social media data for personalized experiences on other platforms.

E-commerce is a significant aspect of digital ecosystems. Platforms like Amazon, eBay, and Alibaba exemplify how interconnected digital environments can revolutionize traditional business models. These platforms connect buyers and sellers from around the world, offering a vast marketplace where users can find and purchase products. The integration of payment gateways, logistics services, and customer support systems within these platforms creates a seamless shopping experience. Additionally, e-commerce platforms leverage data analytics and artificial intelligence to provide personalized recommendations, targeted advertising, and efficient inventory management.

The education sector has also been transformed by digital ecosystems. Online learning platforms like Coursera, edX, and Khan Academy provide access to educational resources and courses from institutions around the world. These platforms integrate video lectures, interactive quizzes, discussion forums, and peer assessments to create a comprehensive learning environment. Moreover, they often collaborate with universities and industry partners to offer accredited courses and certifications. This interconnected approach democratizes education, making it accessible to a global audience and enabling lifelong learning opportunities.

Digital ecosystems have a profound impact on healthcare as well. Telemedicine platforms, electronic health records (EHR) systems, and health monitoring devices are all part of the digital health ecosystem. Telemedicine platforms like Teladoc and Doctor on Demand enable patients to consult with healthcare providers remotely, increasing access to medical care. EHR systems facilitate the sharing of patient information among different healthcare providers, improving the continuity and quality of care. Health monitoring devices, such as fitness trackers and smartwatches, collect data on physical activity, heart rate, and sleep patterns, which can be integrated into health apps for personalized health insights and recommendations.

The concept of smart cities is a prime example of how digital ecosystems can transform urban living. Smart cities use interconnected technologies to enhance the efficiency and sustainability of urban infrastructure and services. This includes smart grids for energy management, intelligent transportation systems, and IoT (Internet of Things) sensors for monitoring environmental conditions. These technologies work together to optimize resource usage, reduce pollution, and improve the quality of life for residents. For instance, smart traffic management systems can reduce congestion by dynamically adjusting traffic signals based on real-time traffic data. Similarly, smart waste management systems can optimize collection routes and schedules, reducing costs and environmental impact.

Digital ecosystems also play a crucial role in cybersecurity. As more devices and systems become interconnected, the potential attack surface for cyber threats increases. Therefore, cybersecurity measures must be integrated across the entire ecosystem. This includes using encryption to protect data, implementing multi-factor authentication, and deploying advanced threat detection and response systems. Cybersecurity ecosystems often involve collaboration among various stakeholders, including technology providers, regulatory bodies, and end-users, to ensure a coordinated and effective defense against cyber threats.

The financial sector has been significantly impacted by digital ecosystems as well. Fintech companies like PayPal, Square, and Stripe have developed platforms that integrate payment processing, financial management, and e-commerce solutions. These platforms enable businesses and consumers to conduct financial transactions seamlessly across different channels. Blockchain technology, which underpins cryptocurrencies like Bitcoin and Ethereum, represents another dimension of the financial digital ecosystem. Blockchain provides a decentralized and secure way to record transactions, potentially transforming various industries by enabling transparent and tamper-proof record-keeping.

Digital ecosystems are not without challenges. One of the primary concerns is the issue of data privacy and security. As more personal and sensitive data is collected and shared across interconnected systems, the risk of data breaches and misuse increases. Ensuring robust data protection measures and compliance with privacy regulations, such as the General Data Protection Regulation (GDPR) in the European Union, is crucial to maintaining trust in digital ecosystems.

Another challenge is the potential for monopolistic behavior and lack of competition. Large technology companies, often referred to as "Big Tech," can dominate digital ecosystems, creating barriers to entry for smaller competitors and stifling innovation. Regulatory measures and policies aimed at promoting competition and preventing anticompetitive practices are essential to fostering a healthy and dynamic digital ecosystem.

Interoperability and standardization are also critical issues. For digital ecosystems to function smoothly, different components and systems must be able to communicate and work together effectively. This requires the development and adoption of common standards and protocols. Efforts like the development of the Internet of Things (IoT) standards and the Open Banking initiative, which promotes the use of open APIs in the financial sector, are examples of how standardization can facilitate interoperability in digital ecosystems.

Digital ecosystems also have significant implications for the workforce. The automation of tasks and the rise of remote work are reshaping the nature of work and employment. Digital platforms like Zoom, Slack, and Microsoft Teams have become essential tools for remote collaboration and communication. The gig economy, facilitated by platforms like Uber, TaskRabbit, and Upwork, offers flexible work opportunities but also raises questions about job security, benefits, and workers' rights. Ensuring that the workforce can adapt to these changes through skills development and supportive policies is essential for a resilient and inclusive digital economy.

In conclusion, digital ecosystems represent the intricate and interconnected web of digital environments and platforms that define our contemporary technological landscape. They encompass a wide range of devices, applications, and services that work together to create seamless and integrated experiences for users. While digital ecosystems offer numerous benefits, including enhanced connectivity, efficiency, and innovation, they also present challenges related to data privacy, competition, interoperability, and the future of work. Addressing these challenges requires a collaborative effort among technology providers, policymakers, and users to ensure that digital ecosystems are secure, inclusive, and capable of fostering sustainable and equitable growth.